STRAIT

Jilong

Sanchong
Taoyuan
TAIBEI
Zhongli
Banqiao
Daxi

Xinzhu

Taizhong

25°

23°

120°
121°
122°

PUBLICATIONS ON ASIA
OF
THE SCHOOL OF INTERNATIONAL STUDIES
UNIVERSITY OF WASHINGTON
NUMBER 35

Sponsored by the China Program
of the School of International Studies

PLOUGHSHARE
VILLAGE

Culture and Context
in Taiwan

STEVAN HARRELL

University of Washington Press

Seattle and London

Library of Congress Cataloging in Publication Data
Harrell, Stevan.
    Ploughshare Village.

    (Publications on Asia of the School of International
Studies, University of Washington; v. 35)
    Parallel title in Chinese characters.
    Bibliography: p.
    Includes index.
    1. Ethnology—Taiwain-Li-she-wei. 2. Li-she-wei
(Taiwan)—Social conditions. 3. Li-she-wei (Taiwan)—
Economic conditions. I. Title. II. Title: Li-she-wei.
III. Series.
GN635.T28H37   306'.0951'249   82-8333
ISBN 0-295-95946-0   AACR2

Contents

Illustrations

Preface

This book is part of a larger project begun by Arthur and Margery Wolf in the late 1950s, with the objective of understanding the society of the southwestern Taibei Basin, the area known as Haishan. As such, it builds on the foundations established by previous published and unpublished anthropological research in that area. In my first year of graduate school in anthropology, when it became clear that I was interested in field research in the Haishan area, Arthur Wolf, with an eye to the comparative, suggested I study a picturesque but poor village of coal miners, situated on a point of land and approached by two suspension bridges. I flatly rejected his suggestion and spent the summer of 1970 in Shitouxi studying lineage organization. During that summer, however, I became intrigued with the question of individual differences in religious belief, and when I proposed a systematic study of such individual differences as a dissertation project, convenience of field work dictated that I work in a nucleated village, of which there are relatively few in Haishan. So in 1972 I set off, with my wife and eight-month-old daughter, to study individual differences in religious belief in Ploughshare village, the very community of coal miners that Wolf had suggested to me two years before.

We all stayed in Ploughshare five months, in three rooms rented from a rather prosperous village widow. My wife and daughter returned home in late 1972 because of the baby's illness, and I stayed on until April 1973. My wife cooked and marketed while she was there, and I took over these duties for myself when she left. For the first six weeks, I employed an interpreter to translate my Mandarin Chinese into the villagers' Hokkien and back again, but when he left to go to college, I interviewed and interacted almost exclusively in the Hokkien language. I started out missing things, but learned fast, out of necessity.

Though my primary focus at the time was on religion, I collected basic demographic and economic data from all the 101 households in the village at that time; it is these data that serve as the base line for the current work. In 1978, I returned to Ploughshare for eight weeks, renting a room from a different widow this time, taking my meals at the new village noodle shop. During this visit I collected data on family economies and how they had changed since my previous work. I also did some interviewing of local factory managers and made a few exploratory trips to a remote mountain village to compare its stagnant economy with Ploughshare's booming one. I visited Ploughshare again for four days in the summer of 1980, but I did not do any systematic interviewing—I just visited and gathered rough impressions.

This study has depended on cooperation from many people. Foremost among them are the people of Ploughshare, and although I cannot thank them all individually, I should like to single out Tan Chiu-kun, Li Zien-sui, the late Tan Bieng-kui, the late Huan Cin-ik, and my landlady Li Pou-cng. All of them did more than just cooperate with my inquiries, and went out of their way to help.

The patience and cooperation of my teachers were no less essential. G. William Skinner first stimulated my interest in things anthropological and systemic. Arthur Wolf got me interested in Taiwan, and kindly allowed me to use his connections and his data, both essential to the results of this research. Renato Rosaldo taught me what I needed to know about religion. Wang Shih-ch'ing taught me not only Hokkien language but also a lot about Haishan history and Taiwan in general.

During my two stays in Ploughshare, I was first a visiting researcher, then a visiting scholar at the Institute of Ethnology, Academia Sinica, Nankang. I received much help and encouragement from teachers and colleagues there; I am particularly indebted to Professor Li Yih-yuan and Professor Wang Sung-hsing.

At various times in the field, I received hospitality and encouragement from other friends and colleagues, and I should like to thank them: Emily Ahern, Katherine Gould-Martin, Robert Martin, Robert

Weller, Robert Weiss, Jane Chu, Lung-sheng Sung, Margaret Mian Yan Sung, William Speidel, and William H. Newell. Zhou Yujing (Eugene Chou) was an able interpreter and has been a constant friend.

Several people have been helpful with comments on various drafts of this manuscript, in whole or in part: James Townsend, Jack Dull, Arthur Kleinman, David Spain, James Palais, Susan Greenhalgh, and Edgar V. Winans. Wilhelmina Savenye printed the pictures to look better than the photographer deserved, and the publications office of the School of International Studies has made the production of the book smooth and efficient. This is owing particularly to the editor, Lisa Kennedy; Rose Fishman, who did the composition; and Jeanne Woo, the cartographer.

The 1972-73 research was supported by an NIMH predoctoral fellowship, and the 1978 research by an ACLS-SSRC grant for the study of contemporary China.

I would like to thank Mouton Publishers who have kindly given me permission to reprint a portion of my article "The Ancestors at Home: Domestic Worship in a Land-Poor Taiwanese Village," in *Ancestors,* edited by William F. Newell (The Hague: Mouton, 1974).

Barbara Harrell shared in the field experience, and did not complain when, on my second field trip, I sold her typewriter.

A NOTE ON ROMANIZATION

The people of Ploughshare speak almost exclusively the Anxi dialect of Quanzhou Hokkien; scholarly discourse in and about China uses almost exclusively Mandarin Chinese, known in Taiwan as Guoyu. In this book I have tried to compromise.

Romanized in Mandarin, according to the Pinyin system, are:

—all place names, with the exception of a few names referring to parts of Ploughshare, which are in Hokkien, preceded by an (H);

—terms that refer to official, government functions;

—terms that are standard in the ethnographic literature on China.

Romanized in Hokkien, according to the Bodman system, are:

—all personal names, with the exception of mainland Chinese, which are in Mandarin, preceded by an (M);

—terms characteristic of Ploughshare discourse.

The glossary gives Chinese characters for all place names and general terms, but not for personal names, as these are all fictitious.

PLOUGHSHARE VILLAGE

Introduction

About twenty-five kilometers south of Taibei City, along the road that leads from the rather sleepy market town of Sanxia through the mountains to the old river port of Daxi, a small, unnamed stream cuts a deep gorge as it emerges out of the nearby hills. It twists and winds, and finally debouches into the broad bed of the Sanxia River, which usually contains only a small stream, but fills up to its banks in a whirl of mud when the typhoons come. The point of land where the two rivers come together, when looked at from the top of the nearby brush-covered hills, has a shape resembling the iron share of the plow used by the local rice farmers to till their fields. So the first settlers, who came here from Anxi County, Quanzhou Prefecture, Fujian Province, just across the Taiwan Strait on the mainland of China, called this place Lei-ci-be, or Ploughshare Point. The village that grew up there took on the same name and is called that, informally at least, today.

Ploughshare had over 700 inhabitants in 1973, and a hundred more in 1978, almost all of them speakers of the Anxi dialect of Hokkien Chinese. They, like nearly everyone else in the Sanxia area, can be told

Looking across the small stream to farmland in Blacksmith Gulch, 1972

readily from speakers of the other Quanzhou dialects and still more easily distinguished from Zhangzhou speakers, by the pronunciation of certain words: tail, for example, is not *bue* or *be,* but *bə*; student is not *hak-se:,* as in the Zhangzhou dialect, but *hak-si:;* fish is neither *hi* nor *hu,* but *hə*; and so on. Native speakers of the various dialects of Hokkien can understand each other with no trouble, and find it rather amusing when an overanalytical foreigner points out the distinctions to them. But the distinctions, along with certain ritual practices, are the only remaining signs of the division between the Anxi settlers who inhabit the area around the Sanxia and Yingge, extending northward to the edge of Shulin town, and the Tongan, Sanyi, and Zhangzhou people who flank them on both north and south.

Ploughshare is approached by two wooden suspension bridges—one across the Sanxia River from Dapu and a shorter, wobblier one across the smaller tributary from Blacksmith Gulch (Pha-thi-khi:), the strip of inhabited land between the stream and the mountains to the north of it. There is also a concrete road bridge across the small stream about one hundred meters upstream from the short suspension bridge. Motorcycles can approach the village from Dapu across the long suspension bridge, but cars and trucks have to come in by way of Blacksmith Gulch. Most of the houses are arrayed in neat rows along the streets that run the length of the village from the lower, or north end, where all the approaches are, to the upper end at the south. Before World

War II, most of the houses, built of sun-dried mud and straw blocks or of pounded earth walls, faced toward Dapu, giving the west or Dapu side of the village the designation of *thau-cieng* (the front), while the houses on the eastern side are referred to as *au-pia:* (the back). The pushcart railway, which used to run along what is now Back Street, was replaced in 1961 by a gravel road, suitable for trucks, and since then most of the brick and stucco houses that have replaced the old adobe ones in that part of the village have faced the street. So the terms *front* and *back* have ceased to describe the orientation of the village; in fact all eight commercial establishments in Ploughshare now face Back Street. This street was paved in 1968 by the paper company that runs a factory in Shisantian just above and to the south of Ploughshare, and Front Street was paved and concrete gutters added, crossed by sturdy motorcycle ramps, as part of a local construction project sponsored by the Taibei County government in 1972. Between the two streets runs a network of concrete lanes, connecting Back with Front and providing access to houses lying between the two streets. In all, Ploughshare is a very compact village. It is only about four hundred meters from the intersection of the two streets at the lower end to where they meet again at the top, and most villagers can walk to each others' houses in three minutes or less.

Most of the houses are new. In 1973, there were only fourteen families living primarily in mud-brick houses, and a construction boom between 1973 and 1978 produced forty-eight new houses or major additions to existing houses, and left only three structures of mud-brick. By 1978, almost all houses were built in the style known as *tiam-khi* (store construction), and those adjacent to streets invariably faced them. The front door of a *tiam-khi* house usually leads to the *thia:;* or parlor, a room containing the family altar, chairs for visitors (plastic upholstery, preferred in 1973, had largely been replaced by carved hardwood with marble seats and backs by 1978), and, in the days when few people had them, the refrigerator. By 1978 refrigerators were so common they were nothing to show off, and had almost all been moved back to the kitchen. In a one-story house, a door to one side of the altar leads to a corridor, flanked by bedrooms on one or both sides. These are appointed with wooden sleeping platforms, sometimes topped by Japanese-style tatami mats, with quilted cotton coverlets folded in the corners of the platforms, and with portable wooden bureaus and closets. At the back of a typical *tiam-khi* the corridor opens out into the family kitchen, which contains the brick stove *(cau)* symbolic of the unity of the patrilocal family. The stove is fired with wood or coal, and its two woks *(tia:)*, each seventy centimeters or more in diameter, serve to boil water for baths, steam large fowl and puddings, and in a very few cases to stir-fry the vegetable and meat dishes accompanying the polished white rice that is the staple food of all three daily meals. By 1978, most families used the brick stove only to boil water and cook large festive dishes, doing their everyday cooking on two-burner portable gas ranges, fed from propane tanks delivered on motorcycles from several outlets in Sanxia. Rice itself is always prepared in electric cookers with automatic timers; many younger villagers were astonished, in 1972-73, that we could cook rice in an ordinary pot over a low gas flame. Almost all families also have running water in the kitchen; until the summer of 1978 it was invariably pumped with electric motors *(mo-tha)* from one of the village wells or from the spring located halfway down the river embankment at the southwest side of the village. In August 1978, many villagers took advantage of the opportunity to hook up to the newly installed public water system that now serves the entire southern Taibei Basin. Drinking water is always boiled: I once observed a group of village children playing a gambling game in which the loser's penalty was to drink a glass of water straight from the tap. Many new houses contain bathrooms with pebble-tiled Western-style bathtubs supplied from coal-stoked water heaters; people in older dwellings must content themselves with washing in a plastered closet, using water heated over the brick stove. The old wooden outhouses that still served a few families in 1973 were gone by 1978, replaced by some Japanese-style and some Western-style flush toilets. Gone, too, from most homes at least, were the pigs in the pens adjoining the old toilets. Only ten families still kept pigs in 1978.

In 1973, most housing was one story, with seven two- and one three-story buildings in the village. But even then, the newer houses had flat roofs that would allow addition of a second story at a later date. And the building boom from 1973 to 1978 was as much upward as outward. By 1978 there were twenty-three two-story houses and three three-story ones, and others would have added another story had it not been for the stringent zoning regulations, which were beginning to be enforced seriously. Most of the two-story houses have balconies facing the street, and many of them have their parlors on the second floor, immediately inside the balcony. Some of these houses are built to accommodate projected expansion of the family in the future, and the first floor may be unpartitioned, with all the bedrooms on the upper story.

There are a few open spaces within the village housing complex, and in 1972-73 many of these were vegetable gardens or patches of dirt where laundry could be hung on bamboo poles to dry. By 1978, many of these empty spaces had either been built on, or concreted over to

The front of a typical *tiam-khi* house, with its flat roof, 1978

Ploughshare's Front Street, 1972

look just like the concrete rice-drying grounds in front of the houses of the nineteen families who grew rice. This gave the village an almost urban appearance, despite its small size and bucolic surroundings. But Ploughshare remains a village in terms of its position in the society of the southern Taibei Basin, a community that itself supports very little commercial activity, but whose inhabitants have long played roles as cash-agriculturalists, wage laborers, and small-scale entrepreneurs in a commercial economy. As such, it differs considerably from most other communities in the ethnographic literature on Taiwan.

The social organization of Ploughshare, the pattern of behavior of community members who stand in certain defined relationships with each other, both resembles and differs from the social organization of other Chinese communities in the southern Taibei Basin and elsewhere. Similarities include patrilocal marital residence, and hence a family developmental cycle that includes a patrilocal joint phase; equal patrilineal inheritance; indirect dowry in wealth but not in land or capital goods; authority within the family of males over females and older over younger generations; and a wide range of kin- and nonkin-based dyadic ties as bases for forming both single-stranded and multistranded relationships between families. Differences (and here I mean differences from the statitistical norm of Chinese communities, since every community shows some differences from every other) include a higher incidence of the alternative uxorilocal form of marital residence; statistically earlier breakup of patrilocal joint families; a significant weakness of the separation of male and female roles and of the authority of males and seniors; and a virtual absence of corporate, polyadic groups, kin-based or otherwise, as elements of social organization. The aim of this study is to explain these similarities and differences.

Social organization, as defined, is an aspect of behavior and must be explained by the same causative factors that explain any aspect of behavior. Since almost all human behavior is motivated rather than instinctive, we can begin with the assumption that people behave as they do in any situation for two basic reasons: either they have always done it that way, and therefore do not question that that is the proper way to do it, in which case the behavior becomes a habit or a custom, or they assess the situation and decide that a certain way is the best way to behave. Habitual or customary behavior of course differs greatly from one community to another; insofar as any behavior is totally habitual or customary, it is determined by that set of shared principles for structuring reality that we ordinarily call culture. Behavior in response to assessment of the situation, on the other hand, is determined by the set of alternatives presented to the actor by that situation, and it is this set of alternatives that I choose to call the

context of that behavior. In reality, almost no behavior is totally determined either by culture or by context, because culture delimits and
influences the actor's perception of the context, while responses to
context shape the possibilities for the formation and change of culture.

Since social organization is an aspect of behavior, it follows that
it also is determined by an aspect of culture and an aspect of context.
That aspect of culture consisting of shared principles for the structuring
of social reality I refer to as *social structure*. That aspect of context
relevant to making decisions about social behavior I refer to as the
socioeconomic context. It is the thesis of this book that social organization, the actual patterns of social behavior, can only be understood as
a process of interaction between social structure and socioeconomic
context.

If we posit social structure and socioeconomic context as causes
of social organization, we need to examine them more carefully. Social
structure, as defined above, is a set of shared principles for structuring
social behavior. All humans learn these principles, consciously or
unconsciously (and always somewhat idiosyncratically) as they progress
through the life cycle. When people are faced with the necessity of
interacting with someone (engaging in social behavior), what they do
will be partly determined by the principles of social relationships they
have consciously or unconsciously learned. Thus people in Ploughshare
commonly have sexual relations with their spouses, send their children
to the store to buy cigarettes, or borrow money from their affines
because of culturally learned principles about relationships between
spouses, parents and children, or affines. At this level, context has
very little to do with it. Similarly, behaviors of longer duration, such
as marrying virilocally if such a marriage is available, forming sworn
brotherhoods with unrelated men of one's own age, or organizing
an annual festival for the local deity Cieng-cui Co-su on the sixteenth
day of the first lunar month, are influenced by cultural, learned patterns of what is customarily done. None of these is the only possible
solution to the problem of marital residence, of forming useful business
contacts, or of organizing for reciprocal feasting.

If social structure, as an aspect of culture, shapes behavior in this
way, socioeconomic context also influences behavior, including in
particular social organization. By socioeconomic context, I mean the
sum total of exogenous, given factors to which people with certain
cultural rules have to adapt their social behavior. This context has
a physical aspect consisting of what Marxists would call the forces of
production—the natural environment, the available technology, and
the human population of producers and consumers. Its social aspect
consists of the larger social systems in which behavior occurs. Depend-

ing on the unit studied, these can comprise anything from the family system to the world economy. For an individual, the entire social system is context; for a nation, the world system is context and everything internal is its own organization. For Ploughshare, the social context includes all the larger systems of which the village is a part. (The particular manner in which I describe these systems is outlined below.) The total context thus includes both the physical side—natural environment, technology, and population—and the social side—the larger systems—and it sets limits on behavior, or social organization. In certain cases these limits may be very narrow, and we can say that context determines certain kinds of behaviors. In other cases, the limits are wide and the behavioral choices many.

To return to the simple examples discussed above, it is possible for most people to have sexual relations with their spouses partly because the demographic parameters of Taiwan's current population allow a spouse for most young and middle-aged adults; people can send their children to the store to buy cigarettes because they are available in Taiwan's economy and the store is close enough to assure that children will not get lost or run over on the way; and people can borrow money from their affines because Taiwan's is a money economy. Who the spouse is, why they send children to the store instead of going themselves, and why they turn to affines for loans are all culturally determined. But without the enabling context, these behaviors would be impossible.

To turn to less obvious examples, when people from Anxi came to Ploughshare and began to cultivate tea on the mountainsides, they did so because it was the only way of making a living, given the physical and social context in which they had to live, and their social organization reflected the necessity of organizing for the production and sale of tea, rather than the production and direct consumption of rice and sweet potatoes, for example. But organizing in patrilocal families with certain kinds of dyadic links between them was not the only possible way of organizing for the production and sale of tea; rather it grew out of an interaction of the social structure that these people had carried with them as Hokkien-speaking Chinese from Anxi County, Fujian, and the context, both natural and social, in which they found themselves having to produce to make a living. The context sets limits on their behavior, while culture provides guidelines within which to act.

This view of socioeconomic context and social structure as formative factors in social organization is still an approximation, however, because it does not allow for the influences that each one, through the mediation of social organization, can have on the other. It is obvious how social organization, particularly of production in the narrow sense, can modify the context, both physical and social; the people of a community are actors in an ecological and a social system, and as such modify both their natural and their social context. But at the same time, social structure changes as well. If social organization is the adaptation of social structure to a particular context, those who grow up in such a context will learn at least some of their principles, their model for behavior, from the social organization that they participate in. Social structure for the next generation may well be different from what it was for the previous one, and indeed it may change for a particular individual over time.

In this way, behavior itself becomes a mediator between culture and context. If behavior changes in response to contextual change, that behavior will eventually become a basis for modifications of the principles according to which people operate. If enough people, for example, marry their daughters in the formerly culturally devalued minor fashion, in which the future daughter-in-law is adopted by her husband's family while she is still a small child, that form of marriage may become part of the principles that form the basis of peoples' decisions about marriage (Wolf and Huang 1980, p. 282). Conversely, behavior shaped by cultural principles can change the context. For example, the web of sworn brotherhoods, patron-client ties, and political factionalism of the Sanxia elite determines who gets elected to local office and how much of the local government funds go to activities that do or do not contribute effectively to building up the economic infrastructure. When flood-control funds were used to build villas in the late 1960s, this had a direct effect on the ecological aspect of the socioeconomic context for many Haishan people. We can thus diagram the interaction between social structure, socioeconomic context, and social organization in figure 1.

All this may seem an obvious point. I belabor it not only because it is part of the theoretical basis for the empirical study that follows, but also because there are those who would like to ignore the role of either culture or context in shaping behavior, as well as the reciprocal effect of behavior on both culture and context. On the one extreme we have Harris (1979, for example) and his followers, who would like to explain social organization entirely from the interaction of technology and environment (Harris 1968, pp. 4-6). The best they can do, it seems to me, is produce a statistical model, which will generate a better than random fit with empirical findings and correlations between techno-environment and social organization. But I am interested in neither correlations nor statistical models, except perhaps as intermediate heuristic devices. I am interested in mechanical models and in explanation, and I am convinced I can never explain such facets of

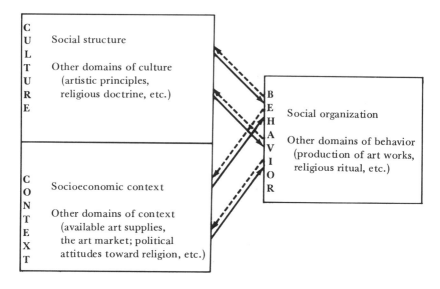

Fig. 1   Interaction of culture, context, and behavior

Ploughshare social organization as exchanging incense with the bearer of a god's image in procession, equal inheritance, or sworn sisterhoods merely by the interaction of technology and environment. Technology, and particularly the physical and social context, can tell me a lot, but they can only tell me in a historical sense why Ploughshare's social organization developed as it did if I begin my history with, as Sahlins has aptly put it, "a culture already there" (1976, p. 23).

At the same time, there is an equally disturbing trend at the other extreme, exemplified in Kelly's tour-de-force explanation of Etoro social structure (1977), in which he denies the ability of contextual changes to effect changes in social structure (ibid., p. 174). Principles, he maintains, are impervious to changes brought about by such contextual forces as demography; observed changes in patterns of behavior arise from contradictions between various principles that have to be resolved by violating one principle or the other. In a static analysis, this principle of contradiction can explain a lot, but it falls down as a historical explanation, because we know that structure ultimately does change. To return to the example of minor marriages, people do not use the minor marriage principle anymore because young couples, who have now gained changes in employment because of the changing context of Taiwan's economy, refuse to be married in this way. I have no quarrel with the assertion that cultural principles do not change automatically, and reflexively, in response to contextual changes. But neither is culture immutable. How long it takes to change in a particular case is an empirical problem.

The point in all this is a simple one: people's behavior is shaped by learned principles and by the possibility of adaptive choice, and how they behave affects both the observed behavior that is part of the basis for learning the principles and the possibilities for future choices. This point is also a very abstract one and outlines an approach for explaining social organization only in a very general way. To apply this approach to the specific problem of explaining why Ploughshare's social organization differs from that of neighboring communities in particular ways, we need to formulate some specific guidelines for describing the socioeconomic context and the social structure of a particular Chinese community. The context of Ploughshare I take to be a series of nested social and economic systems. Each of these has a physical and a social aspect, the latter being conceived of as the social division of labor between component parts. Each system contains parts that may constitute systems at lower levels, and in turn each system is part of larger systems, culminating in the world economy, which now includes almost all the world's human societies (Wallerstein 1974, pp. 397-98). The significance of the context for any component (such as the village of Ploughshare) is thus the part played by that component in the social division of labor that is the larger system. Now the division of labor in such a system can be according to one of two modes: complementary, which is described in a sectional model, and dominance-subordination, which is described in a core-periphery or concentric model. For example, tea growers in the hills might sell their tea and buy rice marketed by lowland cultivators. If this exchange involved an approximately equal living standard in the two areas and no power of one area to determine the fortunes of the other, we might analyze this system according to a sectional model. If, on the other hand, tea producers sold at lower prices, enjoyed a lower standard of living than the rice farmers, and were dependent on the vagaries of an external market controlled by people living in the rice region, then the rice region would become a core and the tea region a periphery. My analysis of Ploughshare's context involves its shifting from a model with both sectional and concentric characteristics in the nineteenth century, to the periphery of a concentric model in the Japanese colonial period and finally to the core of a concentric model since 1960.

Assumptions regarding the description of social structure are more difficult: since it is rare that informants verbalize the rules of their social structure, this structure must be inferred from other sources. To describe social structure in Ploughshare, I proceed on the assumption that there is such a thing as Chinese social structure, a set of principles shared, with variations, by members of all communities that call themselves Chinese and live in Chinese societies (overseas Chinese exhibit extremes of variation for which this approach, though workable, is less useful). That the variations exist testifies to the historical process of change in a people with a common cultural origin who have adapted to widely diverse contexts. That the variation is on a single set of themes testifies to the existence and persistence of cultural principles as a basis for behavior.

This approach to describing and explaining the social organization of Ploughshare dictates the order of presentation of this book. It begins with three chapters that are mostly context. The first describes Ploughshare's place in the series of socioeconomic systems of which it is a part, as it has changed from the founding of the village in the nineteenth century to the present day. The second describes the changing nature of work available to the villagers of Ploughshare. Already here we see the interaction of culture and context, for the Chinese family system shapes the way in which work is organized. But context is predominant; villagers have little say in determining the kinds of work available, or how much they pay. The third chapter concerns social inequality. The system of inequality is both context, in that it is part of the larger system, and organization, in that it is partly an aspect of social relationships within the community. But the analysis of inequality is placed with the context chapters because the nature of inequality in the village is shaped primarily by the villagers' place in the larger system of social classes in Taiwanese society as a whole.

The second half of the book concerns the social organization of Ploughshare itself, explicable only in terms of interaction between social structure and context. I consider three aspects of social organization in this section: that of the community, the family, and that of religion. In each case, I first describe the principles of Chinese social structure that shape that particular domain of social organization, and then show how Ploughshare's context has led the villagers to apply those principles in a way that results in the particular aspects of Ploughshare's social organization.

To do this, we have to derive principles of Chinese social structure from a conjunction of a variety of Chinese communities' social organization.[1] But there is a problem here because the further apart in time and space are the communities whose social organization is being

---

1. This does not imply that a structure is merely an epiphenomenon of organization, but merely that the investigator must derive principles, rarely verbalized by the natives, from the study of organization.

compared, the more likely the social structural principles themselves will be different, and the less certain we can be about differences in social organization being attributable to contextual differences. This difficulty can never be eliminated, but it can be minimized by making comparisons as close in space and time as possible. The most valuable comparisons are thus those between Ploughshare and other Hokkien-speaking villages in the southern Taibei Basin in the 1960s and 1970s, and these will be relied on wherever possible. Other Taiwanese examples, especially Hakka communities, and systems in other parts of China, while they will be used, should be taken with considerable caution.

Ploughshare in the Socioeconomic System

Ploughshare has never been an isolated community. Neither, for that matter, have any significant number of other Chinese villages in historical times. Even in periods of the most intense economic and coercive closure (Skinner 1971), any community in a complex society will have relationships of trade, taxation, or conflict with the larger social system and its component parts. But Ploughshare has never even been relatively isolated; its particular place in the social division of labor as a village of people who have produced for the market or sold their labor, or both, means that most of its families have never even known the relative self-sufficiency of the peasant household that produces most of what it consumes and consumes most of what it produces. The tie between Ploughshare and the larger systems of which it is a part is thus the logical starting point for an analysis of Ploughshare's social organization.

Throughout its history, Ploughshare has been part of a hierarchy of social and economic systems. At any one time, such systems exist at many different levels, but some of the levels will be relatively more closed or integral systems than others, and therefore more useful for analysis. The importance and degree of integration of particular levels also changes over time; I describe for each time period the most salient. In general, we can see Ploughshare as part of a local system, which includes all the communities for whom the basic-level market, and later administrative center, has been the nearby town of Sanxia. This local system is, in turn, part of a regional system, including all of the Chinese-inhabited parts of Taiwan from Taoyan and Zhongli in the south to Jilong in the north, with its market and administrative center at the twin cities of Megjia and Dadaocheng, which later became Taibei. This regional system, likewise, is part of an island system of Taiwan as a whole. And Taiwan is part of the world system. To understand Ploughshare, then, we must trace the evolution of this hierarchy of systems from the nineteenth century, when Ploughshare was founded, to the present day. This chapter analyzes the political and economic relations of this hierarchy of systems in three periods: the late Qing dynasty, the Japanese colonial period, and the postwar industrialization of Taiwan.

THE LATE QING DYNASTY

Taiwan

Taiwan has been inhabited since prehistoric times by aboriginal peoples of Malayo-Polynesian ancestry, and there has been some Chinese settlement in the island since the Song dynasty. Migration from the Chinese mainland to the island was rather restricted, however, until the late sixteenth century, and it was not until the period of nominal Dutch sovereignty (1624-62) that there were a large number of Chinese settlers. During the Dutch period, Chinese settlers around present-day Taiwan grew rice and sugar, and both crops were exported. There was a major influx of Chinese during the turmoil accompanying the dynastic turnover from Ming to Qing, greatly accelerated when the Ming loyalist Zheng Chenggong (known in Western accounts as Koxinga) retreated to Taiwan from the mainland, drove out the Dutch colonial forces, and settled much of his army as farmers in the southwestern part of the island. By the time Zheng's successors were conquered and the island nominally included in the Qing Empire as a prefecture of Fujian Province, there were Chinese farmers as far south as Dagou (later Gaoxiong) and as far north as Yunlin (Ho 1978, p. 10). Northern Taiwan was settled later and more slowly; it was not until the eighteenth century that the southwestern part of the Taibei Basin, in which Ploughshare is located, was opened up for Chinese cultivation. By 1811, Ho estimates that there were about 2,000,000 Chinese in Taiwan; this number probably increased by another million during the rest of the nineteenth century (ibid., p. 11).

During the eighteenth century, northern Taiwan in particular was largely a frontier outpost of southeastern China. Immigrants, primarily from Quanzhou and Zhangzhou prefectures in Fujian, and secondarily from the Hakka areas of northeastern Guangdong, were not permitted to settle permanently in Taiwan until the middle of the Qianlong period, in the mid-eighteenth century. Although there was some settlement prior to this date, settlers were not allowed to bring their families with them, so many of them crossed the straits to Taiwan in the spring, planted a crop, stayed until the fall harvest, then returned again.

After the mid-1700s, immigration became permanent, and a settled Chinese society, with villages of farming families, began to form (Wolf and Huang 1980, pp. 42-43). The island was an exporter of rice and sugar, primarily to northern China. Society, however, was still far from being a carbon copy of the relatively peaceful, orderly countryside of eighteenth-century society on the mainland. The Qing government was unable or unwilling to exert much direct political control over the island, and local communities thus became virtually self-governing under the rule of locally powerful families (Meskill 1970). These "fledgling gentry," as Meskill calls them, organized irrigation works, clearing of land and, importantly, defense against hostile aboriginal peoples being driven slowly back into the island's mountainous interior by the spread of Chinese agriculture in the western plains and foothills. As the island's good agricultural districts gained population, military feuds between Fujianese and Hakkas, or between Fujianese of diverse origins on the mainland, became ever more frequent, culminating in the great battles in the mid-nineteenth century (Wang 1976, p. 73; see Lamley 1981, p. 309).

In the mid-1800s, Chinese society in Taiwan had lost some of its former wild frontier character, and the opening up of Danshui, Jilong, and Anping as treaty ports placed Taiwan in a position of a trading partner not only with the Chinese mainland and Japan, as previously, but also with the Western powers, particularly England, the Netherlands, and the United States (Ho 1978, pp. 13-15). Its traditional exports of rice and sugar continued, and the important camphor trade of northern Taiwan was supplemented by tea after the 1860s. Its imports consisted primarily of consumer goods, by far the most valuable of which was opium. Wang (1976, p. 74) speaks of British ships at Jilong exchanging opium, not produced in Taiwan but rather widely used, for camphor during this period. The total volume of trade was rather small, however, for most of Taiwan's rural folk were engaged in production for personal consumption, mainly of rice and sweet potatoes, selling only a small surplus on the market.

Taiwan was thus only marginally included within world political and economic systems throughout most of the Qing. Ignored by its own nominal government, producing mostly for its own consumption, much of the population was relatively self-sufficient. There are, however, important exceptions to this generalization. There were extensive sugar-producing districts, primarily in the south, and tea districts in the north, whose economy was totally dependent on foreign trade. Ploughshare, as we shall see, was one of these exceptional communities.

The first real attempt to develop Taiwan's polity and economy came under the late Qing governor Liu Mingchuan, who ruled from 1884 to 1891. An official with considerable experience in various posts on the mainland, he took over with the Qing court's decision to raise Taiwan from the status of a prefecture of Fujian to a province in its own right, and he proceeded apace with schemes of political and economic reform. With the help of foreign engineers, he laid plans for China's first railroad, to run the length of the island from Jilong to Dagou. He began the dredging of Jilong harbor so that Taiwan would gain its first deepwater port. He adopted a policy of entering the mountains and governing the aborigines, who continued to be at war with Chinese settlers, particularly camphor workers (Davidson 1903, p. 405). For this purpose he set up local militia and organized military expeditions into aborigine territory. And Liu set about political reform, issuing an ambitious series of regulations for village government designed to make local officials responsible to the Qing bureaucrats and to break the power of impromptu justice (Wang 1976, p. 66).

Few of Liu's plans amounted to much, however. The railroad, beginning at Jilong, never got past Xinzhu, and even that stretch was primitive and inefficient (Davidson 1903, p. 751). The dredging of Jilong harbor never got anywhere, and the military expeditions to pacify the aborigines often had the opposite effect, finally ending inconclusively. There is little record of the impact of Liu's political reforms, but it was not long before he was dismissed from his post (supposedly because of factional opposition at court) in 1891, and the Japanese takeover in 1895 brought about a much more thoroughgoing political control than Liu had ever envisioned. Liu Mingchuan tried to turn Taiwan into a political and economic system in the 1880s, but was stifled in his efforts; almost all of his plans would be fulfilled under the Japanese.

The Northern Region

The process of permanent settlement in northern Taiwan was very different from that in the south. The south, settled earlier, was opened up to a large extent by the efforts of Zheng Chenggong's forces, but the north remained a backwater during Zheng's tenure as ruler. When large-scale permanent settlement came about in the eighteenth century, it was by means of the government's granting of patent, or *dazu*, rights to wealthy entrepreneurs, some of them from Amoy and others from South Taiwan. These patent holders were given rights as tax farmers on large tracts of land, and in turn they contracted with large gangs of laborers, usually recruited from Zhangzhou and Quanzhou prefectures, to clear the tropical rain forest that covered the land and convert it to cultivation of rice or other crops. Sometimes the clearing workers would then bring their families over to settle on the cleared land; sometimes other settlers would be recruited. These settlers, in turn, paid a small percentage of their crop to the patent holders, and were free to sublet their lands, usually at rental rates of 40 to 60 percent (Wickberg 1981, p. 213) to tenant farmers who actually cultivated the land. Three tiers of land rights developed: the patent holders, the landlords proper, and the tenant cultivators. On some land, and this seems to have been the case ordinarily with tea land,[1] there was no intermediate landlord, the smallholding peasant cultivating his own land and owing a small portion (usually 10-15 percent) of its crop to the *dazu* holder.

As agricultural society emerged in the eighteenth century, settlers from different parts of China tended to settle in different areas of the north. In the southwestern Taibei Basin, Yingge, Sanxia, Dingpu, Shitouxi-Ganyuan, Shanzijiao, Pengcuo and Xizhou were all settled by people from Anxi County of Quanzhou Prefecture. To the south, near Taoyuan, were Zhangzhou people, who also inhabited Banqiao and Zhonghe. Finally Shulin was an ethnic mixture, with Anxi, other Quanzhou, and Zhangzhou people all represented (Wang 1976, p. 72). There was some strife in this area, culminating when the great battle of 1856 over control of the port at Mengjia spread to the surrounding countryside and most of the Zhangzhou people who remained within Anxi areas were driven out.

The north of Taiwan has neither the rich soils nor the extensive plains of the south and center of the island; thus in the nineteenth century the economy of the north developed important sectors that were given over to the growing of cash crops and to some secondary industries associated with the agricultural products. Before the 1860s, the principal among these was camphor, produced by distillation from the wood of a large tree that grows along the lower slopes of Taiwan's

---

1. Wickberg (1981, p. 213) mentions that the three-tiered system, with the *xiaozu* landlord in between the patent holder and the cultivator, was most common on paddy land.

interior mountains. Camphor workers were, of all Chinese, the most likely to be involved in fighting with aborigines; the grisly raids and reprisals on both sides testify to the motivation of the settlers for an income from this product and to the determination of the aborigines not to concede an inch of territory without a fight (Davidson 1903, p. 405). The most important camphor center in North Taiwan was at Dakekan (later Daxi), which was reported to have over 20,000 camphor stills in 1870—Sanxia had about 150 (Wang 1976, p. 75).

Tea, on the other hand, was a relative late-comer to Taiwan's economy. Some had apparently been grown before the 1860s, but it was only when the British trader John Dodd introduced cuttings from Anxi in 1865 and 1866 that the tea industry became important. Once introduced, it grew rapidly. In 1866, Taiwan exported 82 metric tons of processed tea leaves; by 1888 that total had grown to over 8,000 metric tons (Ho 1978, p. 21). Tea was grown in the hilly areas all over northern Taiwan from this time on—Sanxia is frequently mentioned in old sources as one of the more prominent tea districts (Davidson 1903, p. 398). It was grown primarily by small holders with about a hectare of gardens each, employing mostly family labor, and by a few larger farmers with six or eight hectares, which required large numbers of laborers, mostly unmarried women, to do the picking. The tea was allowed to ferment somewhat, giving it the characteristic flavor of Oolong, and dried in local processing plants, then shipped to the merchant houses, both Chinese and foreign, of Dadaocheng (present-day Yanping district in Taibei). There it was further cleaned, dried, and boxed for shipment, usually transshipment through Amoy and on to the American and, to a lesser extent, European markets. Formosa Oolong, as it was called, was considered a superior grade of tea to what was produced in China, and was thus intended for a high-priced market in America (Davidson 1903, p. 372).

By the 1880s, northern Taiwan, not so well-endowed for rice agriculture as other parts of the island, had developed a considerable cash-cropping sector, dependent on foreign trade for its prosperity. Davidson (ibid., pp. 375-76) describes well the rising and falling fortunes of local growers and processors as they reacted to the ups and downs of the speculators in the Dadaocheng market. This dependency did not link the tea districts of North Taiwan into an island-level economy; rather it integrated them into the world economy, with apparently very little trade taking place with the center and south of Taiwan. North Taiwan had at this time become underdeveloped in a sense: it exported primary products to a world market over which it had very little control (Chirot 1977, pp. 34-36).

Sanxia in North Taiwan

The economic hinterland of Sanxia, which in the nineteenth century seems to have included, for some purposes at least, nearly all the Anxi areas in the southwestern Taibei Basin, is divided ecologically into two zones. In the flood plains of the Dakekan and Sanxia rivers, and in a few foothill plateaus, the land is flat and rice can be grown. In these areas, such as Ganyuan-Shitouxi, Longenpu-Liucuopu-Maizi-yuan, and the lower part of Hengxi, it appears that rice growing was the major occupation of most of the inhabitants in the nineteenth century (Ahern 1973, pp. 11-13; Harrell 1981c). Along the mountain slopes and in the upper reaches of the river valleys, however, the terrain is unsuitable for rice cultivation and must be put either to cash crops, such as tea, or used for various kinds of forestry, such as distilling camphor or manufacturing charcoal. It is the character of this second ecological zone that gave Sanxia its special place in the economy of nineteenth-century northern Taiwan.

The first zone was opened earlier. Most of the plain between Sanxia and the Dakekan River was under rice cultivation before the middle of the eighteenth century, and it is recorded that Sanxia itself was already a considerable town in 1786 (Wang 1976, p. 50). Even the flatter areas to the south of the town were brought under cultivation in the eighteenth century: Jiaoxi in mid-Qianlong (1760s); Bazhang and Zhongpu in 1756. Areas at higher elevations, though penetrated by Chinese in the 1700s, were not fully opened up until the late Jiaqing and early Daoguang periods—the 1810s and 1820s. Most of the Chinese in the area were still rice farmers, though a few appear to have supplemented their income by working nearby forests for camphor or rattan. In the 1820s, indigo plantations were established on the hills near Chengfu by a wealthy merchant from Mengjia who imported workers from Fujian. A dyeing industry then grew up in Sanxia town, persisting until the twentieth century. Most of the dyed cloth was exported to Fujian (Wang 1976, p. 74). With this one exception, the hills remained aborigine country. Chinese guarded against attacks but rarely ventured far into the mountains (Ahern 1973, pp. 12-13).

The transport system of Sanxia shows a similar temporal development. Roads from three to ten feet wide connected Sanxia with Yingge, and thence Taoyuan; with Ganyuan and thence Shulin; with Hengxi; and with Dakekan by way of Zhongzhuang by the end of the Qianlong period (1796). But roads leading to Chengfu, Dapu, and other points in the hills were not built until the early nineteenth century. It was in 1840 that the road from Hengxi through Chengfu and Ankeng connected Sanxia with Xindian on the other side of the mountains (Wang 1976, pp. 70-71).

The development of the mountain areas of Sanxia did not really come until the introduction of tea in the 1860s, and then it came very quickly. Hengxi and Chengfu in particular, and the mountains surrounding the plateau of Ploughshare and Shisantian as well as the districts around Mayuan and Tudigongkeng, seem to have received large influxes of tea planters in the last half of the nineteenth century.

By the 1880s, Sanxia was anything but a self-sufficient economic system. Its forests produced some camphor and much charcoal, as well as wood for a furniture industry that grew up in Sanxia town. Cash crops, first indigo and then tea, were grown for eventual export, and tied a considerable portion of Sanxia's population into the international economy. And when, in the late nineteenth century, the Lim family of Banqiao, the wealthiest family in the southern Taibei Basin, bought great tracts of land in Ganyuan-Shitouxi and parts of Hengxi, it meant that much of the rice produced by Sanxia's fertile plains was also exported from the area. The town itself boasted a wide range of commercial establishments, many of them dealing in the products of the nearby countryside, and the population of the area is estimated by Wang to have been about 2,000 households, or perhaps 10,000 people, in 1895 (Wang 1976, p. 64). Probably about 40-50 percent of these households grew tea.[2]

Ploughshare

The relationship between ecology and the social and economic position of Ploughshare is a paradoxical one. With its neighbor Shisantian, Ploughshare is situated on one of those plateaus that are extensions of the lowland, rice-growing zone of the Sanxia system. But its economy, and thus its place in the system, are controlled, unlike those of Shisantian, by the characteristics of the upland zone. This seems to have come about in the following way.

The first mention of Ploughshare in any historical source comes in the 1760s, when a Chinese family settled there and cultivated crops on the nearby mountainsides, probably those to the north of Blacksmith Gulch. Formal *dazu* rights to Ploughshare and Shisantian were given by the aboriginal patent holders to a Chinese in 1779, but the land does not appear to have been cleared at that time (John Shepherd, personal communication). Around 1800, the area was divided into three "camps" of lowland aborigines who began to clear the land in about 1816. By the 1820s, most of the land was cleared, and the *xiaozu* (landlord) rights were under the control of three separate landlord families living

2. In a 1900 survey of all Haishan, one-third of farming households grew tea. The proportion must have been much higher in Sanxia than in Yingge or Shulin (Wang 1976, p. 97).

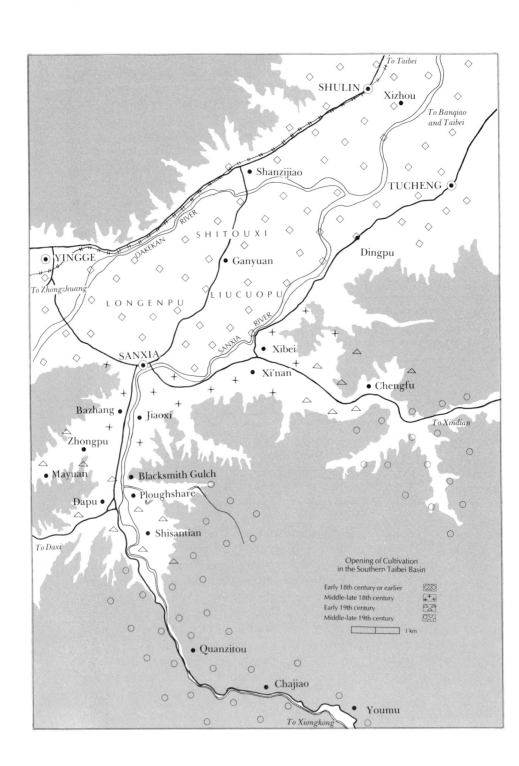

SHULIN

Xizhou

To Taibei

To Banqiao
and Taibei

TUCHENG

Shanzijiao

SHITOUXI

Dingpu

DAKEKAN RIVER

YINGGE

Ganyuan

To Zhongzhuang

LONGENPU

LIUCUOPU

SANXIA RIVER

SANXIA

Xibei

Xi'nan

Chengfu

To Xindian

Bazhang

Jiaoxi

Zhongpu

Mayuan

Blacksmith Gulch

Ploughshare

Dapu

Shisantian

To Daxi

Opening of Cultivation
in the Southern Taibei Basin

Early 18th century or earlier
Middle-late 18th century
Early 19th century
Middle-late 19th century

1 km

Quanzitou

Chajiao

Youmu

To Xiongkong

in Sanxia town (ibid.) and of an Ong lineage—whose first ancestor moved to Shisantian during this period—that held about one-fourth of all the rice land in the area. There seem to have also been people in what is now Ploughshare, but if so, none of their descendants survives in the village today.

The first families whose descendants remain in Ploughshare came in the 1840s and 1850s, at a time when the landlord rights to the entire plateau had long been parceled out among the Sanxia landlords and the Ong lineage. The first ancestor of a villager of whom I have records was the great-grandfather of Ong Cai-lai—he settled in Ploughshare around 1840 and grew rice. He probably owned his land—we know that he was a member of the association for the worship of the deity Sieng-ong Kong, which owned the land from the upper part of Ploughshare to the lower stretch of Shisantian after 1847. His family did not, however, continue as owner-farmers. The original settler had no sons of his own and bought a boy from a roving peddler. The boy did not turn out well, and within a few years of his majority had sold or mortgaged all his land to pay for opium; as a result, his descendants were not lowland farmers, but were reduced to manufacturing charcoal in the mountains, an occupation more typical of Ploughshare families in the nineteenth century.

Ong Cin's grandfather was another very early settler. He came to Ploughshare from Anxi sometime around 1850, and built the mud-brick compound that still stands beside the Dapu suspension bridge. He had seven sons, the fifth and sixth of whom managed to acquire, in the late nineteenth century, two parcels of rice land—one in nearby Jiaoxi and the other in Dakekan. They became the only Ploughshare residents to own land at the time of the Japanese cadastral survey in 1905, and remained the wealthiest family in the village until Ong Hieng made money in the tea-processing business in the 1930s. One of the original settler's daughters took in as an uxorilocal husband a man from Anxi who came to Taiwan in the 1880s. He was surnamed Ti:, and became a tenant on some of the rice land owned by the Sieng-ong association. His son, Old Ti:, was the oldest man in Ploughshare in the early 1970s, dying in 1977 at eighty-one. He remained a rice farmer until his retirement in the 1960s.

At least one other family with descendants remaining in the village today were lowland farmers; there also must have been other families, now lost to the village, who managed to acquire such rights, since there were nine heads of households listed as rice or mixed rice and dry-crop lowland farmers in the Japanese household survey of 1905. But the first large influx of population to Ploughshare came in the 1870s and 1880s, at the time when the tea trade was expanding, and most of the families who settled in the village were tea growers or charcoal burners. Tea and charcoal were, of course, not grown in or around Ploughshare itself, but on the mountains behind Shisantian and upstream toward Baiji. But the settlers could not live in the mountains, especially the high peaks behind Shisantian. This was a period of increased military confrontation between Chinese and aborigines, due principally to expansion of cultivation on the mountainsides and later on to Liu Mingchuan's aborigine policy. Even after the Japanese takeover, at least one villager was killed in the mountains while picking tea.

So the newly settled mountain farmers and workers came to live on Ploughshare Point. Of the ancestors of today's village families who immigrated from the late 1850s to the 1880s, eight were tea growers, three charcoal makers or casual laborers, one a tenant rice farmer, and one opened up a butcher shop in a house near the lower end of Ploughshare.

Descendants of these 16 households constitute 58 of the 107 families in Ploughshare in 1978.[3] But these were certainly not the only people living in Ploughshare in the latter decades of the nineteenth century. In addition to what may have been a rapid turnover of population, especially among those families who had no permanent rights to rice or tea land, the Japanese invasion induced emigration from the area. About 200,000 Chinese are reported to have left Taiwan at the time of the invasion (Davidson 1903, p. 561), and resistance to the occupying armies in the Sanxia area meant retribution. Ploughshare was apparently one of the centers; it was burnt to the ground by the occupying forces. Ong Tho's mother, eighty-three years old in 1973, remembered the time well—she was about five, and fled with her mother to the foothills back of Shisantian. There they remained for a few days (lucky it was warm weather, she says, as there was no shelter available), until it looked as if there would be no more trouble; then they returned to the village.

Not everyone who fled at that time returned. One Ploughshare family's ancestors altogether left the village to settle elsewhere, but returned a few years later. Others never came back, but were replaced by new immigrant families in the first few years of Japanese rule.

It can be surmised from this brief account of its early social and economic context that Ploughshare has never been anything like what is often described as a typical peasant village. Scott, for example, talks

---

3. By contrast, in Xi'nan, a neighboring group of lineage-based, rice-growing communities, 130 of 171 households resident in 1970 were descendants of settlers who came before 1800 (Ahern 1973, p. 20).

about peasant villages as producing primarily for subsistence, paying rent to landlords or taxes to government, but otherwise remaining clear of economic interaction with outside forces (1976). Popkin, doubting the harmony and benevolence of the traditional peasant community, nevertheless assumes a transition from production for subsistence to production for the market as the important transformation of the village community during modernization (1979). Now we have known for a long time that Chinese villages have fit this model only imperfectly, and then only at certain periods of closure, at least since the commercialization of rural society in the late Ming and early Qing, and probably long before that (Skinner 1971; Elvin 1973, pp. 166-67). Even in the eighteenth century, approximately 35 percent of the agricultural production of China entered into local or long distance trade, some of it through rent or taxes, but a sizable proportion through direct marketing by the peasant producers themselves (Perkins 1969, pp. 114-15). But Ploughshare, from the beginning, has not simply been connected to the market—the village in a very real sense has been the creature of a market economy. Like certain other areas of China, notably in the lower Yangzi macroregion (ibid., p. 145), northern Taiwan had important cash-crop agriculture all through the late Qing period. And Sanxia, whose hinterland is located partially in the upland agricultural zone, in which only cash crops are profitable, grew up as a trading and manufacturing center for products of this cash-crop agriculture. Ploughshare, in turn, was settled by people intent on making their living from such market-oriented pursuits as tea growing and charcoal manufacture. On a spectrum of Chinese villages, from those oriented to subsistence to those oriented to the market, Ploughshare belongs at the latter end: at least three quarters of its production has been oriented to the market from the beginning. In this it contrasts with nearby communities, such as those located on the Dakekan-Sanxia river flood plain, including Shitouxi (Harrell 1981c), and certain others located along the edges of the mountains, including Hengxi (Ahern 1973, 1976) or even its own southern neighbor, Shisantian.

The implications of Ploughshare's location and early dependence on the market are two. First, its history during the later periods, particularly during Japanese rule but also during Taiwan's postwar industrialization, has been different from that of farming communities. More people from Ploughshare participated in wage labor than was typical of most rice-growing communities. Second, Ploughshare's own social organization, throughout its entire history, has been influenced in certain important ways by its nature as a village producing first cash crops, then wage labor, for the larger economic systems of which it is a part. Its population has been more mobile, less tied to the land, and organized in different ways than the population of even nearby rice-farming communities. These differences are treated fully in the later chapters of this study.

THE JAPANESE COLONIAL PERIOD

Taiwan

Taiwan was a spoil of the Sino-Japanese War of 1895, ceded to Japan in the Treaty of Shimonoseki. Upon hearing the news of the cession, some Taiwanese gentry and intellectuals proclaimed the Democratic Republic of Taiwan (Taiwan Minzu Guo). It was, however, short-lived and mostly on paper, as Japan moved promptly to occupy the island militarily. The Japanese met considerable resistance from militia units organized by local gentry in various parts of the island, but their superior firepower prevailed within a few months, and they set to the task of colonial development.

The object of Japanese colonial policy was to turn Taiwan into a supplier of agricultural products for the home islands and a market for certain Japanese manufactured goods. Whatever benefits the colonial regime brought to the people of Taiwan—and these were considerable in many areas—must be seen in light of this policy: every change in the economic system, every educational, public health, or construction policy or project, even every action of police control, were directed toward integrating Taiwan into the imperial system, and in turn strengthening the position of the Japanese Empire in the world system that it had entered so dramatically, becoming a major power between the overthrow of the Tokugawa Shogunate in 1868 and the victory over Russia in 1905.

Taiwan, then, was to supply agricultural commodities, primarily rice and sugar, to Japan. To do so efficiently, the colonial government had to ensure four things: (1) enough production to assure a marketable surplus; (2) local facilities for refining sugar; (3) a transport network that could get the products from the field to the port in the case of rice, or to the refinery and thence to the port, and from there to Japan, in the case of sugar; and (4) stable political order under which the production, marketing, and processing of these important commodities could go on in an orderly manner. Japanese agricultural policy was shaped by those four goals.

Japanese plans for production first divided the island into two rough economic zones; the north and central parts were to specialize in rice, while the south, with warmer winters, was to produce sugar. The economic arrangements in the two zones were somewhat different. Rice continued to be grown by small peasant farmers, and the only major reform in the land tenure system was the abolition of the patent or *dazu* rights, which in many cases had become nominal by the end of Qing rule anyway (Wickberg 1981, p. 216). Considerable attention, however, was paid to improving methods of cultivation. At the beginning of the Japanese period, some lands were still available to be cleared for rice cultivation, but they were soon used up, and any increase in production to feed the home islands had to come from increased yields. These the Japanese promoted by a program of rural credit and extension services, along with the introduction after 1920 of a series of high-yielding varieties of rice known as *penglai* that, like other, more recently developed "Green Revolution" varieties, is highly sensitive to increased inputs of water and particularly fertilizer. Chemical fertilizers were both imported from Japan and produced locally in Taiwan. By the 1930s, Taiwan was already producing 36 percent more rice per capita than it had in 1900, though less was being consumed locally, with 45-50 percent of the harvest being exported to Japan (Ho 1978, pp. 31, 68, 316, 357).

Sugar, unlike rice, has been a plantation crop in many parts of the world. Although most sugar-growing in Taiwan continued to be done by small farmers under the Japanese, many of these were tenants on the extensive land of the Japanese-owned sugar companies. Other company lands were worked with hired labor in a plantationlike manner. Japanese-owned refineries processed the sugar, 90 percent of which was then exported, the rest going for domestic consumption. Improved varieties of sugar cane and methods of cultivation were also introduced, but the effect was not so dramatic as with rice (Ho 1978, p. 31).

Transport was another important requisite for the extraction of an agricultural surplus from Taiwan, as well as for efficient political control. The Japanese wasted no time in establishing a modern transport network: Liu Mingchuan's experimental railroad was torn up, and a modern line put in, completed all the way from Jilong to Gaoxiong by 1908. Spur lines were also built, and in the 1920s and 1930s the main line was double-tracked. Country roads were made into modern, paved highways, facilitating both truck transport and, increasingly throughout the twenties, bus lines to most of the major market towns (see Wang 1976, p. 91, for examples from the Taibei Basin area).

A stable political situation was a final requisite for facilitating the production and extraction of an agricultural surplus. Pacification was accomplished within a few years of the original colonial occupation, and both a census and a cadastral survey were completed by 1905. In this same year, the Japanese also set up a permanent system of police registration, in which each household had to report to the police station any change in its composition, to facilitate local control over the island. Local government institutions were also maintained; Japanese regional officials appointed heads of administrative villages and townships, and also included some Taiwanese officers in the police. Many Taiwanese, perhaps disgusted with the well-known corruption and petty crime of the Nationalist era, look back on the Japanese period as a time when they never had to lock their doors. Whatever the truth, the administration was efficient, corruption practically nonexistent, and corporal punishment swiftly and liberally applied to petty wrong-doers. Taiwan was an extraordinarily peaceful colony.

Extraction of an agricultural surplus was only half of the Japanese colonial policy. The other half was creating a market for Japanese industrial goods and a limited industrial sector in Taiwan itself, which could produce some things locally more efficiently than they could be shipped in from the home islands. Imported Japanese goods were of two kinds, consumer goods, especially clothing and textiles, and producer goods intended for use in agriculture, such as fertilizer, transport equipment, and agricultural processing machinery. Agriculture itself was insignificantly mechanized during this period. Japan thus established a "triangular relationship" (Ho 1978, pp. 27-31), in which agricultural products of Taiwan were sold to Japan, industrial goods from Japan were sold to Taiwanese industrial and business sectors who sold them back to Taiwan's agricultural producers. It is important to realize that this relationship worked in favor of the Japanese. The value of the exports of agricultural products always exceeded that of the industrial imports, so that even though there was considerable capital formation in agriculture, and to a lesser extent in industry during the colonial period, there was a net drain of capital from Taiwan (ibid., pp. 29-32).

At the same time, if the Japanese can legitimately be described as extracting goods from Taiwan to their own advantage, they cannot be accused of keeping the island economically backward. Where it suited their purposes, they both fostered the development of a small, nontraditional industrial sector in Taiwan, and introduced extensive measures that, if aimed primarily at raising the productive capacity of the Taiwan economy, also meant improvements in the quality of life for most Taiwanese, at least until the beginning of the Pacific war. The industrial sector in Taiwan consisted primarily of food processing, and that mainly of sugar refining, though the processing of other traditional crops, such as tea, and of newer products such as fruits and vegetables, was also carried out in modernized establishments. The rest of Taiwan's modern industry involved the processing of local nonagricultural raw materials—the ceramic industry, already established at the end of the Qing, grew markedly, and a chemical industry producing mostly fertilizer emerged. In keeping with colonial policy, most such large-scale modern industry was Japanese-owned, often with large numbers of shares held by the great financial combines of Japan—the Zaibatsu (Ho 1978, pp. 70-90). In addition to industry, mining also became important to the Taiwanese economy. Taiwan's principal mineral resource is coal, which served both industries and railroads, and some gold was also mined on the northeast coast of the island.

It was also in the Japanese colonial interest to have a healthy and at least minimally literate population in Taiwan—even farmers can benefit from literacy, especially once modern agricultural methods are introduced, and although most of the higher managerial posts remained in Japanese hands, Taiwanese increasingly took part in management of industrial and government concerns at lower levels. Public health measures were begun early in the period of colonial rule; the Japanese ended not only smallpox but foot-binding, a severe health problem for nearly one half of the Chinese population. Six years of primary education in Japanese was gradually made available. Admission of Chinese to higher level schools was rarer but not nonexistent, and Taihoku Teikoku Daigaku—Taibei Imperial University, later to become National Taiwan University, graduated some Taiwanese, particularly in the field of Western-style medicine. By 1930, it was estimated that 27 percent of the Taiwanese population was literate in Japanese (Ho 1978, p. 322).

The effect of Japanese colonial policy up to the early 1930s was to make Taiwan into an integrated economic system, dependent for its livelihood on commercial agriculture (over 70 percent of Taiwan's rice crop was marketed by the thirties) and industrial imports, together with a small domestic industrial sector. This system was connected by an efficient modern transport network of roadways and railways. At the same time, Taiwan as a whole was brought into the world economy in a way that only certain small sections of the island had participated in previously. Its position, in many respects, was that of a typical peripheral region (Chirot 1977, pp. 34-36), an economy that depended on the export of primary products in exchange for industrial manufactures, at a loss. But because of the nature of Japanese colonial policy, many other typical features of an early twentieth-century peripheral society were weakened or even absent in Taiwan. The typical "radial" transport system, centering on ports of international trade, did not develop, probably because the narrow west coast plain of the island is best served by a trunk line, and towns and trading centers off this line were easily linked by roads. The Japanese themselves controlled both economy and government closely down to the local level, preventing the rise of a significant comprador or "broker capitalist" class

(Schneider and Schneider 1976, pp. 10-14) that would siphon so much of the economy's fruits into its own pockets. Labor intensive production of primary products, along with extreme population pressures on the land, may have prevented coerced labor or the formation of an agricultural proletariat. And finally, even though a Japanized elite did form, its identification with Japan was never particularly strong, and widespread schooling, even in the countryside, meant that this elite did not have a monopoly on literacy or the skills arising from it. As long as Taiwan remained in such a colonial relationship with Japan, it was bound to remain a peripheral society, but it had the physical and human capital that would enable it to grow rapidly, even with the continuation of a certain type of economic dependency, once the direct colonial yoke was shed.

With the expansion of Japan's imperial pretensions and war preparations in the early 1930s, colonial policy toward Taiwan changed somewhat. First, a wider effort at industrialization of the island was undertaken, although it was still in its beginning stages when it was halted by the more urgent requirements of the Pacific war. Second, during the war years, a last-ditch effort to Japanize the population took place—people were even urged to take Japanese names, speak Japanese exclusively, and change from Chinese to Japanese forms of religious worship. Neither of these policies, being short-lived, had much effect on the island, but the war years became difficult as both manpower for the Japanese army and increasing percentages of Taiwan's rice crop were exported. In addition, Allied bombing raids knocked out much of Taiwan's fledgling industrial plant. By the end of the war, all sectors of the economy were suffering, and living standards had declined dramatically since the mid-thirties, as they also had in Japan (Ho 1978, p. 103). But the capital plant and the human resources remained, giving Taiwan a considerable advantage in the postwar economy.

The North

The northern region, already commercialized because of its tea and camphor production in the late decades of Qing rule, continued along this road under Japanese colonial rule, and by the 1930s was still one of the most commercialized parts of the entire Taiwan economy. Taibei, including the formerly rival cities of Dadaocheng and Mengjia, had been made the provincial capital under Liu Mingchuan, and Jilong was one of Taiwan's more important ports. But it was under the Japanese that the north became the true core region of the island economy. Much of the Japanese population, engaged in government and large-scale trade, resided in Taibei and to this day the city has districts made up almost entirely of Japanese-style homes. Taibei had a university, as well as most of the government offices, and continued to be the major trading center of the island. Its population grew from an estimated 59,000 in 1900 to 287,000 in 1935 (Davidson 1903, p. 598; Ho 1978, p. 318).

Not only the metropolitan functions of Taibei itself, but also the agriculture in the north attest to the commercialization in this region during the Japanese period. Wickberg (1981, pp. 230-31) shows that in one probably typical rice-growing district that included part of Shulin town, several indicators of a commercialized economy were higher than the averages for Taiwan as a whole during this period. For example, over 50 percent of households were tenants, in contrast with 43 percent for Taiwan. Also, the wealthiest cultivators were tenants, because all the best and largest parcels of land were in the hands of absentee landlords holding the land as a source of cash income. Over 90 percent of rice land was under tenancy. In addition to the commercialization of rice, which is also a subsistence crop, we should remember that the commercial crops of the north in the Qing period, while they declined as a portion of Taiwan's agricultural output or its surplus, did not decline in absolute amounts during this time—there were as many tea cultivators in Haishan in the 1930s as there had been during the tea boom fifty years earlier.

Sanxia

At the beginning of the Japanese period, Sanxia was the largest market town in the Taibei Basin between Banqiao and Taoyuan—with 158 households and 715 people dependent on its industry and commerce for their livelihood, it was larger than either Yingge or Shulin (Wang 1976, p. 89). It served a hinterland with a population of around eight to ten thousand (exact figures are not available until the administrative changes of 1920) that, as mentioned before, was composed of rice and cash-crops cultivators, along with a few hired laborers in agriculture and primary processing of its products. Although Sanxia declined in relative importance when the railroad bypassed it in 1901, nearly all aspects of the economic activity of the town and its hinterland grew in the Japanese period, and significant new activities, particularly coal mining, were added during that time.

Rice cultivation in the lowland parts of Sanxia's hinterland appears to have increased during the Japanese period; in addition to milling, which was electrified beginning in the 1910s, the town continued to specialize in the manufacture of *mifen,* or rice noodles, which were sold all over northern Taiwan, including the large stores of Taibei City (Wang 1976, p. 115).

More important for our analysis are the industries connected to primary production in the hilly areas of Sanxia. Wood from the forests was made into fine furniture, which was sold in Taibei and Jilong. The dyeing industry, begun almost a century earlier, continued to flourish at the beginning of the Japanese period, and there were reportedly 500 camphor stills, located primarily in such deep-mountain areas as Chiajiao.

The tea industry, during the late Qing already a mainstay of Sanxia's economy, continued and expanded somewhat under the Japanese. New gardens were brought under cultivation in the remoter areas of the hills, especially along the upper Sanxia River valley from Quanzitou up to Youmu and Shuangxi, and the processing industry continued to flourish in the 1910s and 1920s. It is interesting, however, that much of the tea from Sanxia underwent its final processing not in Sanxia but in Shulin. Despite Shulin having very little tea land, over twenty tea-processing plants, most of them fairly small, opened in Shulin between 1910 and 1930. Sanxia itself had fewer processing plants. There were small, Chinese-owned and -operated ones at Tudigongkeng, Chengfu, Ankeng, Shanyuantanzi, Baiji, and Erjia; some of them were up to 100 hectares of land, worked by hired labor. But in addition to these smaller plants, two large factories were etablished with Japanese capital: one was located at Chajiao, the other at Zhulun. These, like the smaller plants, both had their own land worked by hired labor, and bought tea from small holders; although they, like most processors, made the traditional Formosa Oolong, they also specialized in the production of black tea, which requires a longer fermentation process. Most of the black tea was exported to Japan.

Tea thus continued to occupy a large percentage of Sanxia's population, particularly in the upland areas. A survey of 1936, for example, showed 1146 households engaged in the production of rice, while 1490 households grew tea. The total yearly production was about 600 metric tons, or around 8 to 10 percent of Taiwan's total tea production (Wang 1976, pp. 106-8, 111-14).

New industries that were important to the economy of Sanxia and surrounding communities were wine-making and mining. Wine-making was primarily a specialty of Shulin, where in the first decade of the twentieth century a pre-existing winery was modernized and taken over by a Japanese state monopoly, and became the largest winery in Taiwan, producing rice wines that were sold all over the island, and even exported to Japan (ibid., pp. 109-10). At the same time, there were at least two small wineries in Sanxia, both producing for more local markets.

Mining was more important. There are two coal fields in the southern

Taibei Basin area, one near Shanzijiao and the other, larger one, in the hills stretching from Mazutian through Hengxi to the upper Sanxia River valley, extending as far as Xiongkong. There had been mining at Mazutian as early as 1870, but mines really got underway in earnest with the outbreak of the First World War, which cut short needed fuel supplies for Taiwan and Japan. Between 1914 and the early twenties, at least eight large coal mines were established in the Sanxia area, at Wujia, Quanzitou (two mines), Chengfu, Chajiao, Wuliao, Baiji, and Xiongkong. Most of these employed a hundred workers or more; by the early 1930s, over a thousand men were employed in the mines. Most of the mines were Taiwanese-owned, and coal mine owners joined landlords and tea merchants in Sanxia's dominant local elite (Wang 1976, pp. 115-17). The mines were tied partly to Taiwan's export economy, and their fortunes fluctuated widely. At the time of the Great Depression, many miners were put out of work, and mining wages declined precipitously (Ho 1978, p. 336). When Japan introduced the general industrialization policy a few years later, however, the mines flourished as never before, and wages once again increased (ibid.).

All the economic activity of Sanxia was thus involved in some way with the market and with trade, and both the merchant population of the town and the transport network expanded greatly in the Japanese period. In 1900, Sanxia town had about 158 households engaged in commerce; by 1937, there were 329 stores, including establishments selling such diverse goods as clothing, shoes, grains and flour, meat, bean curd, liquor, tea, ice (a summertime treat with bean sauce), tatami mats, hardware, fuel, drugs and cosmetics, and lumber and bamboo. Small marketing centers also grew up in some of the larger settlements around the periphery of the Sanxia area—there were several stores each at Dapu, Xibei, and Chengfu by 1933 (Wang 1976, p. 91). Credit was also an important function of the town. The first credit cooperative was established in 1920, making it much easier to get loans than when one had to approach private moneylenders (ibid., pp. 120-21).

All the goods of Sanxia's commercial agriculture, mining, and industry of course had to be moved, and the Japanese period, here as elsewhere, witnessed an enormous growth of the transport system. Under the Qing, there was a flourishing system of river transport and goods originating as far away as Dakekan, as well as in the hinterland of Sanxia itself, could go all the way to Mengjia by river, where an estimated eighty junks plied the course at the beginning of this century. But modern transport gradually displaced the old river route. The north-south railway passed through Banqiao, Shulin, and Yingge on its way to Taoyuan in 1901, and it quickly became the preferred transport. Sanxia was bypassed, but it still was easier to move goods from Sanxia overland to Yingge, and thence northward by train, than to use the old river transport. The Sanxia-Yingge road was widened in 1905, and the following year a graded road was built into the upper river valley as far as Chajiao. In 1910, the first pushcart railway was installed between Sanxia and Yingge; by the twenties, similar lines ran to Hengxi and Chengfu, and up the Sanxia River valley through Ploughshare and Quanzitou as far as Xiongkong, the site of the most distant coal mine. In 1920, the Sanxia-Yingge stretch was double-tracked (Wang 1976, pp. 93-94).

Nor were roads neglected. The major ones were paved in the early thirties and the bridges strengthened, so that bus service connected Sanxia and Banqiao in 1929, and extended to Taibei in 1932. A road built in the 1930s also connected Jiaoxi, Dapu, and Quanzitou, and another ran from Jiaoxi through Blacksmith Gulch to Baiji (ibid.).

The development of the Japanese colonial economy and society thus markedly transformed the economic system of Sanxia. Its connection with the larger system of northern Taiwan, built on the export of primary products or processed agricultural goods, became more central to its economy and expanded greatly. More of Sanxia's products were being exported, and modern transport facilitated this, though it meant a decline in Sanxia's importance in comparison to Yingge and Shulin, both situated on the railroad. The internal structure of the Sanxia system, however, was transformed. Previously there had been a lowland and a highland zone, one growing rice primarily for subsistence, and the other growing cash crops. While the two zones were previously linked in a dependency relationship, the asymmetry and dependence increased with the colonial system of economic transportation. The division between zones was transformed into one of core and periphery: the lowland core, containing the good roads, the rich land, and the growing towns, became wealthier and more dominant over the highland periphery, whose cash crop producers and, increasingly, mining and transport laborers began to constitute a lower, exploited class merely by virtue of residing in the periphery. There, transport was still primarily by walking, houses were built mostly of mud, and education was less readily available than in the market centers. There was also, naturally, a greater class differentiation in the core area, where wealthy landlords and mine owners often lived alongside impoverished small tenants and agricultural laborers. In the periphery, on the other hand, as we shall see later, everyone was poor, though poverty in the Japanese period, with somewhat better health measures and rural electrification, and the end of banditry and feuding, may well have been a step upward from the conditions of the late Qing.

Ploughshare

The disruption of the population of Ploughshare at the time of its resistance to Japanese occupation was apparently rather brief. As mentioned, several families moved out, and others moved in to replace them in the next few years. In addition, eight men from Ploughshare who were active in the resistance were taken to Sanxia by the Japanese and beheaded. Their bones were buried in a collective grave at the upper end of the village, and this grave soon became a shrine. Villagers to this day refer to it as Pueq-lang Kong, or the venerable eight men, and still make offerings there in the seventh lunar month, when ghosts and other malevolent spirits are thought to be about, or when they have a special reason to seek the favor of these powerful if somewhat illegitimate spirits (Harrell 1974b). And in 1896, the Japanese set up a police station in the village as part of their meticulous program of local control. It remained there until it was moved to Dapu in the general governmental reorganization of 1920.

From colonial household registers and informants' accounts, we can piece together a fairly complete picture of Ploughshare in 1910, in the beginning decades of the colonial period.

Ploughshare in 1910 had fifty-four families, living on twenty-eight different house sites. Of the fifty-four families, only twenty-two are identifiable as having descendants living in the village today. There were the sixteen permanently resident families who came before 1895, of whom two had divided by 1910, and four more families had moved in and were destined to make Ploughshare their permanent residence. Of the other thirty-one families living in Ploughshare in 1910, we know very little. Ten were still there at the beginning of the Second World War, but have left in the meantime. Of the remaining twenty-one, two were single-member households, which ceased to exist when they died in 1922 and 1927, while all the rest moved out sometime between 1910 and 1935. At least eighteen of them probably rented housing, for we know that they were living on the same plots of land as more permanent residents.

A full account of what I know about the economic livelihood of villagers at this time is given in chapter two; suffice it to mention here that there were a few tenant rice farmers and lowland dry farmers, but that most of the village families either grew tea, made charcoal, or engaged in miscellaneous wage-labor. They were poor, all of them except the one family of Ong Cin, who owned rice land, and most of their families were small. Because they were poor and often were not attached to the land, it is not surprising that many of them resided in the village only briefly.

Throughout the period of Japanese rule, most Ploughshare people

A pushcart railway at the entrance to a coal mine

Picking tea, the nineteenth-century occupation of many Ploughshare villagers

remained poor, but the economic and social changes that transformed Taiwan and the Sanxia system as a whole also had their effect on the village. In particular, the new occupations, which came with the further commercialization and beginning industrialization of the economy, presented opportunities for Ploughshare villagers to take steady, reasonably well paying if arduous jobs. Foremost among these was coal mining: all but three of the major mines established in the Sanxia coal field in the 1920s and 1930s were within reasonable walking distance of Ploughshare, and many village men took jobs there. Most of the older and middle-aged men living in Ploughshare today served some time in the coal mines, and during the Japanese period and the early postwar years, Ploughshare was known to outsiders as a coal miners' village. In addition, a few villagers found employment in more distant mines, particularly in Taiwan's only gold mine, at Jinguashi on the northeast coast of the island. At the same time, many villagers became cart pushers on the Xiongkong or Chajiao to Yingge route; this work is described more fully in chapter two. Many people also continued in their old pursuits of growing tea, now occasionally supplemented by oranges or, in a few cases, rice.

Changes in living standards during this period were slight but significant. Suspension bridges for the first time connected Ploughshare with Blacksmith Gulch and Dapu, replacing the bamboo rafts that had previously acted as ferries, and there was also the pushcart railway bridge on the site of the current concrete road bridge. In the 1930s, the village got electric lights; people seem to have taken readily to this innovation. And education touched at least some families in the village. Some village men went to primary school and became literate in Japanese, but by no means all of them—a significant number of men over forty-five in 1973 were illiterate. And education for girls, though it existed in Taiwan, extended to only one woman who married into Ploughshare in the Japanese period—the daughter-in-law of the landlord Ong Cin. One other older woman, the mother of the storekeeping Iap brothers, was literate at the time of my first visit but she had simply taught herself. I have no information on the schooling of village daughters who later married out, but I strongly suspect their situation was like that of Lou Lan, who married within the village. She once told me with a smile that *"Gwa pua: ci m bat"*—"I don't know half a character."

During the Japanese period, the inhabitants of the village continued to change rather rapidly. In addition to the twenty-two families who resided in the village in 1910, but were gone by 1935, there were sixteen families who moved in during that time. Of these sixteen, four apparently found little opportunity to make a living in or near Ploughshare, for they moved out again sometime before 1935. Of the twelve who were still there at the beginning of Japan's military adventures, nine are not identifiable as having descendants in the village today: there at the beginning of the war, they have left in the meantime. Finally, we have three families who moved in and whose descendants remain. Two originally came as tenant farmers and the other family, which gained no access to land, as coal miners and cart pushers. The net outmigration of Ploughshare families between 1911 and 1935 (twenty-one families left or died out and sixteen moved in, of which four left again) was partially balanced by the division of families that remained. Five divisions created nine new households in the village between 1910 and 1935. It is remarkable, however, how few family divisions took place in this period. Families grew in size; where there were fifty-four families averaging 5.39 members in 1910, there were only fifty families, but averaging 8.66 members, in 1935; the village had a total population of 433 people.

Growth seems to have accompanied a relative prosperity in the twenties and early thirties, for although only two families were well off, others seem to have had steady employment. The wealthiest families were those of landlord Ong Cin and tea processor Ong Hieng. Hieng, who was appointed village head by the Japanese in the mid-1920s, became so wealthy that he built a house out of fired brick, the first in the village to be constructed out of anything but adobe or bamboo and thatch. Most people were of course much poorer. Of the twenty-seven other families whose occupations are known, eight were tenant farmers, four were tea growers, one both tenant farmers and laborers, thirteen were laborers in the mines or on the pushcart railway, and one was a storekeeper.

In the last ten years of Japanese rule, the demographic pattern of the village changed somewhat. Between 1935 and 1945 no fewer than seven families underwent division, nine moved out, and four more moved in.

During the final years of the war, villagers also became directly involved in the hostilities. Taiwanese men, including at least four from Ploughshare, were drafted to serve abroad in the Japanese armed forces. Two villagers never returned, and the two who did still occasionally talk about New Britain and other theaters of war. American air attacks caused a certain amount of evacuation of the towns and cities, which was the occasion of the settlement of the four immigrant families mentioned. Finally, for a short period American prisoners of war, presumably captured in the Philippines, were housed somewhere in the mountains to the south of Ploughshare. They were employed as forced labor on the pushcart railway, and the villagers, some of them quite proud to be able to tell me that they used to slip cigarettes to these unfortunates, nevertheless report that with the bad food and general debilitation of prison camp life, it took five or six Americans to move a cart that is generally pushed by two healthy Taiwanese.

It is clear to me that, insofar as the Sanxia system developed a definite core-periphery pattern with the growth and increased commercialization of the Japanese period, Ploughshare belonged to the periphery. Its lack of rice land pushed its inhabitants into cash crops and wage labor, both occupations associated with dependence on market forces out of one's control. It is perfectly true that, in some situations, agriculturalists may switch to cash crops not out of desperation, but as a way of increasing earnings, as a response to a positive opportunity. And I have no proof that tea was a worse crop than rice in the early twentieth century. But tenant rice farmers were more prestigious than either laborers or tea growers (Wolf and Huang 1980, pp. 54-55), and both mining and tea were subject to the vicissitudes of changing markets in ways that rice, both a staple locally and a necessary import for Japan, was not. In addition, Ploughshare was peripheral because it was geographically somewhat distant from the centers of local power. The bus lines and modern roads reached this area rather late, and transportation to Sanxia and on to major urban centers was thus quite inconvenient. Finally, Ploughshare's population was nearly uniformly poor and had little access to the benefits of colonial development, with the exception of improved health and a very marginal amount of primary education. Ploughshare in the Qing had belonged merely to an upland zone, now it belonged to a dependent periphery. The story of the 1960s and 1970s is the story of how Ploughshare joined the ever-expanding core of Taiwan's modern economic system.

POSTWAR INDUSTRIALIZING TAIWAN

Two themes stand out in the history of Taiwan since 1945, unusually rapid economic growth and dictatorial one-party rule. There seems to be a definite connection between the two. The state was able to enforce, among other things, certain kinds of economic policies that may have been unpopular but later led to rapid and sustained growth.

In 1945, with the defeat of the Japanese Empire, Taiwan reverted to Chinese rule and was handed over to the occupying forces of the Guomindang, or Nationalist party. Its economy was in shambles, after being milked dry by the war effort and bombed by American planes; industrial output in 1947 is estimated to have been less than half that of 1937 (Kuznets 1979, p. 33). During the immediate postwar years, the Guomindang did very little to improve the situation since it was occupied with its struggle against the Communist party for control of the Chinese mainland (Ho 1978, p. 103). Certain Guomindang officials, however, followed the pattern set in their takeover of formerly Japanese-occupied areas on the mainland (Pepper 1978), and operated more in their own interest than in that of the island or its population. The result was a revolt of Taiwanese in February 1947, after which an estimated 20,000 rebels were killed (Amsden 1979, p. 350). The political situation then stabilized, but there was little economic growth or reconstruction until after 1949. In that year, the main forces of the Guomindang were driven from the Chinese mainland by the victorious Communist armies, and retreated en masse to Taiwan, setting up Taibei as the temporary capital of the Republic of China. With the Guomindang exodus came an estimated one and a half million mainland Chinese, slightly less than half of them army officers and soldiers. At the same time came the realization that the Guomindang was stuck in Taiwan, at least for a while. If they never gave up their cherished aim of reconquest of the mainland (somewhat whimsically to outsiders, it remains part of sacrosanct official dogma to this day), they realized that their survival was now dependent on the development of a secure base in Taiwan. When, with the outbreak of the Korean War in 1950, the United States Seventh Fleet occupied the Taiwan Straits and prevented a Chinese Communist naval expedition against the island, the military security was at least there, and the Guomindang turned to the tasks of political control and economic construction.

Political control is the simpler topic for us to explain. Essentially, the Guomindang maintained on Taiwan the same political system that they had developed in their final years of rule on the mainland. Although the Guomindang constitution for the Republic of China includes rules for democratic elections and guarantees of civil liberties, these are all suspended indefinitely during the period of the bandit (Communist) emergency. Thus all posts of substantial power are held by party appointees, and such elections as exist are confined to local officials (county and township executives, and provincial assembly representatives). Parties other than the Guomindang are banned, although candidates are allowed to run as independents. Neither political candidates nor the press, however, are allowed to criticize the major dogmas of Guomindang rule—the saintliness of the ruling Jiang family and the eventual return to the mainland. As a result, elections never involve conflicts over issues, but are "patronage" contests in which the candidate who has given or can promise the most political favors (including cash for votes) to constituents will win the elections. This is true of both Guomindang and opposition (independent) candidates.

Politics consist of a hierarchy of central and provincial government and party officials giving orders to executives at lower levels. The power of the center is supported by its emergency regulations, which make such acts as assembly for peaceful purposes potentially seditious, and by an effective secret police system, backed up by military trials and extensive political prisons that effectively prevent any articulate political opposition. But it is important to note, at the same time, that this close police control of intellectual and political opposition has very little effect on the life of the average person, who has probably only heard one version of Chinese history and politics—the official Guomindang version taught in the schools and reiterated in the newspapers— and for whom political participation means being receptive to the maneuvering for votes that goes on at election time.

Another, and for our purposes, more salient result of such tight political control by the government is its ability to set economic policy and, in fact, to control economic development of the country. Taiwan's is not a planned economy in the sense that such exist in the socialist countries today, but government regulations and manipulations set the direction in which a primarily, though not entirely, privately owned capitalist economy can go. So the history of economic growth is at least partly a history of certain measures taken by the government to stimulate such growth. Whether we believe that the state's role has lain primarily in direct, state-capitalist involvement in the economy (Amsden 1979), or in allowing economic liberalization after a short period of controls (Ho 1978), the role of the state remains strong in all analyses.

Like growth during the Japanese colonial period, growth in the 1950s in Taiwan was dependent on increases in agricultural production and on extraction of enough surpluses from the agricultural sector to help fuel a fledgling industrial sector that was still absorbing, rather than creating capital. The initial move in this direction was the land to the tiller program of 1949-53. In this program, both rents and de facto local political power were taken away from noncultivating landlords. Peasants were sold land for cultivation at a low price and on easy mortgage terms (ibid., pp. 159-74), and the rural elite, a potential rival of the Guomindang for power, was eliminated as a serious threat. Thus a measure with important economic effects was carried out for political reasons. On the mainland of China, where a land reform law had been on the books since 1933, but where the support of the rural elite was vital to the Guomindang, no significant amount of land was ever redistributed to peasant families.

With the landlords out of the way, the government then moved in to extract the surplus from agriculture itself by three methods, an increased tax on agricultural production, compulsory purchases of rice at below market price, and a government monopoly on chemical fertilizer, which could only be obtained by bartering rice at a rate unfavorable to the cultivator (Ho 1978, pp. 180-81; Wang and Apthorpe 1974, p. 75).

Part of this extracted agricultural surplus went to feed the million or so government employees and dependents, including soldiers and their families, and part to government efforts to stabilize prices on the open market. But part of it also went to subsidize industrialization, which in this period no longer formed part of a triangular colonial relationship; instead, the government aimed to stimulate industrial development by a policy of primary import substitution (Ho 1978, p. 187; Amsden 1979, p. 364). Imports of consumer goods were severely restricted, although raw materials and capital goods could be imported much more easily. The result was that by 1956, despite substantial increases in industrial production, private consumption had risen hardly at all; most of the increased production went into savings (Ho 1978, pp. 226-29).

Import substitution in the 1950s promoted domestic savings, but it did not have much effect on the total balance of payments, since imports of raw materials and capital goods were still high, and exports at this time were confined primarily to agricultural and processed agricultural goods. Taiwan's growth would then have had to be financed by inflation, had it not been for economic aid from the United States. This aid, given for essentially political purposes (containment of the Communist Bloc), accounted for over 35 percent of Taiwan's gross domestic capital formation every year from 1952 to 1962 (Ranis 1979, p. 250). At the same time, private foreign investment never accounted for more than 4 percent of capital formation in this period (ibid.). Thus Taiwan's relationship with the world system in the 1950s was an unusual one: a core power, the United States, saw it in its political interest to subsidize the development of a peripheral country, Taiwan, and this political interest was more important than any direct economic desire to extract capital from Taiwan's economy at that time. And since Taiwan's government could control imports and to an extent industrial production, Taiwan was able, during this period of fledgling industrialization and heavy American aid, to build up its industrial sector, primarily in manufacturing, to a level where growth could become self-sustaining in the mid-1960s.

In the late 1950s, however, the domestic picture began to change. Easy import substitution, as Ho puts it, was over, and Taiwan's economy had to shift to a policy of export promotion, which was accomplished by the early sixties. In promoting exports, Taiwan's comparative advantage lay in labor-intensive goods such as textiles and, later on, electronics. With rather stagnant income levels from agriculture and rising employment opportunities in industry, this meant the beginning of a fundamental restructuring of Taiwan's economy. First, there was a rapid decline in the percentage of the labor force employed in agriculture, from 60 percent in 1953 to 30 percent in 1978 (Galenson 1979, pp. 387-88). By the early 1970s, only in a few areas did farm families depend entirely on agriculture for their income; almost everyone had one or more children working in factories. This entailed substantial migration from rural to urban areas during this time: Taiwan's five largest cities had 18 percent of its population in 1951 and 27 percent in 1972. Also, many rural communities developed permanent ties to certain sectors of the industrial economy, and networks of remittances from urban laborers to their rural families were set up (Gallin and Gallin 1974). Thus urbanization did not involve dual development in which the countryside is cut off from the benefits of rising urban employment and wages. In addition, the small size and efficient rural transport system of Taiwan, combined with relatively low land prices in rural areas, have meant that much of Taiwan's industry has been located outside the urban centers, and rural communities, formerly agricultural, have been able to shift partly to industrial employment without losing population (Ho 1979). Thus the economic changes associated with the shift from agriculture to industry as the largest economic sector have not been accompanied by social changes of as great a magnitude, though they have been considerable. Rural communities still exist and function as communities in today's industrialized Taiwan.

Industrialization in Taiwan has thus had three important characteristics: it has been disproportionately rural (Ranis 1979, p. 222); it has been labor-intensive; and it has been increasingly oriented to the export of manufactured goods. The impact on the lives of the people has been both positive and negative. The rural character of industrialization has probably had an almost wholly positive effect. Large cities have grown much more slowly than their counterparts in Korea or Indonesia, for example, and the formation of extensive slums and other urban problems have been less severe in Taiwan. Also, as mentioned, most rural communities have survived relatively intact. Finally, it has been suggested that, since rural industries are typically more labor-intensive than urban ones, the dispersal of Taiwan's industry contributes to its labor-intensive character (ibid., p. 232). The effects have been, at least since about 1972 or 1973, to raise wages in comparison to prices. Even though savings continue to increase as a proportion of income, wages are still rising, because there is, at least in the more industrialized areas, a real labor shortage. This may also contribute to what are described as better working conditions than, for example, in South Korea (Little 1979, p. 469). The need for labor has also pushed up wages for women and moved more of them into the labor force; about 40 percent of females over fifteen years of age were employed in 1978 (Galenson 1979, p. 368), and a subculture of young, female factory workers has developed in recent years (Kung 1981). If it is true that income distribution in Taiwan is more equitable than in most countries (there is a controversy over whether it is becoming more so or not, but it is probably not becoming less so—see Kuznets 1979, pp. 103-6), this is at least partly attributable to the labor-intensive nature of the export-oriented industry and the consequent rise in wages. In any case, the rising living standards that the people of rural places like Ploughshare have enjoyed have been possible because of the nature of the industrialization process.

But what of the effects of the export orientation? It seems, in the first place, that Taiwan, as a small island poor in raw materials, especially minerals, must import if it is going to manufacture, and that these imports must be balanced by exports, as they have been since the late 1960s, even without substantial aid. And exports, which constituted 41 percent of the gross domestic product in 1971-73 (ibid., pp. 86-87), have probably become even greater since then. The market has been the core nations, primarily the United States and Japan, and most exports have been labor-intensive manufactures, such as woven and knitted textiles and clothing and electronic equipment and components. If wages in Taiwan reach too high a level, it seems probable that there will be a shift to more capital-intensive production, with consequences for employment, and a need for new export markets. But more important, the emphasis on exports ties Taiwan into the world trading system in a dependent way. Taiwan does not suffer from the kind of dependency characteristic of many Third World countries, where foreign investment and thus foreign repatriation of products or profits represents a predominant part of the economy; foreign investment, though significant, is hardly predominant. But merely exporting so much makes Taiwan dependent on the continuing existence of outside markets for its goods. It seems likely that the United States economy could exist with minor adjustments if the supply of Taiwanese sweaters, shoes, radios, and Raggedy Ann dolls were cut off, but the consequences for Taiwan would be much more serious. Given its size and resources, however, this kind of dependency seems inevitable. As long as growth and relatively equal income distribution are maintained, an export economy is the price Taiwan will have to pay for its prosperity.

The Northern Region and Sanxia

By the postwar period, or at least by the 1960s, because of the modernization of transport, Sanxia and its hinterland had ceased to be the kind of economic system that would merit a separate level of analysis, though it still had considerable political and ritual importance. Therefore, I will include it with the northern region for the postwar period.

The most important special characteristic of the northern region, from Jilong to Taoyuan, is its rapid and dispersed industrialization. The north has long since ceased to be a primarily agricultural region, and even in its rural areas, factories stretch the length of roads, taking up former farmland and former farm labor. The rural character of Taiwan's industrialization is perhaps best exemplified by this. Sanxia zhen had over 140 registered factories in 1975, and they employed about 10 percent of its total population and 30 percent of its population over 15 years of age. Almost no families in the area still subsist entirely on farming.

At the same time, the northern region has thus experienced considerable temporary and permanent in-migration. In addition to the capital city of Taibei, which has absorbed migrants from agricultural areas all over the island for a long time (Gallin and Gallin 1974; Speare 1974), almost all factories in the northern region employ some local labor and some labor from the less industrialized regions to the south. (There are industrialized regions in the south as well, notably around Gaoxiung, Taiwan's second largest city.) But northerners refer to everything from Xinzhu south collectively and condescendingly as *e-kang*, or the "lower port." Within the northern region, there is considerable migration up the hierarchy of economically central places, but in all but the most peripheral regions, migration out seems to be balanced by migration in.

If the north represents the core, or at least a core, of Taiwan's industrialized economy, there is still significant variation within it; specifically, it can be divided into an industrialized core and a still agricultural periphery. This was, of course, true of the Sanxia system during the colonial period, but the difference is that now, with the continued expansion of highway transport, and the accompanying spread of private motor vehicles, as well as convenient public transport to and from work, the boundaries of the core, the industrial zone, have expanded. In the southern Taibei Basin, the core not only includes the plains and inner foothills, as it did previously, but many formerly peripheral areas, such as Ploughshare and Chengfu, that have been brought into the core by easy access to transport for both labor and goods, allowing industries to locate in this area or to put out piecework profitably to cottage industrialists such as the knitters so common in Ploughshare. It is only five minutes from Ploughshare to Sanxia on a motorcycle, and thence one can get anywhere in the Taibei Basin within an hour. One can thus live in Ploughshare and participate fully in the industrial economy, either as a laborer or as a small-scale entrepreneur.

The industrial zone of the northern region does, however, remain a core: it leaves a periphery that has not been able to benefit so directly from industrial development. Areas like the upper reaches of the Sanxia River valley, from Chajiao to Xiongkong, exemplify the remaining periphery. A few mornings of observation and interviewing in Youmu, a community in this area, enabled me to understand the plight of such communities. Youmu has its own center, a group of houses along the main, unpaved road into the valley, but most of its inhabitants live in farm compounds strung out along a series of trails that follow tributaries of the Sanxia River upstream along the mountainsides. People who remain there grow tea and oranges. In the late 1970s, a family could make a living from tea, though market fluctuations made this chancy, but oranges, which had glutted since 1975, were examples of the danger of relying on cash crops. But agriculture of any sort no longer provides a decent living or opportunities for expansion in northern Taiwan. Anyone who wants to keep up with the urban, or at least core, rise in living standards, must engage in industry. In a place like Youmu, however, small-scale investment is out of the question; transport distance is too great to induce even the putting-out system. In the entire *li,* or "administrative village" of Youmu, there is not one small factory or even a knitting machine. And the old tea factory at Chajiao is closed down. So anyone living in Youmu who wants to engage in industry must do so as a worker, but even to work in a factory means a long commute. It is forty-five minutes on the bus to Sanxia, and many people live on the hillsides thirty minutes to an hour and a half from the Youmu bus stop. So it is difficult to remain at home and one must migrate, temporarily or permanently. Temporary migration seems to be the rule, but lots of people move out altogether. The *li* lost about 10 percent of its population between 1970 and 1978, and the loss was proportionately greater in the remoter mountain neighborhoods. By contrast, Sanxia zhen as a whole had a stable population from 1973 to 1976, and Ploughshare's grew about 12 percent between 1973 and 1978. It is not only convenience of work that induces people to leave places like Youmu, however; it is almost impossible to maintain a decent living standard there. People do not have motorcycles because they cannot get them up the mountainsides, even if they can afford them. A refrigerator would probably require four strong men to move it up one of those trails, and it is virtually impossible to persuade a repairman to come fix it if it breaks down. Life in Youmu, once probably as comfortable for a tea grower as elsewhere, can no longer compare with life in any part of the industrial core of the region.[4]

There remains, then, a periphery in the northern region, a zone that is underdeveloped in the sense that development in the core has been partially the cause of the misery of the periphery. And the core absorbs labor from the periphery, as people from places like Youmu move to places like Ploughshare or to more central ones. What seems to me noteworthy about the northern Taiwan regional system in the postwar period is that the periphery is so small, that good transport and partially rural-based, labor-intensive industry have allowed so many people to enjoy the rising standard of living of the industrial core. I have not been able to investigate the extent of the core and periphery in other parts of Taiwan, but I would assume that peripheries might be somewhat larger in less industrialized regions. Still, when we think of the classic model of a developing country where only suburban agricultural areas and the cities themselves benefit from urban industrial growth, and where rural to urban migration is massive and creates sprawling urban slums, we can appreciate the special nature of Taiwan's industrialization.

Ploughshare

Not much is said in the village about the immediate postwar years, the years of the restoration of Taiwan to the Nationalist Chinese government, except that times were hard and there was very little to eat, and some families blame the deaths of their members on not having enough money to consult a doctor or buy medicine. There was something of a recovery at the end of the 1940s, and throughout the 1950s, Ploughshare continued much as it had been before the war—the administration was Chinese, instead of Japanese, the rural district boundaries were drawn differently, but the people lived in the same ways, by coal mining, cart pushing, and a small amount of farming. A big change did come for the tenant farmers in the village with the land to the tiller program; eighteen of the nineteen farming families in the village today are the result of division of families who received land at that time. But as the land reform program did not really enrich farmers anywhere, it did even less for the rather marginal farmers of Ploughshare. Only two village families built brick houses before the latter part of the 1950s. Ploughshare remained a poor

4. For a fuller account of the contest between Ploughshare and Youmu, see Harrell 1981b.

village. Its only landlord, Ong Cin, had sold his land in panic at the prospect of having it taken away, and tea processor and village head Ong Hieng also saw confiscated the small bit of good paddy land he had managed to purchase with the profits from the family business. And most people were still doing what they and their parents had been doing since the 1920s or before.

Since the early 1960s, however, things have changed—Ploughshare has participated in northern Taiwan's industrial development. Factories have become a source of employment for young girls, who could do little but pick tea previously, and for male wage earners as well. This meant ruin for small tea merchants like Ong Hieng: the girls would no longer risk suntans and chipped fingernails when they could earn the same amount of money for indoor labor. For men, this was simply another form of wage-labor, one which did not pay quite as well but was much safer than working in the coal pits. If the qualitative change was minor, however, the quantitative change was enormous, especially in the hiring first of large numbers of young girls, and in the middle seventies of large numbers of young boys who had not yet served in the armed forces. This meant that the percentage of working-age people employed increased (a decrease in Taiwan as a whole has to do with increased high-school attendance, which did not become impor-tant in Ploughshare until the late 1970s) and family incomes rose as a result. The changing connection between wage labor, stratification, and social class is examined in chapter three.

The other major change was the rise of the cottage knitting in-dustry. Textiles and knit goods were among Taiwan's primary growth industries with the development of the export orientation, and many knit-goods companies operated on a kind of double system, using some in-factory labor and some labor recruited through the putting-out system. Ploughshare's participation began when Ong Cin-hieng, a newly retired cart pusher, sent his two eldest sons, recently returned from their compulsory service in the Nationalist army, to learn the trade of machine knitting in a factory on the outskirts of Taibei City. They did learn, and managed to save up enough money to buy a ma-chine of their own. Around the same time, Ong Lou, another young man just out of the army, scraped together enough cash to buy a machine in partnership with one of his elder sisters' husbands, a man living in Shisantian. One used the machine in the daytime and the other one at night. From these rather humble beginnings, the knitting industry has expanded to employ, as owners or wage earners, sixty-five villagers in the late 1970s and to provide a major source of income for village families.

With these economic changes came general prosperity for Ploughshare, interrupted in this period only by a brief recession at the time of the world oil crisis in 1973-74. In addition to the building boom mentioned, acquisition of consumer conveniences has proceeded apace. In 1973, 60 of 101 families owned television sets, two of them color. By 1978, only a few families were without sets, and color outnumbered black and white by a wide margin. About 20 families had refrigerators in 1973; by 1978 virtually everyone had one. Motorcyles were owned by 40 families in 1973 and by nearly all in 1978. Even cars were becoming relatively common by the date of my last visit: there were seven for private use and five taxis in the village in 1978.

Along with economic growth has come population growth: from 50 families and 433 residents in 1935, the village grew to 101 families and 716 residents in 1973, and to 107 families and 826 residents in 1978. Part of this growth has come from expansion and division of existing families, part from recent immigration. For example, the descendants of a 1901 settler surnamed Lou now number 7 house-households; those of 2 nineteenth-century settlers surnamed Tiu: and Ong, number 8 each. In addition, there have been recent immi-grants. Several of those newly arrived in 1973 were already gone by 1978, but many others were still there and seemed destined to stay. Fifteen families came after the end of World War II and remained at least until 1973, 11 more came in the next five years, while 12 resident families moved out. Most of the postwar immigrants came to Plough-share as manual laborers of one sort or another, but there were at least 2 business families. Po Hok-lai, a wealthy businessman from a Sanxia landlord family, bought a large building along Ploughshare's Front Street in the late 1960s, where his family lived and managed a cosmetic-basket workshop. In 1976, however, his family followed him to Hong Kong, where he has built up a travel business. Kou Hieng, originally from Baiji, came to Ploughshare and opened a butcher shop in 1966. By 1973, he seemed destined to stay and was building his own house on Back Street. In the next few years, however, he went heavily into debt, and he and his family left the village suddenly one summer afternoon in 1978. So it is impossible to predict who of the new immigrants will leave and who will stay, but it is evident that people are readily accepted into the village community when they arrive, and it is probable that in the near future a large percentage of the village population will continue to consist of recent immigrants.

Among recent arrivals must be mentioned the several mainland Chinese men who moved into Ploughshare at various times after the retreat of the Nationalist forces to Taiwan in 1949. Popular accounts of Taiwan usually speak of mainland Chinese as a business, government, and educational elite, and it is true that mainlanders are overrepresented, at least in government and education (Gates 1981). But it is important to realize that the million and a half mainlanders who came over with the defeated Nationalist forces in 1949 also included an army remnant of several hundred thousand men. The enlisted men and noncommissioned officers among them usually were not able to bring their families with them; in addition, most of them were poor, and many of them illiterate and unskilled. This sort of mainland man has often married into poor rural Taiwanese families. There were twelve of them in Ploughshare in 1973, eight married uxorilocally into village families, most of them to women with no brothers, and the other four in technically virilocal marriages[5] but living in Ploughshare. By 1978, two of these had left and two others, both virilocally married, had moved in. Mainland men are not especially appreciated in rural Taiwanese communities, but as individuals their reception and status varies according to their own personalities and their own willingness to conform to local ways. In this regard they vary widely. Zhang Xiaoyi, a Hunanese married to a village woman, is a man who will not learn Taiwanese, at least not so that anyone can understand him, and scoffs at local religious customs. He also has a reputation for meddling in people's affairs, because he was a policeman. He is universally disliked and feared in the village, and serves to reinforce the stereotype of mainlanders as haughty and untrustworthy. On the other hand, a man like Gao Sihui, who lived in Ploughshare for six years in the 1970s, made a very different impression. He was a sergeant in the army, stationed at Yingge, then retired and bought a house in Ploughshare from a village family who moved to Dapu. He was from Jiangxi, but married a Taiwanese woman and learned to speak the language fluently, almost without an accent. He and his wife participated in local festivals, he worked alongside Taiwanese men in the mines, and he was generally well liked despite his origins. Other mainland men fall somewhere between these two extremes: not considered totally obnoxious but not held in any great affection either.

From this brief historical account, we can see how the position of Ploughshare evolved with the nature of the local and regional systems of which it was a part, and how they in turn evolved as part of the island system of Taiwan, which had its own position in the world economy. Ploughshare was founded, or at least became a recognizable community, in response to the expansion of commercial tea cultivation in the mountain zone of northern Taiwan; it became part of the under-

---

5. These couples were living with the wives' parents, but had a separate hearth and budget, and all the children took the husband's name. They were referred to with the verb *chua* "to take in a wife" rather than *ciou* "to take in a husband."

developed periphery as its inhabitants shifted partially to mining, which began as an adjunct to Taiwan's colonial industrialization, and it moved into the industrial core zone during the rapid expansion of Taiwan's postwar industrial economy.

Although Ploughshare's place in the systems of which it is a part has changed through the course of its history, it has some characteristics that have persisted across the changes. There are the commercial, rather than subsistence, nature of almost all family economy and the mobility, both geographical and occupational, of the population. These two characteristics, as common to the tea growers of Ploughshare of the 1880s as to the knitters and factory workers of Ploughshare in the 1970s, have had profound effects on the village's social organization, which is the subject of the second part of this study. To understand these effects more fully, however, we must first turn to more specific aspects of the political economy of Ploughshare, the nature of work and the kinds of social inequality found within the village and between it and other communities.

The Changing Nature
of Work

The work Ploughshare villagers do has always been constrained and influenced, if not totally determined, by the village's place in the political-economic system of which it is a part. In the late nineteenth century, this meant that the majority of Ploughshare people, denied access to good flatland, grew tea, made charcoal, or worked as agricultural laborers. Tea was introduced to the Haishan area by British and Dutch interests in the 1860s (Wang 1976, p. 74), and charcoal was an important fuel for the pottery industry of Yingge. Even though Ploughshare is located a half-hour's walk or so from any substantial mountains, its people early on depended on these mountains for their living.

Tea *(Camellia sinensis)* is a species of camellia that, unlike its more ornamental cousins, produces only small, if attractive, white flowers in the wintertime. It can be grown on quite steep slopes, and for that reason has been an important cash crop in several hilly or mountainous regions of China for many centuries. There is only one variety of tea plant, and its different flavors depend on such factors as climate, soil, season of picking, size of leaves, and, most important, processing. I have no direct account of tea picking from the nineteenth century, but now it is a rather simple process. The only parts of the plant considered good for drying (and therefore the only kind a grower or picker can sell to a processor) are the tender new leaves, up to about seven or eight centimeters long. When growth starts in early April, pickers ascend the mountains with narrow-necked baskets on their hips, pick off the tender leaves with both hands, and put them in the basket. Full baskets are dumped into larger ones suitable for attaching to carrying poles that will transport the leaves down the mountains. In the old days, tea picking used to be quite convivial, with boys and girls singing teasing, lamenting, or happy songs across the ravines in a musical repartee. Leaves must be processed within twelve hours or so of the time they are picked or they begin to wilt, which renders them useless, so pickers would often make several trips per day down the mountain to sell their tea. Since many of the tea gardens are a half-hour to an hour's hike from the lowlands, tea picking could be an arduous occupation in spite of the relative easiness of picking. Growers were paid according to both quantity and quality of leaves. The smaller and newer the growth, the higher the price per *jin,* but the more labor it would take to pick an equivalent weight.

Tea plants continue to produce in this part of Taiwan until mid-October, and the number of pickings per plant per year depends on the location and the amount of fertilizer applied. Nowadays some plants can be picked as many as seven times, but traditionally it was more like three. The quality of tea, and hence the price paid by processors, also varies by season: spring tea is considered to be the best, because of the energy stored in the roots during the cool winter when there is no new growth. Fall tea is second best, and summer tea, the rank growth from too much heat, is the lowest quality, suitable in modern teamen's eyes only for making flower tea, known to mainland Chinese as *xiangpian,* and to Westerners as jasmine. Spring tea, on the other hand, is made into the best quality Formosa Oolong, which when drunk without sugar has an initial sweet taste and a sweet aftertaste that can linger for as long as an hour.

Producing charcoal was the other way to make a living from the mountains in those days. I do not know much about it except that villagers would cut wood from unowned tracts of mountainside and burn it in special ovens under low-oxygen conditions, which yielded charcoal that they sold.

Along with agricultural labor, these seem to have been the major occupations of Ploughshare villagers in the nineteenth century, except for the few families who had tenancy rights to flat land and grew rice, or rice and sweet potatoes. A survey taken by the Japanese colo-

nial administration in 1905 shows the primary occupations of Ploughshare households (see table 1).

TABLE 1

OCCUPATIONS OF PLOUGHSHARE HOUSEHOLD HEADS, 1905

(Japanese census)

Tea grower	18	Militiaman	1
Tea picker	1	Bridge builder	1
Rice farmer	4	Boatman	1
Mixed farmer	5	Bamboo worker	1
Miscellaneous coolie	8	Fruit seller	1
Daily wage worker	6	General storekeeper	1
Cart pusher	2		

During the remainder of the Japanese period, there were some
significant changes in the nature of work. First, tea growing was supplemented by the introduction of mandarin oranges. These are a very
sweet variety about the size of California tangerines, but more wrinkled.
They, like tea, can grow on slopes that are difficult to terrace and
usually impossible to irrigate for rice, and in the early twentieth century many previously uncultivated patches of mountainside were
planted with orange trees. These have the added advantage of a season
almost exactly complementary to that of tea—they begin producing in
November and finish in March. They, too, have to be carried down the
mountain, but unlike tea, they are very heavy. A strong young man
carrying a load of oranges down a mountain with a carrying pole in the
ten degree centigrade or cooler temperatures of a North Taiwan winter
will be drenched with sweat by the time he reaches the flatland. In
fact, this is considered the most physically demanding of all work,
although the fresh air makes it still preferable to coal mining. So people
in Ploughshare in the 1970s, when they speak of *co-sua:* (literally
"working the mountain"), mean the cultivation of winter oranges and
spring-to-fall tea.

Also in the Japanese period, the coal mines, opened in the 1920s
and 1930s, took away one common Ploughshare occupation and added
two. Charcoal was no longer used once fossil coal could be mined, and
charcoal burning ceased to be a source of livelihood. The mines did
offer jobs as miners to men, and as cart pushers to men and women.
The work of a coal miner is described below, as it is still important as
a job for Ploughshare villagers. Since cart pushing has disappeared, I
will describe it here. The mines were connected to the river ports and
the north-south railway by a pushcart railroad *(khieng-pien-chia)* sys-

tem. The trunk line, going from the most distant mine at Xiongkong and the nearer ones at Chajiao, Jinmin, and Quanzitou, ran along what is now Back Street in Ploughshare and the main road of Shisantian. Hence it was natural that many villagers took up cart pushing as an occupation.

Cart pushing, like mining, was hard work, although not as dangerous as working in the coal pits. The pushers used to get up at around 2 A. M. and walk to Yingge, where they picked up empty carts, to be pushed as far into the mountains as needed. They then returned to Yingge with carts full of coal. The carts, rather like wooden packing crates on wheels, took two people to push them, and the pushers made from one to three round trips per day, depending on whether they merely went as far as Quanzitou (the nearest coal mine), or whether they would farther into the mountains to Chajiao, or even to Shuangxi and Xiongkong. They would finish their daily shift, for which they were paid slightly less than coal miners, around noon or one in the afternoon, and return home to take a nap and spend the rest of the day around home, until it was time to go to bed (usually shortly after dusk since they rose at two the next morning).

Even though specific jobs changed, work was more or less what it had been in the nineteenth century: physically hard, uninteresting, often dangerous, and offering almost no opportunity for expansion of one's economic base, or mobility into another stratum. Most of the people of Ploughshare were either *co-sua:-lang* (mountain workers), *than-ciaq-lang* (wage earners) or, in a few cases, *co-chan-lang* (lowland agriculturalists).

This situation has continued in some sense to the present day, and most people are still wage laborers. The expansion of the economy, the beginning of opportunities for small-scale investment, the spread of primary and, increasingly, of secondary education, all have greatly changed the economic structure of Ploughshare, and its place in the regional society and economy in the twenty years since the start of Taiwan's large-scale industrialization. But even though the economic significance is vastly different, the majority of people still work long hours for wages, still are *than-ciaq-lang*.

The predominance of wage earning and the secondary importance of small-scale entrepreneurship are illustrated in table 2, which lists the occupations of all employed and self-employed adults in Ploughshare as of January 1973, and again as of July 1978.

It is evident from this table that the work of Ploughshare villagers changed somewhat even from 1973 to 1978. But the changes in the occupations themselves have not been as great as those in the pay and working conditions. I shall examine each of the major occupations

TABLE 2

Occupations of Employed Persons in Ploughshare

OCCUPATION	1973 Men	1973 Women	1978 Men	1978 Women
Wage labor				
Apprentice	5		8	
Bus conductor		2		
Coal miner	30		25	
Construction worker	6	3	3	4
Cook		1		
Factory worker	16	40	58	53
Janitor	2	2	2	2
Knitting mill worker	9	13	8	10
Nurse		2		
Shop assistant[a]		5		
Trades (skilled, semiskilled)[a]	14		8	
Total	82	68	112	69
Salaried positions				
Minor government official	3		3	1
Policeman	1			
Private managerial			7	
Private office job				5
Total	4		10	6
Business and cottage industry				
Barber	1	2	2	2
Knitting machine repairman	1			
Knitting mill owner	2		2	
Knitting mill owner/operator	25	16	32	16
Proprietor of business[b]	7	6	10	9
Proprietor of business[a]	5	2	8	7
Salesperson	3	1		
Snake catcher	1		1	
Taxi driver	2		5	
Total	47	27	60	34
Agriculture				
Farmer only	8		6	
Farmer and factory worker	1		9	
Farmer and mason	1		2	
Farmer and miner	5		2	
Farmer and odd jobs	1		1	
Tea grower		1		
Rice growing helper (busy seasons)		4		4
Total	16	5	20	4
Prostitution		2		1
TOTAL EMPLOYED PERSONS	149	102	202	114
		(251)		(316)

[a] Outside Ploughshare
[b] In Ploughshare

pursued by Ploughshare villagers, describing the nature of the work, the pay, and the incentives for working as they changed from the economy of 1973 to that of 1978.

WAGE LABOR

The Coal Mines

Coal mining is no longer as important a source of income for Ploughshare men as it once was, but it is still a common way of earning wages. Five large mines account for most of Ploughshare's miners. Three Zhongyi (formerly Haishan) mines were originally the property of the deified Ng A-cang but are now transferred to his erstwhile partner, the wealthy Tan Then-su of Sanxia. These are located at Hengxi, Baiji, and Quanzitou. The Sanxia coal mine, located a mile or so up the road into the mountains on the other side of the river, and the Jinmin mine, also on the other side of the river but farther upstream, also each employ several Ploughshare men.

All the mines work on the same principles. Any fifteen-year-old male can work there, and there is no upper age limit. The mines are deep, sometimes requiring an hour or more's journey by foot and elevator to reach the face, and are reported to be nearly unbearably hot. The miners therefore wear nothing but their lighted helmets while working in the mine, showering before they return home. Work at the face is usually done in teams of from two to ten or more miners, depending on the size of the face and the amount of coal being extracted. Typically, two or four members of a large crew push the railway carts full of coal out from the face while the rest work with pick and shovel. Their pay is based on the amount of coal each team extracts, and the total sum is divided equally among its members. Other miners work at blasting and are paid by the length of tunnels they clear. Whether blasting or digging coal, miners in 1973 could expect to earn between NT$120 and NT$140 for a day's work, usually 4 or 5 hours. Other workers not directly involved in the extraction of coal were paid less. Both those who tended the ventilation system and those who built the wooden frameworks supporting the tunnel roofs were paid a flat wage of NT$90 per day. In 1978, when retail prices had approximately doubled, mine wages, like other wages, had more than kept up with the trend. Average piecework rates were reported to be about NT$300 to 400 per day, with several hundred more possible for overtime or unusually productive workers.

No worker is required to work on a particular day. If he doesn't show up, he is simply not paid for that day, so the membership of the mining teams varies from day to day, though the miners generally work with neighbors or friends when possible. If a miner without any medical condition does not appear for ten working days in a row, he loses his insurance protection, which pays for injuries sustained in the mines and also pays survivors a flat rate in case of fatal accidents.

It seems at first glance that coal mining, with its high wages and short hours, might be a desirable occupation for an uneducated man willing to work hard, but it is universally despised, even by the men who have spent all their days doing it. First, the work is miserable in the extreme, hot, dark, and sweaty. "A four-hour shift," one miner said to me, "doesn't seem like very long to work, but when you are in that mine you can't tell how long it is." Many miners take half-gallon jugs of tea with them but drink them up by the time they have been down for two or three hours. As the shallower mines have been played out and tunnels are dug deeper and deeper in search of coal, these problems have become exacerbated. Wages are already adjusted to the discomfort of the particular site, so that the workers in the deepest part of the Zhongyi mine at Quanzitou, the closest to Ploughshare, for example, are paid the same amount for a two- and one-half-hour shift as other men earn for five hours of work in cooler tunnels. I do not know how long this will continue before mining becomes either totally unbearable or unprofitable to the operators.

Second, there is a great danger of injury and death. Thirteen Ploughshare men have been killed in the mines in the past twenty-five years, and there is hardly a miner who has not sustained a temporarily disabling injury. Not only cave-ins and explosions, but bad ventilation is often responsible for mine deaths: one supervisor from Ploughshare was killed in 1965 when he went down to check the quality of air in a particularly sensitive place to see if it was safe to allow miners in the area, and suffocated. The entrance to each mine contains, in addition to a large sign reading "Safety First," a shrine to the earth god, Tho-te Kong, and the miners worship both him and the ghosts of people killed in accidents. Even though the men go to the mines nearly every day, they always go fearing accidents.

Third, wages are deceptive because of the men's ability to work. A young man in his twenties, strong and vigorous, can work twenty-five or more days in the mines each month and earn a quite comfortable living for himself and his family, but debilitation and often black lung disease come early. By the time he is fifty, when his family is still likely to need support, he will be lucky if he can spend fifteen days in the mines, and his income will be considerably less. I have known men over sixty who went into the mines more often than that, but they are the exception. Most miners, even if they live that long, are unable to do much work by the time they reach such an age.

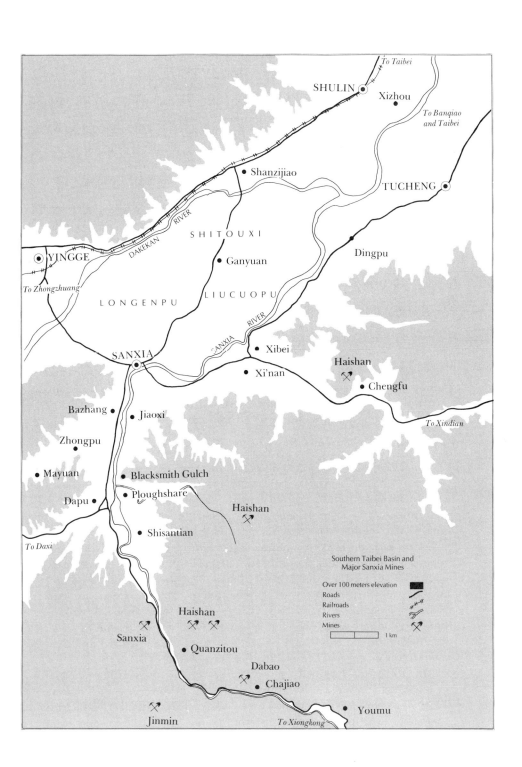

To Taibei

SHULIN

Xizhou

To Banqiao
and Taibei

Shanzijiao

TUCHENG

SHITOUXI

Dingpu

DAKEKAN RIVER

YINGGE

Ganyuan

To Zhongzhuang

LONGENPU

LIUCUOPU

CANXIA RIVER

SANXIA

Xibei

Haishan

Xi'nan

Chengfu

Bazhang

Jiaoxi

To Xindian

Zhongpu

Mayuan

Blacksmith Gulch

Dapu

Ploughshare

Haishan

Shisantian

Southern Taibei Basin and
Major Sanxia Mines

To Daxi

Over 100 meters elevation
Roads
Railroads
Rivers
Mines

1 km

Haishan

Sanxia

Quanzitou

Dabao

Chajiao

Jinmin

Youmu

To Xiongkong

Because of all these factors, it appeared in 1973 that the mines would soon face a severe labor shortage. Young men just returned from military service at age twenty-one or twenty-two were no longer entering the mines, preferring to take knitting or factory jobs, and even experienced miners in their thirties and forties had begun to leave the mines for other occupations. Factory labor, where it was available, paid about NT$110 for an eight-hour shift, while knitting paid the same or a little more for a ten- to eleven-hour workday. But longer hours for less pay seemed a small price for getting out of the coalpits, and many men were willing to take the cut in return for the relative safety and not-so-dismal future in the factories and knitting mills.

As table 2 on page 58 indicates, the decline in mining labor from Ploughshare has not been as precipitous as predicted. Mining wages (higher than factory pay to begin with) rose slightly faster in the intervening period, and knitting labor, for reasons discussed below, became somewhat less attractive. In three cases, men with fairly well-established knitting businesses saw the floor fall out from under their labor supply with the rapid rise in female factory wages, and had to return to the mines to support their families, while substantially reducing the size of their knitting operations. For all these reasons, not many men left the mines, and a few former miners even went back. But still almost no young men are entering the mines after military service, and attrition of older workers seems destined to bring the once-delayed labor supply crisis to the mine owners after all.

Factories

In 1973, factories ranked second to coal mines as a source of wages for men. In 1978, there were more than twice as many men employed in factories as in coal mines (see table 3). In fact, a great percentage of the increase in absolute numbers of employed Ploughshare men is due to the relatively new phenomenon of young boys working several years in factories before they enter military service at age nineteen. In both 1973 and 1978, factory work was the primary source of wages for Ploughshare women. But the economic structure of factory work for both sexes changed notably between my two visits to Ploughshare, and this change has affected other aspects of family economy and wage labor generally. To understand this, we must examine the economics of factory employment in 1973 and then analyze the changes in the ensuing five-year period.

In 1972-73, unskilled factory labor for men was rather unusual in northern Taiwan, but many Ploughshare men worked in the Xinfeng Paper Company, a five-minute walk away in Shisantian. The factory was built in 1969 on a piece of former rice land. It is owned by a consortium of Sanxia and Taibei businessmen including Tan Then-su, primary owner of the Zhongyi coal mines. The factory produces heavy rolls of brown paper, used in manufacturing cardboard cartons, from recycled waste gathered in Hong Kong and shipped to Taiwan. Because the company hired only males and paid substantial wages (averaging NT$110 per day) for the physically taxing work, many Ploughshare men had already, in 1973, left the coal mines to work there. They put in an eight-hour shift, rotating weekly from day to night to graveyard, and received one day off every other week.

Factory labor for women in the early 1970s was of quite a different order. The numerous electronic, textile, and other factories that began to dot the North Taiwan countryside since the early 1960s were at that time dependent on very cheap labor, which was abundantly available from women, particularly young, unmarried women. Since the only reputable traditional source of income for these girls was tea picking (prostitution paid more, but people had to be desperate to send their daughters to be prostitutes—see M. Wolf 1972, p. 207), and since tea picking was a low-paid, arduous task, young women readily flocked to the factories; even the low wages they were paid at this time were more than they could have contributed to family income any other way.

Unlike their male counterparts, female factory workers in 1973 were young, low-paid, and temporary.[1] They were expected to work only until marriage, or perhaps until the birth of their first child. For a day's work they were paid a starting wage of NT$30 to 35 a day, less than a third of what the paper workers at Xinfeng earned, possibly because they were peripheral to the main income generation of their families—because in a sense their income was extra, rather than essential, to their families' livelihoods. Most of their earnings they turned over to their parents as part of the *jia,* or household, budget, but some were allowed to keep a small amount for spending money, or as savings toward their dowry when they eventually married.

A minority of women workers were older. Very few young mothers worked in factories, except out of absolute necessity, but women whose children were school age or older often found factory work an attractive prospect for the small amount of extra income it brought in. Even grandmothers took up some of the less taxing jobs.

What the factory women actually did seems irrelevant to their place in family and society—they did any sort of unskilled or semi-skilled light work, from tending machine looms to soldering electronic

1. For accounts of the transitory nature of female factory labor in contemporary Taiwan, see Diamond 1979 and Kung 1981.

components. In 1973 several Ploughshare women worked at the TRW electronics plant just outside of Shulin, a company that provided bus transportation to and from work, and recruited from different areas of the countryside for its different shifts. The four Ploughshare women employed there worked from 4 P.M. to midnight, returning home at about one in the morning. They included a woman in her late forties with nine children—the youngest already of school age—her sixteen-year-old daughter, a young mother of two whose husband was killed several years before in a mine accident, and a fifteen-year-old girl who was the main source of support for her wretchedly poor, blind, and aged grandfather. They said that the work in this factory was comparatively interesting but they thought they would always earn the same wages, with no chance of promotion or transfer to a better job. Still, it was worth it. Even their pay of NT$900 per month was a significant increment to their family incomes. Other village women worked in factories producing textiles, synthetic leather boots, wooden shoe heels, and hypodermic needles.

By 1978, the situation had changed. Factories had continued to sprout up on the local landscape. Seven small plants were built even in relatively remote Shisantian between 1973 and 1978, and two more large ones were beginning construction at the time of my 1978 visit. All of these factories, small and large, old and new, were in need of labor, causing a general labor shortage in the area. Six of the seven factory managers I interviewed in summer 1978 said they were from 10 to 20 percent short of the ideal number of workers, and indeed one could see help-wanted signs posted in front of nearly all the large factories on the floor of the Taibei Basin. One plant even listed starting wages for various types of work on a billboard by its main gate. This labor shortage has meant two things, a rise in real wages, particularly for female workers, and the hiring of teen-age boys, previously thought undesirable as workers because they would leave at age nineteen for military service.

The increase in wages has been variable. If we count prices as having only approximately doubled in the interval, we can see that wages for men have only slightly more than kept up. The starting wage at the Xinfeng paper plant—about NT$90 a day in 1973—was slightly over NT$200 in 1978. Wages in a nearby automobile-jack plant that employs mostly pre-army boys start at NT$130 a day for those with a junior high-school education or NT$145 a day for those who have been to high school. Still, this is a sizable contribution to a family income, especially considering that young boys were virtually unemployable except as apprentices in 1973. For women, on the other hand, the wage hike has been dramatic. Where a beginning electronics worker received from NT $28 to NT$35 in 1973, she now can expect to start at about NT$110, and through salary increases for seniority and working overtime she can easily double that wage. Her contribution to the family economy, while still less than an adult man's, has now become substantial. This has had important effects on the cottage knitting industry (which has lost workers), and on the family developmental cycle and its relationship to family economy.

Building and Other Trades

A number of Ploughshare men work at skilled trades both inside and outside the village. Some families send their sons, recently graduated from elementary or junior middle school, to be apprenticed to tradesmen in other communities. They are paid a token wage plus room and board for the few years of apprenticeship, after which they begin to bring in earnings commensurate with those of coal miners, male factory workers, or wage earners in the knitting mills. Those who have completed their training usually remain in their trades. There are young men from Ploughshare working as cabinetmakers, tailors, and auto mechanics, among other trades. Apprenticeship does not, however, always turn out as planned. The fourth son of Ong Tho, apprenticed to an electrician in Taoyuan in 1972, was back in Ploughshare working with his father as a construction worker in a coal mine in 1978.

Tradesmen also operate within the community, primarily in construction. Because of the boom in construction throughout the seventies, with new factories and houses being built all the time, and older houses being renovated, the construction trades were among the most lucrative occupations for relatively uneducated men. Ploughshare now has three masons. One is Tiu: Chin-ong, who had been a coal miner but who killed two men in self-defense in a dispute with a neighboring family, and was sent to prison for twelve years. He was, however, a model prisoner and learned to lay bricks while serving his time. Released on parole after only six years, he returned to Ploughshare to take up his newly learned trade. Another mason is Li Hieng, also a former coal miner. A third is Chiu Tau-bieng, a father of five who also works a small plot of rice land in Shisantian. All these men are often aided by their wives (in the case of Li Hieng, who is divorced, by a woman who had started out as his assistant and later moved in with him), who serve as hod carriers and general helpers, and by another village woman who does the same thing. In 1972-73, the masons earned NT$130 a day and the hod carriers NT$70. By 1978, the masons made over NT$300 and the hod carriers over NT$200 a day. At either time, this constituted a respectable income for a village family, and unlike seasonally employed construction workers in the United States, they were never short of work. In fact, people wanting to build houses had to wait two or three months before the services of the village masons were available. Tiu: Ching-ong, anxious to salvage both his reputation and his family's economic fortunes after his years in prison, put in 380 workdays in 1972. He took off only New Year's Day and major holidays, and frequently worked extra hours in the evening. By 1978, he had become essentially a contractor and would build houses for a flat rate determined by the floor space. People complained that he would make extra profits this way, but there was little they could do about it if they wanted new houses or new additions built, as most everybody did.

These occupations, together with a few miscellaneous jobs such as shop clerks, bus conductors, and janitors, made wage earning the source of income for about 60 percent of the employed people in Ploughshare in both 1973 and 1978. The image of Ploughshare as a workers' village is thus reasonably justified.

BUSINESS AND COMMERCIAL ACTIVITY

Knitting

Another major source of wages for both men and women is in the local knitting mills, but since these are for the most part owned and operated by the villagers themselves, I will discuss them here. Business and commercial activity is the second largest source of income for Ploughshare villagers, and it supports the village's wealthiest and most influential families. By far the most important business is the knitting of sweaters, an activity that deserves detailed description.

As most Americans undoubtedly know, large numbers of knitted goods sold here are imported from Taiwan. What most have probably never thought about, is that a great portion of these knitted goods are produced not in the large factories of Taibei and Sanchong, employing several hundred workers each, but at least partially in small-scale, cottage-industrial plants. Practically every rural and urban community in the Taibei Basin sports at least a few of these knitting mills, but in Ploughshare and some other places they form a major component of the village economy. The knitting industry in Ploughshare, like other aspects of the local economy, changed greatly between 1973 and 1978.

In 1973, from early morning until late at night, the streets and houses of Ploughshare gave forth the characteristic sound of the knitting machines, an alternating whishing rhythm caused by the shuttle moving back and forth. These machines are steel frames, about five feet high and five feet wide. The knitters stood on the ground, or on makeshift platforms, and moved the shuttle back and forth to the tune of loud imitation Japanese rock music. Every few passes they stopped to rearrange the stops on the machine, producing colored patterns as well as ribknits and other fancy effects. Knitters were of either sex, and from about eighteen to around fifty years of age. Boys and girls under eighteen were thought to be too weak to move the heavy shuttle back and forth ten or eleven hours a day, six or seven days a week, and most people over fifty can no longer see well enough to manipulate the stops on the machine accurately. The skill takes several months to learn and, typically, workers were paid no wages during this time. Once they learned the trade and could knit on their own, they were paid on a piecework basis. This probably accounts for the seemingly frantic pace that they sustained for so many hours and days in a row.

The economic structure of the knitting industry was quite complex. With the exception of the village head, all the machine owners in the village worked on consignment for large companies with offices and factories in the various urban centers in and around the Taibei Basin: Banqiao, Taoyuan, Zhongli, Sanchong, and so on. These factories sent representatives in panel trucks out to the villages and towns where the mills were located, and gave out raw yarn and instructions to follow. The owners of the machines were paid a piece rate based on the complexity of the work to be done. At a specified time, the factory representatives called again to pay the machine owner and pick up the knitted pieces, which were sewn into finished garments by low-paid women at the factories. The machine owners, in turn, paid their workers a similar piece rate, deducting a certain percentage as their own margin.

There were thus several possibilities for village families engaged in the knitting industry. The simplest was to have one or more family members employed as wage laborers in the neighbors' mills. These laborers earned between NT$90 and NT$110 for a ten- to eleven-hour workday—considerably less than coal miners, but for a safer job.

Other families had managed to buy a knitting machine or two for themselves. New machines ranged in price from NT$14,000 to $18,000. The more expensive ones were from Japan and said to last longer. Used machines were often available for a few thousand Taiwan dollars. Families with only a few machines sometimes did not deal directly with the factories, but absorbed surplus work from families with more machines. The large operators usually farmed out work to the small-owner families free of charge as a neighborly gesture. I have never heard of them taking any kind of cut. A worker who used his or her family's own machine made approximately NT$140 per day.

Other families owned from five to ten machines and hired labor, as well as working some of the machines themselves. Laborers were hired both from Ploughshare and from outside the village. Many of the outsiders were young boys and girls from villages farther in the mountains where it was uneconomical for the factories to transport yarn and pick up finished goods. Those who lived inconveniently far from the village often boarded in the homes of their employers, who deducted the monthly room-and-board charge of NT$300 from their wages. In addition, there were Ploughshare villagers who worked outside the community, though fewer in number than those coming in. Families with several machines, and hired as well as family labor, could truly be said to be in the knitting business. They were usually quite knowledgeable about economic affairs and were expecting to expand their operations.

A typical family knitting operation was managed by Lou Khieng-hun, the third of six brothers. His two elder brothers had taken out their shares of the family property individually. His mother and uxori-locally married father, a retired farmer, took no part in the knitting. Khieng-hun and his next youngest brother, Khieng-sieng, each operated one of their seven knitting machines. In addition, Khieng-hun carried yarn and finished pieces back and forth to the factory on his motorcycle, obviating the need to have the factory representative call, and making it easier to get work. Their next brother was just learning to knit, so they hired labor—two young women from the village and three outsiders, none of whom boarded with them. They took the full profit from pieces they knitted themselves on two of the seven machines, paying the workers who operated the other machines about NT$100 each.

Like the smaller-scale operations, full-fledged businesses like the Lous' often traded work. Operating under the pressure of deadlines and with unsteady supplies of materials, but steady supplies of labor, one family was often short of work while another had more than it could do. In this case, the arrangement was an informal one, in which the family farming out the work simply turned over the pay for that work to the family who actually did it, with either its own or hired labor.

This kind of small-scale enterprise paid well. Even the investment in a new machine was paid off in approximately four months with family labor, or in a little over a year with hired labor. It is not surprising then that, with the growth of Taiwan's exports in the early 1970s, many knitting families were expanding rapidly and others were getting into the business whenever feasible.

Nevertheless, this kind of entrepreneurship represented only an intermediate stage on the way to the ultimate goal of having one's fully independent knitting business, of no longer being tied to a putting-out relationship with a large factory. In 1972-73, this had been achieved only by the village head, Ong Cin-hieng. He bought the yarn directly from the manufacturer; one of his sons drove the family car to pick it up, and it was reeled and knit in his large house in the village. Another of his sons both knitted and managed the other knitters, while a third worked another of the machines. The remainder of the twenty-one machines were worked by hired laborers, most of them from Ploughshare. None of them, as far as I know, boarded in their house that, while spacious, had to house both the knitting operation and the fifteen-member family. Cin-hieng's wife and one of his daughters-in-law were in charge of a large group of village women who worked upstairs in their house for low wages, sewing the pieces together into finished garments that were sold to exporting firms during the summer months. During the winter, the Ongs sold them in a store they had recently purchased in the Wanhua (formerly Mengjia) section of Taibei City. One of Cin-hieng's unmarried daughters took charge of the store most of the time, and the family head himself sometimes spent several days helping out during busy seasons. In addition, Cin-hieng often put out work to other village families on the same system used by the larger factories, paying a fixed rate for a certain number of pieces.

All during the ten months I spent in Ploughshare in 1972-73, the knitting industry was growing. People were giving up other jobs to go into knitting; young boys and girls were learning the trade; families with a little extra cash were investing in their first machines, and families who already owned machines were purchasing more. This occurred in spite of the sizable investment required, the exacting work, the long hours, and the pay, which was less than a grown man could earn in the mines or in a construction trade. I think the reasons for this, however, can be found in the potential long-term benefits of the knitting business.

In the first place, knitting is preferable to mining in every way but the wages paid and the hours worked. While many miners are killed and others disabled by injuries or black lung, there seem to be no comparable occupational hazards associated with knitting. Also, even with the long hours, knitting is a lot more pleasant. Transistor radios blare, breaks are taken in the sunshine or in the houses rather than in the black tunnel and, at the very least, it isn't as hot as in the shafts. And since young men and women work together at knitting, there is an opportunity to meet prospective spouses, or to flirt and joke around.

But anything is preferable to coal mining. Why was knitting more popular than, say, construction work or steady factory jobs? The answer seems to lie in the possibilities for expansion. Once a family amassed the capital to buy a machine, the investment paid off in a relatively short time and as long as the industry was expanding in Taiwan as a whole, there appeared to most villagers to be an indefinite opportunity for growth. So even if knitting became impossible when one's sight weakened with age, a young man of twenty-five buying his first machine could look forward to being manager of a large operation by the time he was forty. If everything went well, he should not have to work the machines himself when he reached a certain age. This is quite unlike the prospect of a young coal miner who, when forced to slow down because of black lung disease or another disability, will have nothing to fall back upon but the wages earned by his sons and unmarried daughters. Even the relatively safe work in the paper factory did not carry with it any opportunity for promotion or expansion, nor did the skilled and reliable work of a bricklayer. So people flocked to the knitting machines.

The knitting business was a source of wages as well as a field for entrepreneurship. In 1972-73, both these aspects were attractive. Knitting paid as good a wage to men as anything but the undesirable coal mine work. For women, it paid approximately three times what they could earn as a starting wage in a factory, and over twice what they could make as experienced factory workers. As a field for entrepreneurship, the possibilities looked almost limitless. And the two aspects were connected: entrepreneurship was attractive because there appeared to be an unlimited supply of workers, and work there was made more attractive because it was a possible avenue toward ownership of machines, and eventually a comfortable living as an entrepreneur.

But by 1978, all this had changed quite radically with the continuing labor shortages and the consequent rise in factory wages, especially for women. Knitting income rose between 1973 and 1978, but not as much as factory income. A knitter working for wages made approximately NT$200 to $300 a day—about the same as an experienced adult male factory worker, or around twice as much as a beginning female worker. So it is still advantageous, at least for young women, to knit rather than work in factories, but the advantage is less than it once was and the work is much more difficult. It still requires ten or eleven hours a day in the mills, while the standard factory workday is only eight. One can get an additional half-day's pay for three hours of overtime work, making the pay for eleven hours of relatively easy factory labor comparable to the pay for eleven hours of difficult knitting. So girls from families that are not economically struggling (and few are, these days) have left the knitting mills for the much easier work of the factories. And while the ratio between knitting wages and factory wages for men has not diminished sharply, factory work is now generally more available for young men who are correspondingly tempted to take the easier jobs. It has now become difficult for owners of several knitting machines to find workers. In 1978 when I returned to the village, I found only two intermediate-sized knitting mills still in operation. Others had only a few machines that could be worked by family labor and perhaps a few ambitious hired workers.

As a consequence, at least three former knitting operators had returned to their previous work in the coal mines to support their families. But to those with considerable available capital, there was another alternative: electric, semiautomated knitting machines. These knit sweater pieces according to a pattern that is simply encoded by means of stops on a rotating plastic belt. An operator has only to set the pattern, replenish the yarn supplies when they run out, and check the machines every once in a while to make sure nothing has gone wrong. The shuttle moves leisurely back and forth by itself, and the finished pieces pile up steadily at the foot of the machine. Such a machine is a considerable investment, a good one costing at least NT$300,000, but it can make its owner NT$400 or $500 a day, or more if it works nearly around the clock, so that the investment can be repaid in two to three years. And there is no problem whatsoever with hired labor since an owner-couple can easily manage six to eight of these machines without help. Two will easily support a medium-sized family, and more than two can produce large profits once the initial loan is paid off.

In 1978, five families in Ploughshare had managed to acquire automatic machines, and one other had bought semiautomatic machines, six of which could be tended by three brothers. Of all the knitting operators, Kou Pou-ban had made the largest investment, both borrowing money and selling farmland to acquire six automatic machines. Other families had one or two. As of this writing, it all seems a gamble. Will the automatic machines—for those who have been able to afford them—bring in enough profits for long enough to offset the large investment necessary to acquire them? If so, they will probably become more widespread; if not, it may spell the end of the knitting industry as a major source of income for Ploughshare villagers.

One knitting operator who has continued to expand through all this economic change is former village head, Ong Cin-hieng (his son took over in August 1978, having run unopposed in the last election). Most of the twenty-one manual knitting machines he owned in 1973

After butcher Kou Hieng fled the village, a family from Shisantian began selling pork in their newly built house, 1978.

A young entrepreneur showing off one of his automatic knitting machines, 1978.

are sitting idle and he has only two automatic machines. But his whole-sale and retail business—mostly for domestic consumption—has con-tinued to grow. He sells both to retailers in other parts of the island and directly to the public at his store in Wanhua. Most of the actual work is done by machine owners in and around Ploughshare. Cin-hieng has taken over the role of the factories that contract the labor out, and so far he has been able to find people with both manual and automatic machines sufficient to supply his needs.

Storekeeping

Not counting the two barber shops, there were five stores in Plough-share in 1973 and six at the beginning of my visit in 1978, one of which folded while I was there. Various others were there in the past but were abandoned for diverse reasons. Ciu Hieng-ik's grandfather sold pork in the house on the point until World War II, and Ong Cin-hieng's grandfather had a small general store on the site of the present village activities center in the 1920s, but it lasted only a few years, and old-timers were quite scornful of its limited selection. All the stores now operating were established after the end of the Second World War.

The largest and most prosperous store in 1973 was run by the Iap brothers at the upper end of Back Street. The older brother, Bu-kiet, and his wife occupied the upper section of their store-front house, where they sold fresh fruits and vegetables. Bu-kiet went every morning at about six to buy new produce on his motorcycle, sometimes only to Sanxia and sometimes as far as Banqiao. In season, his store stocked a wide variety of fresh fruits, including bananas, pineapples, papayas, mangoes, pears, lichees, oranges of various sorts, pomelos, dragon-eyes, guavas, and other fruit, as well as such fresh vegetables as onions, bean sprouts, string beans, spinach, several other varieties of greens with no English name equivalents, cabbages of assorted shapes and sizes including the kind we usually refer to as "Chinese," carrots, turnips, potatoes, sweet potatoes, broccoli, cauliflower, green peppers, hot chili peppers, tomatoes, bamboo shoots, water chestnuts, ginger, long thin eggplants, and mushrooms. In addition, there were usually several kinds of small salt-water fish, often squid or octopus, occasionally chicken breasts and legs, and frequently a small mussel best enjoyed raw. Bu-kiet also stocked a small quantity of pork for people too lazy or hurried to make the thirty-second walk to the butcher down the street.

Next to Bu-kiet's produce market is the general store run by his younger brother, Tiek-iek, with whom he shared a common budget in 1973. In 1974, they divided their households, putting the stores under separate management, and in spring 1976, Tiek-iek was killed, leaving the operation of the store to his widow, A-mui. This store stocked nearly everything anybody needed on a daily basis. Bins in the middle contained brown and white sugar, flour, noodles, various kinds of dried peas and beans, bean pastes of different consistencies, garlic and other spices, and eggs (duck slightly cheaper than chicken)— all sold by weight. Shelves around the outside were filled with bottles of soy sauce, dark and light vinegar, sesame oil, oyster sauce, and all the others necessary for Chinese cooking on one side, and alcoholic drinks—beer, several grades of rice wine, plum wine (which tastes like prune juice), and an herb liqueur (which tastes like herbs)—and various soft drinks, most of them sweeter than their American counterparts. On the lower shelves sat all sorts of ritual articles—incense, paper money, and firecrackers in strings of various lengths. Jars near the counter held candies and salted plums, while a large crock at the back was used to hold the peanut oil that the storekeeper dished out (bring your own bottle) with a long-handled ladle. Rice came from the back room. Drawers in a desk held postage stamps, patent medicines, and a few antibiotics, and cigarettes were displayed prominently on glass shelves above the desk. There was usually at least one customer in the Iaps' stores, and the brothers' crotchety mother used to sit in front and bark at the children.

Iap Tiek-iek told me he expected to make about a 5 percent margin on the items he sold, and his overhead was minimal, since the brothers operated out of their own house and needed to pay only the costs of the motorcycles used to transport merchandise and the fees to keep their liquor and tobacco licenses issued by the provincial government monopoly. Probably their most serious problem was that many of the poorer villagers customarily bought everything on credit, and some of them are kin or affines, so the brothers found it difficult to deny credit or to press for repayment of arrears. But they still did reasonably well and were among the better-off families in the village.

Ciam Lien-ki, uxorilocally married son-in-law of Ong Cai-lai, runs another store, also on Back Street but at the south end of the village. Like Iap Bu-kiet, he sells fresh fruits, vegetables, fish, and sometimes poultry, and he also runs a general store, but without a liquor and tobacco license, although he has a somewhat better selection of stationery than Iap Tiek-iek. By 1978, his business seemed to have expanded and was about equal in volume to the Iaps'.

Another general store with a wide selection is located on Back Street immediately above the shorter suspension bridge. It belonged to the youngest of six brothers named Tiu:. Since his death in 1975, it has continued to be operated by his wife, two sons, and two daughters-in-law. They have had their store longer than any of the others and sell approximately the same selection of dry goods as Iap Tiek-iek, but do not deal in fresh fruits and vegetables. In 1973, they sold a small amount of pork, approximately one pig every two or three days; by 1978, their meat business had expanded. Their store also contained the only rice mill in the village, and they sell quite a large quantity of rice to nonfarming families, who of course compose the bulk of Ploughshare's population.

Quite successful in 1973 was the young butcher, Kou Hieng. He moved to Ploughshare in about 1965 from his ancestral home in Baiji. Only as I was leaving the village in 1973 did he build his own house, in the rice fields next to Tiu: Sui. At that time, Kou Hieng sold most of the fresh pork that villagers consumed. In mid-1972, he bought a live pig, usually weighing around 100 kilograms, nearly every day, took it in a cart pulled by a motorcycle to the slaughterhouse in Sanxia, killed it with a long knife, paid the tax to the government inspector (who applied highly decorative meat stamps to the pig's skin), then brought it back to the village where he cut and hung it up for sale to villagers making their morning rounds. Pork is eaten fresh, and most people disdain day-old meat. In fall 1972, the provincial government decreed that the local slaughterhouses were no longer to be used, and that all butchers had to take their pigs to central slaughterhouses where they would be killed by electric shock, and the butchers compensated with an equivalent weight of frozen meat from the storehouse. This was supposed to be more sanitary than the old method, but people universally disliked the frozen meat, and Kou Hieng and other butchers resorted to numerous subterfuges to try to provide their customers with fresh pork. For a while they took the pigs deep into the mountains where no policeman would hear their screams, and then later organized large caravans to transport the pigs to Taizhong County, where knife-slaughter was still legal, and bring them back for sale. Finally, after a few weeks, the government relented and butchers went back to open use of the old methods.

For some reason unclear to anybody in the village, Kou Hieng's business went bad in the years between 1973 and 1978. He had few customers and began to go deeply into debt, bidding money out of rotating credit societies and then not being able to put it back in. He was forced to sell his house in 1977 but continued living in it, and after a while attempted to peddle pork on the streets of Xinzhuang town while his wife sold a little at home. Then, one afternoon in July 1978, they told neighbors they were going to some friends' house for dinner, got on their motorcycle with just a few belongings, and were never seen again. Now villagers will have to buy pork either from the Tiu:s' store by the bridge, or from one of several butchers across the river in Dapu.

Ciam A-chun's general store and grocery, 1978

The life of a shopkeeper is both easier and more difficult than other peoples'. It is easier because there is little hard physical labor involved other than lifting heavy crates or killing, hanging, and butchering pigs. But it is difficult as well, for the shopkeeper almost never rests. There are customers from the time the doors open at about seven in the morning until they close at ten o'clock at night, and even during the slack periods in the mid-afternoon and late evening there are always little chores to be performed, such as checking inventories, balancing accounts, or straightening up the store. Shopkeepers spend a lot of time out on buying expeditions. Even the general storekeepers, who are relieved of the necessity to go to the vegetable market every morning, still have to be dashing here and there to restock this and that. Still, shops once established provide a fairly reliable source of income, probably more so in the long run than the knitting mills, whose profits are subject to the world economy, or the coal mines, where workers are so likely to become disabled.

Besides these storekeepers, there are three barbers in the village, all outsiders. Two women run a shop at the corner of Back Street and the road from the concrete bridge, and a divorced Hakka man from Meinong in South Taiwan has a small business in a shop rented from Tiu: Pun-iek, the storekeeper by the small suspension bridge. In addition, Peq Hieng-bieng, a former coal miner, opened up a small restaurant in his house on Back Street just a few weeks before I left Ploughshare in 1973. He hired as cook a mainland Chinese woman who made *jiaozi,* the probable Chinese ancestor of ravioli, and Hieng-bieng also served various kinds of noodles and meat dishes, as well as keeping a large supply of beer and stronger liquor on hand. In 1978, the restaurant was still there, though somewhat transformed. It no longer sold *jiaozi* and was run exclusively by Hieng-bieng's son A-iong and his wife. They served all manner of rice and noodle dishes, as well as conventional Chinese meals of fried dishes and steamed rice. A-iong is a good cook and seemed to be doing a good business, though his income was supplemented by his father's coal mining, and his mother and two brothers' factory work.

In 1976, the village acquired an ice store. Hua Tua-li and his wife Li A-hong had originally come to Ploughshare from Yilan on Taiwan's east coast—he to take a managerial job in the Xinfeng paper factory and she to cook for the domiciled workers in the Hongtong plastic shoe factory near Ploughshare's concrete bridge. When Hongtong folded, they opened the ice store, a Taiwanese version of a soda fountain, selling in the summer dishes of shaved ice topped by various kinds of sweet bean sauces. This is an extremely profitable business, at least seasonally, probably netting NT$600 to 800 per day during the warm months.

There are also several Ploughshare people who run businesses outside the community but who remain part of family corporations *(jia)* in the village itself. For example, two of So A-bieng's sons run noodle restaurants in the port city of Jilong, one in partnership with his father's sister's son, and one by himself. Lou Chun is a highly successful electrician in Taibei, while Chua Ka-hok's eldest son is in partnership with three other men making candy near the city. So far, all these fairly successful businessmen have retained their ties to their own families in Ploughshare. Part of their income comes back to their parents, and they still hold rights in their *jia* estates (Cohen 1970, p. 27).

Taxicab Driving and Other Miscellaneous Businesses

There were two cab drivers in Ploughshare in 1973, both renting their vehicles from fleet owners, but by 1978 there were five, all of them owning their own cabs. They would generally leave the village sometime between seven and nine in the morning, drive all day (mostly on the streets of Taibei City), try to get a fare home again, and return sometime in the evening. For a full day's driving in 1978, they could net NT$600 to 800 per day after gas, but part of this would go to paying off the loans for the present cab, and laying away money for the next one when this one broke down in a few years. Cabs cost in the neighborhood of NT$350,000 to 400,000, so loan payments and savings would diminish earnings considerably. Stiil, cab driving is a good living, if a tiring one.

Finally, there is the Fujianese man who lives with his daughter in a little crooked brick house on the hillside by the small suspension bridge. He can be seen every night, wearing a miner's cap with a lamp attached, heading for the hills carrying a long pole with a hook on the end and a fishnet. He is going to the river to catch water snakes, which he sells to druggists and specialty restaurants.

SALARIED OCCUPATIONS

Bureaucrats

There are no professionals or members of Taiwan's "new middle class" (Gates 1981) in Ploughshare. The village is too poor and has no history of education or white-collar mobility. The villagers who come closest to being professionals are the three men employed as bureaucrats in the local *zhen* (township) government, and several men and women who hold office jobs in private companies. One of the local bureaucrats, who retired in 1973, is Tiu: Ong Bieng, who headed the construction section of the local government, a respected post with a good salary. Since he had not been implicated in the scandal that wiped out many of the personnel in the *zhen* government (including the former *zhen* head), he was allowed to retire honorably with a substantial bonus. Chiu Hieng-ik, the older of the two brothers in the house on the point, held a minor position in the township government in 1973. In 1975 he was promoted to section head of the financial section. Ong A-bi's son works in the household registration office. Both earned good incomes but are far from wealthy. And the village's only college-educated citizen, a young Iap woman, had a job in the Taiwan Provincial Grain Office.

One other government employee was policeman Zhang Xiaoyi, whose beat was neighboring Tianfu li, including Shisantian and Luku. People generally do not like policemen anyway, considering them corrupt representatives of a generally unfair bureaucracy, and Zhang's being a mainland Chinese, openly disdainful of Taiwanese customs, means that he is almost universally disliked and feared. In 1977, he quit the police and took a minor job with the newly formed local water district.

AGRICULTURE

Rice Farming

Despite its nonagricultural majority, there have always been some farming families in Ploughshare. Nineteen owned some rice land in 1973, though not all of these worked their land themselves. Before the land to the tiller program of the early 1950s, all farmers in the village were tenants, and neither of the two landowning families farmed its land. In the 1950s, farmers were given the opportunity to purchase their land from landlords through long-term loans, and the landlords were paid in government bonds to get them to invest their holdings in industrial and commercial ventures. At that time, all of Ploughshare's farming families but one received title to their lands. Lua Pieng-kui, the lone exception because his land belonged to a religious association rather than a private landlord, purchased his land outright in 1964.

Acquiring title to their lands, however, did not mean immediate prosperity for the farmers of Ploughshare or other places in Taiwan, as the land reform program was accompanied by a steady rise in land taxation and stabilization of the rice price, guaranteed by the government monopoly on fertilizer, which farmers had to receive in exchange for rice through the Farmers' Associations. The rice-fertilizer barter program was abolished in 1974, but the troubles of the farmers had been compounded after the industrialization of the early 1960s by a rise in the cost of agricultural labor, as those who could leave field work and go into factory jobs did so (Wang and Apthorpe 1974, p. 123). So today, while Ploughshare farmers still work their land, they gain subsistence income but little profit from it. It must be worked because the taxes are due anyway, but no family's land is sufficient to provide it with all its income. What most farmers hope for is to be able to sell their land. In contrast to the low returns on farming, the price of land has skyrocketed recently because so many industrial firms are willing to pay high prices for relatively large tracts of land on which to build factories. Lou Phieng, for example, was a farmer until 1968, when he sold his four-fifths of a hectare (eight *fen*) to the consortium of local businessmen who built the Xinfeng paper factory. The NT$800,000 he received for it were sufficient to let him retire and capitalize his son's knitting mill. And I have already mentioned Kou Pou-ban, whose sale of three *fen* of land was enough to allow him to convert from manual to automatic knitting machines.

But whether Prince Charming appears in the form of a wealthy industrialist looking for a factory site depends on luck and on the location of one's land; it is doubtful, for example, that any factories will be built in the area known as Khei-ciu-a, on the alluvial land next to the Sanxia River, below the southwest corner of Ploughshare. This area is inconvenient. Not only does one have to go through narrow Front Street to reach it, it is also subject to flooding in major typhoons. The three families who own Khei-ciu-a thus have the choice of farming the land or letting it lie fallow and taking a loss on the taxes. No one will buy land to farm because farming simply has no future, especially in what was always a marginal agricultural area, on hillside land that would appear fairly unsusceptible to the consolidation and mechanization schemes now being put into effect in the rich agricultural areas of central Taiwan. If no industrialist offers to buy, there is the possibility that wealthy people from the city will purchase small amounts of land for gravesites, as these are becoming increasingly unavailable close to the city. Lou A-sieng sold about a *fen* of land to someone from Taibei who wanted to bury his parents on it, and realized a small profit, although the new arrangement meant that he had to spend the whole winter of 1972-73 rearranging the rice terraces and their irrigation system.

So people who own land generally farm it. They grow two crops of rice per year, one planted in March and harvested in July, the other planted in July and harvested in November. The practice of growing a cash crop of turnips in the winter season has practically died out recently. Most fields lie fallow between the November harvest and the beginning of plowing in late February—the ones close to the village make good baseball fields.

Of the nineteen landowning families, only four, the only full-time farmers in the village, own more than one hectare of land. So Ban and Tiu: Ong each own about two hectares, and Ong Po-chiu and Png Thuan-lai each own well over one. Neither So Ban nor Tiu: Ong has ever done anything else for a living, and indeed they are both busy most of the growing season. Po-chiu has worked in other occupations, but since he got his land in the land reform that is all he has done. He was seventy-one years old in 1973 but still worked in the fields regularly, although he left the heaviest tasks, such as plowing, to his son. By 1978, he had retired and his son had taken over the farming entirely. (The others who work only as farmers are old men with smallish holdings who no longer really do anything full time.) But even a man who farms full time still cannot support his family entirely from the land. Po-chiu has several grandchildren who work in factories. Tiu: Ong had two daughters working as shop clerks, and one son who was apprenticed until he ran away from home one week after his marriage in fall 1972. So Ban has two sons employed in the Xinfeng paper factory, and one who took up construction work when he returned home from the army.

Other families own considerably less land. Most of them sold little, if any, rice except that exchanged for fertilizer at the Farmer's Association before 1974, or sold to pay for fertilizer since then, and some of them even need to supplement their own production with purchased rice. None of the heads of these families works full time as a farmer. All have other jobs in the coal mines, factories, or, in the case of Chiu Hieng-ik's son, as one of the village's three skilled bricklayers.

Some landowning families do not work their own land. For example, six Tiu: brothers, after dividing their inheritance, ended up with about one- and one-half *fen* of land each. One- and one-half *fen* is really only a tiny plot, and the three youngest brothers have given their land over to elder brothers to work. So eldest brother Sui works his land and his fifth brother's while holding down a foreman's job at Xinfeng, where he recently moved from the coal mines. Second brother A-tieng works his own land and that of fourth brother, Chinong, and sixth brother, Kiet, as well as digging coal. Third brother Hong-kui, also a miner, works only his own land. The fourth brother is a mason, and the fifth and sixth own several knitting machines each, employing, among others, three of the children of their two eldest brothers. The men actually working their younger brothers' land pay no rent but only the taxes and production costs.

In another case, land was still rented out. Old Ti:, Ploughshare's oldest man in 1973, felt that he could retire from farming a few years after his seventieth birthday, especially since two of his sons and his daughter-in-law were bringing in income. But since none of his own children wanted to work the land, he let it out to Lou A-tho, a slightly retarded man who lives at the upper end of the village. A-tho found himself incapable of performing mine or factory work, and his wife, though reasonably intelligent and able to manage their household finances, is blind and unable to hold down any job. So he rented Old Ti:'s eight *fen* of land for a straight 50 percent of the crop. When a few years later Old Ti: decided to sell, A-tho bought a small part of the land that he continues to farm, giving him nearly enough rice to feed his family.

One landowner, Kou Thi-cau, who has about five *fen* of land, had let it out to some agricultural entrepreneurs from somewhere near Taibei to grow *Hiong-kang chai* (Hong Kong vegetable), a plant similar in taste and appearance to broccoli. They sold some of the crop locally and some in more distant markets, and paid a fixed rent. The arrangement did not last long, however, and by 1978 Kou, like his elder brother, was working his land with hired labor.

Farm labor requirements for most families can be met by the family members themselves. Everyone takes a few days off at planting and harvest, the busiest times, and manages to get the crops in. The four full-time farmers with larger holdings employ labor exchange wherever possible, usually drawing on farmers in neighboring Shisantian, which is primarily agricultural. Occasionally they must hire labor, as must those in managerial positions who choose not to work their land themselves. This is expensive at NT$120 per day plus five meals in 1973, and NT$300 a day in 1978. One innovation that year was me-

chanical harvesters that could be hired for about the same rate but
got the job done faster.

It is clear that farming has little future in this area, as little as
work in the mines, though even baking and stooping in the hot sun all
day is more pleasant than squatting in the pits. But unlike coal mining,
farming is difficult to get out of because the land is there and it is
taxed. So people go on growing rice, but very few of them depend on
rice agriculture as a major source of livelihood.

Mountain Crops

Mountain land is no longer of much significance for most village
families, though a considerable number still own some. Tea prices
crashed when industrialization began in the early sixties and in 1973
only one village family worked tea land. Even those who had planted
orange trees now generally let vegetation grow in the orchards, and
simply make one or two treks up the mountainside in the fall to pick
whatever crop there is, which usually brings them not more than a
thousand or two Taiwan dollars. The walk and the work simply are not
justified by the returns.

Only Ong Hui-chin, sixty-three-year-old mother-in-law of policeman
Zhang Xiaoyi, and her daughter still derived any appreciable subsistence
from the mountains in 1973. Hui-chin grew tea on two hectares of her
own land and on two rented hectares. She and her daughter did most of
the picking, but they had to hire labor in peak seasons. Their tea land,
together with the policeman's small salary, gave them an adequate
income. But after Hui-chin died in about 1975, her daughter no longer
grew tea. The crop that was once the primary source of income for
Ploughshare villagers ceased to be of any importance whatsoever.

PROSTITUTION

There were but two prostitutes in the village in 1973, and one of
them, Wa A-mui, was an adopted daughter of people who had just
built a house near the concrete bridge and took little if any part in
village affairs. Only the third daughter of Ong Lou Pik-wa, a widow,
was a member of a family that was really part of the village community.
She went to work after her father died, as her brothers were very
small. She spent most of her time hanging around the village with her
illegitimate daughter. Both she and her mother seemed a little ashamed
of her occupation. She herself appeared somewhat bitter and cocky,
and her mother would rather not talk about her daughter's work, although she did say, "we have to support ourselves somehow." By
1978, her younger brother had acquired a job with enough income
to allow her to stop working, but she retained the rather tough man-
nerisms she had learned from her onetime profession.

ATTITUDES TOWARD WORK

There are marked differences of wealth within Ploughshare, but there is no leisure class; some members of even the richest families are engaged in some sort of physical labor. And most people are constrained by their economic position to work in conditions that would seem appalling to most Americans. So work is part of life and people accept it as a fact.

But it is rather a bitter fact, since practically no one enjoys it. People work because that is the only way they will eat, because, if things go right, they may be able to save enough to do something better. For the villagers the components of a good fate are lots of money and not having to work, two things they uniformly reply when asked. In this respect, almost none of them is successful. Only when they grow old—and sometimes not even then—are they freed of the necessity of daily toil, broken for most of them by only two or three days off each month. But they also feel that things are improving. However hard work is now, it was harder in the past. More people were in the fields or in the mines, many were up several hours before dawn pushing coal carts into the mountains, and the job of a housewife was harder when people had to carry water in buckets instead of pumping it into their kitchens, and when everything had to be hauled on carrying poles rather than on bicycles or motorcycles. If there is very little opportunity for mobility into business or white collar occupations today, there was none for these wretchedly poor villagers thirty or forty years ago, and people who remember the time see improvement not only in terms of material goods but in terms of less work, or easier work, than before.

Along with this resigned dislike of work goes a resentment of those who do not need to, but this stops short of any class consciousness. The goal is not to get rid of the exploiting classes but to join them, not so much in exploiting, but in a life style that is free from so much hard labor. At the same time, people in Ploughshare do not simply look with envy at those they consider more fortunate than themselves. They also see them with an ironic air of contempt. When I appeared in the village only to interview people, take notes, and occasionally care for my daughter, what I did was immediately defined by all members of the elder generation as *thit-thou,* "play," or "frivolous activity." No matter that I was getting paid for it, earning an advanced degree or writing a book (concepts that most of them understood perfectly well), I wasn't working and that was *thit-thou.* It was a sign of good fate that I could do such a frivolous thing and be paid for it, but it was also a sign of a certain kind of inferiority, perhaps an inability to do real work. Farmers would often look at my uncalloused hands with real scorn and say, "never worked a day in his life." If I told them that I had dug ditches for spending money while I was in college, they seemed pleased if unimpressed. This is the attitude villagers generally hold toward people who do not work: fortunate they are, but if they had to work they might not be able to, and we can.

In 1973, resignation toward work was accompanied by a realization that to get ahead, to provide a margin of security for one's family, or to have a chance of moving up to a leisured existence, one had to work extremely hard and be willing to do as much work as possible. Those who went into the mines, those who worked ten or eleven hard hours a day at the shuttle of the knitting machines—people like mason Tiu: Chin-ong, who worked every day for a whole year—all were examples that work means money, money means security or possibilities, and one must take advantage of all available work. After all, people had been working hard for generations, and all but the wealthy would still have to work as hard as possible to achieve their goals.

In 1978, however, especially among the younger people, there was a definite if gradual change in attitude; no longer was making the maximum possible amount of money the only goal of most workers. Probably because, for the first time, families could continue to enjoy their prosperity and even raise their standard of living from the income of several workers doing lower paying but more pleasant jobs. The "quality of life" had become an important consideration for people in the labor market. They wanted a reasonable amount of time off for recreation, good conditions while they worked, and, if possible, some fringe benefits. Factory managers complained about this. They had to spend money on better conditions and fringe benefits if they wanted to attract and keep workers in the labor-short market. Knitting-mill proprietors complained even louder. Even though they could offer workers higher wages, they were losing people rapidly to the more pleasant but lower paying factories. Rural Taiwan was becoming a consumer society, and consumerist attitudes were beginning to develop.

Such consumerism, however, was still in its infancy in Ploughshare in 1978. Further research will be required before we know how fast it is likely to develop. It meant easier work, but easier work was, after all, a continuation of the trend begun with the start of industrialization in the 1960s. And there were still people working as hard as ever, and proud of their ability to do so.

In this way, most villagers of Ploughshare see themselves as *than-ciaq-lang*, people whose wages bring them food. They have a certain pride in this lowly fact, for it at least attests to their mettle. But they would all, without exception, give up this life for a softer one if they had the opportunity.

Social Inequality

MODELS OF SOCIAL INEQUALITY

By any standard, there is social inequality in Ploughshare. Some families have higher incomes than others, enjoy more consumer goods, have a higher educational level, are able to save more of their earnings, and so forth. At the same time, the relationship of different families to the means of production, an important component of the Marxist definition of class, also differs. Some are workers, who sell their labor, some are small property owners, who neither buy nor sell labor (including farmers and owners of small shops and cottage industries), and others hire labor. In addition, certain families live both off their own property and the sale of their labor, or entirely off their own property, but employ both their own and hired labor. Two important questions arise out of such empirical inequalities: how are they best described or analyzed, and how do they fit into the system of social inequality in Taiwan as a whole?

In order to answer either of these questions, we must choose a model for the analysis of social inequality. Ossowski (1963) has delineated three kinds of models commonly used in studies of social inequality. One is the "dichotomic model," in which a society is divided into two mutually antagonistic classes, with one superior to the other in wealth, power, or the exploitation of labor (ibid., pp. 19-37). The second is the "scheme of gradation" (ibid., pp. 38-57; see also Stavenhagen 1975, pp. 19-23), in which people are ranked according to some single characteristic, usually wealth, or according to a synthetic bundle of characteristics. The models of social stratification put forth by American sociologists (Warner 1949) are examples of schemes of gradation. The third is the functional conception, in which social classes are determined by the part they play in the process of production, such as capitalists, farmers, workers, and so forth (Ossowski 1963, pp. 58-68). This is usually taken to be the Marxian view, and is close to that taken by Stavenhagen (1975, pp. 28-32). The first of these three seems inappropriate to the analysis either of Taiwan or of Ploughshare, and I will say no more about it. But the second and third are both applicable to this analysis, though in different ways. The second, the scheme of gradation, leads to a static analysis. It shows how individuals or families rank with respect to each other, but not how they interact, either as antagonists in a relationship between classes, or as members of the same class. The third model, the functional classification, leads to a dynamic analysis of how the social groups interact as part of a total social and economic system. We can conveniently refer to the scheme of gradation as a stratification analysis, and to the functional interaction as a class analysis. As Kraus states (1979, p. 12), the difference between these two models is that "stratification looks at steps on a ladder, whereas classes are defined by their opposition within a system." Also, stratification analyses tend to rank people in terms of consumption, while class analyses look at their part in the production process.

Both of these conceptions are models, rather than hypotheses about empirical reality. We can ask whether stratification, measured by whatever criterion we choose to use, exists in a particular society, and the answer will be "yes" for any complex society. This model is useful, at a certain level, for the analysis of inequality anywhere, but its drawback is that it does not say much about historical or social process. That Ong Sam is richer than Li Si tells us little about how they will interact, or what parts they will play in the social process, unless being rich puts Ong Sam into one group, which acts according to one kind of interest, and being poor puts Li Si into another group with a different or opposing interest. In other words, such an analysis tells us nothing about historical process unless the stratification variable is congruent with class membership, in which case it becomes a class analysis.

A class analysis, then, may seem more helpful in answering our questions, but that is not necessarily true, because, unlike stratification, class, as a system of antagonistic collectivities interacting in a historical process, does not exist in every social system. In some, the prerequisites for class, including at least a common relationship to the means of production, antagonistic interaction with other classes, and group cohesion or potential cohesion (Ossowski 1963, pp. 145-51), simply do not exist. If we had a further qualification, that classes must have a class consciousness, that they must be classes not only *an sich* but also *für sich,* this restricts the field of class analysis even further. If we look at the two social systems that we are considering here, the larger system of Taiwan and the smaller system of Ploughshare, we find stratification analysis applicable to either. But for understanding Ploughshare, a stratificational analysis of Taiwan is not very useful: it does not tell us what factors are acting upon the villagers to constrain their choices of social and economic strategies. If we want to know where the workers, cottage industrialists, and small farmers of Plough- share fit into the larger system, and the effect the system has on con- straining their choices, we had best pursue a class analysis for Taiwan. And such an analysis is empirically justified as well, because the inter- actions of inequality that Ploughshare villagers enter into are all con- tained within the socioeconomic system of Taiwan. The island is, in this sense, a closed system (though the effects of the world system influence the nature of the Taiwan system), in which class forces are at work.

If we look at the village system of Ploughshare, however, we find class analysis empirically inapplicable, for several reasons. First, the interactions of inequality that villagers enter into (selling labor, buying labor, selling products to wholesalers, everyday marketing, etc.) are not restricted to other villagers; in fact, a minority of such interactions are confined within the village. The village is not a closed system, and the classes that villagers belong to are part of the island-wide system. Second, interaction between villagers in many situations must proceed on the basis of equality or balanced exchange, rather than of inequality. Important economic interactions between villagers include mutual feasting, and mutual exchange of labor and credit. Even though villagers do interact on unequal terms, as when they hire rather than exchange each other's labor, interactions on the basis of equality are required as part of the morality of being a village member. Such is not the stuff of social classes. And finally, even though there are wealthy, ordinary, and poor people, and even though there are those whose relationship to the means of production differs, neither of these cate- gories has any common interests within the village, nor is opposed to the interests of others who are related differently to the means of production.

If the village is not a system of social classes, it is still stratified. This stratification has both an emic and an etic reality, that is, it is perceptible both to the natives and to an outside observer. People refer to each other as rich or poor, as farmer or laborer, and these differences exist objectively. They are also correlated with the villagers' respective abilities to participate in the national system as members of one or another social class. So we must investigate the system of stratification in Ploughshare, not only with respect to its origins, partly but not wholly in the class system of Taiwan, but also with respect to the recruitment of Taiwanese, from one community at least, into that system. As Stavenhagen points out (1975, p. 23) stratification schemes, in and of themselves, do not go beyond the level of immediate experience. For the stratification hierarchy of Ploughshare to make sense, we have to relate it to the class system of Taiwan.

In this chapter, I proceed on the assumption that the relative value of the class model for analyzing the salient larger system (first Sanxia, then North Taiwan, and Taiwan as a whole by the 1960s), and of the stratification model for analyzing the Ploughshare system, has remained consistent over time. I will examine the historical development of the class system in the larger society and of its relationship to the stratification system of Ploughshare.

CLASS IN THE LARGER SOCIETY AND STRATIFICATION IN THE VILLAGE, PRE-1970

In the nineteenth century, and for the first two decades or so of Japanese rule, the class structure relevant for Ploughshare was that of Sanxia and its hinterland or, at the widest extent, of the Taibei Basin, and the class structure of the Taibei Basin was one of an agrarian society. There seems to have been much variation in Chinese society in the degree to which the exploiting classes resided in the villages themselves, or were concentrated in the towns (Skinner 1978a, pp. 266–67), but in North Taiwan those who were at the pinnacle of the local class system—the landlords, the tea processors, and the merchants of Shulin, Yingge, and Sanxia—were primarily urban. Before the Japanese occupation, the landlords themselves were legally divided into two groups, the *dazu* or patent holders, descendants of tax farmers given government patents to pioneer land and bring in settlers, and the *xiaozu* or landlords proper, who paid a small rent to the *dazu* and received 50 to 60 percent of the crop, as a fixed rent in kind, from the tenant cultivators (Wickberg 1970, 1981; Wolf and Huang 1980). The Japanese abolished the *dazu* system, establishing a single legal class of landlords. The extent to which tea and other merchants were separate from landlords is not clear to me, but it is my impression that they were often the same families, constituting a town-based upper class. Their income came from a combination of land rents and trade in agricultural commodities, particularly tea, which they bought from small producers, and in part by selling staple foods to those agriculturalists who concentrated primarily on tea or other cash crops. Below this urban landlord-merchant class, there existed a small class of local landlords, living primarily in the more prosperous lowland villages. In the Shitouxi area, for example, these landlords owned a considerable amount of land, while the largest landlord family in all Haishan, the Lins of Banqiao, owned the majority (Harrell 1981a, p. 137). There was one such local landlord family in Ploughshare, Ong Cin's, who owned two parcels of land. Neither of these parcels, however, was in Ploughshare, or worked by a Ploughshare family. The village landlords were generally small landlords, owning enough land to bring in rents that freed them from agricultural toil, but rarely, if ever, operating on a scale commensurable with the wealthy urban families.

The great mass of the population of the southern Taibei Basin lived not by rents or business profits, but by its labor, and most grew rice or other staple food crops, primarily sweet potatoes. Within this group of subsistence farmers, we find two subgroups, owner-cultivators and tenants, with an intermediate group owning some land and renting more. The position of the tenant farmers was an extremely dependent one. They had not only to pay a rent of 50 to 60 percent in kind, but also large rent deposits in advance, and to provide such services as long-term, low-interest loans to their landlords (Wickberg 1981, pp. 217-19). But tenants were not necessarily much worse off than owner-cultivators, since most of the good irrigated rice land was concentrated in the hands of landlords, and worked by tenants (this was partially due to the landlord families' former role in constructing the irrigation systems required for rice cultivation), while owner-cultivators were primarily dry-land farmers, growing sweet potatoes (Wolf and Huang, 1980, p. 51). Of the nine lowland farming families living in Ploughshare in 1905, four were rice growers, five were mixed rice and dry-field farmers, and all were tenants. Their landlord was nominally an association for the worship of the god Sieng-ong Kong, which has its headquarters and shrine in Sanxia, but in fact, it was controlled by the family of Tan Bieng-cun, one of the wealthiest and most prominent in town.

But as mentioned, most of the families who settled Ploughshare in the early years had no access to flat land either as owners or tenants. They had to make their living from the uplands, which meant growing tea or burning wood for charcoal, or from the sale of labor. These people were in a definite position of dependence, even more so than the tenants, because the latter were at least able to grow their own subsistence foods. For the upland farmer or laborer, the food they ate depended on the market price of tea, charcoal, or labor. In the 1905 survey, as shown in table 2, eighteen of Ploughshare's fifty families listed their primary occupation as tea growing, sixteen more were laborers, some of whom were charcoal makers, while the others sold their labor primarily to farmers and owner-cultivators.

In simplified form, then, the class system of Sanxia in the first decades of the twentieth century consisted of three classes: the urban landlord-merchants, including a fringe group of local landlords, who earned their living from the exploitation of labor through rents and mercantile profits; the lowland farmers, who earned their living by producing their basic needs, and included both owner-cultivators and tenants; and the upland farmers and laborers, who earned their living by selling their labor or its fruits on the market. With one exception, the families of Ploughshare belonged to the last two of these classes.

How does this translate into stratification within the village? First, it means that everyone, lowland tenants as well as tea growers, charcoal burners, and casual laborers, was poor. They all lived in single story mud-brick housing with dirt floors, and ate mostly rice and sweet potatoes, with vegetables from their gardens, and meat on special occasions. The one exception was the local landlord family of Ong Cin, who lived off their land rents and had the largest house in the village. Even this house was built of mud-brick, with only a few fired bricks around the doorways and window frames. The poor all seemed to have a very similar standard of living. Their houses, many of which were still standing in 1972, were certainly all alike, although I have not tried to identify any possible differences in food, clothing, and so forth. There was, however, something of a hierarchy, with the tenant farmers standing above the tea growers and charcoal producers. Older people consistently told me that being a farmer was a better life. In addition, as Scott (1976, p. 26) has pointed out, cash-crop farming, as part of an agrarian economy, carries some risk, because of its dependence on market prices, which subsistence-crop farming does not, as long as the rents are not so high or constant as to endanger the peasant's basic livelihood, which they do not appear to have done in northern Taiwan (Wickberg 1981, p. 215). Cash-cropping thus has something in common with wage labor, since even with the same income as the subsistence farmer, the wage laborer has a higher risk of his income dropping below the minimum subsistence level (Scott 1976, p. 210). Although there may not have been a large difference in the income levels of tenants versus tea growers, charcoal makers, and wage laborers, the tenants' incomes were more secure, and their lives were considered more desirable.

With the exception of the one local landlord family, the overall picture is one of fairly uniform poverty, and little internal stratification. The situation seems to have remained much the same during the later decades of Japanese rule. The opening of coal mines in the twenties and thirties added an industrial element to the income of the urban landlord-merchant class, and there were new opportunities for selling labor in the mines and on the pushcart railways. These jobs do not, however, seem to have brought a larger or more stable income than the former alternatives of charcoal making or agricultural labor. People remained nearly uniformly poor, although, as before, there were some exceptions. Ong Cin's family continued to prosper, with Cin and his father opening stores in Taizhong County, and the rents still pouring in. Other villagers, notably the father of current village head Ong Cin-hieng, also tried small-scale shopkeeping, but with little success. One other family did manage to prosper during this period. Once ordinary tea growers, Ong Hieng's family managed to set up a small tea-processing operation in the village, which bought tea from the growers, processed it, and sold it to town merchants. They became quite wealthy by village standards; Hieng became village head, and they built the first brick house in Ploughshare in the 1930s. With carved lintels, a covered porch, and pinkish tile facing on the front walls, it now stands crumbling as a monument to the family's former affluence.

The beginning of industry and economic growth in postwar Taiwan had little immediate effect on the stratification system of Ploughshare. True, the landlords were expropriated in the land to the tiller program of the early 1950s, turning the tenant farmers into owner-cultivators. But because of the structure of agricultural prices at that time, farming did not immediately lead to higher incomes for the poor of Ploughshare (see Wang and Apthorpe 1974, p. 146). It only meant that Ong Cin, who had sold his land cheaply in panic before the land reform program, left the village permanently to settle with his concubine in a shop in Taoyuan, and his family became as poor as the rest of the villagers. Also, around 1960, as industrial employment became available in the urban centers, the price of labor in tea cultivation went up, sending small-scale processors like Ong Hieng into bankruptcy. Thus the changes in the economy of Taiwan during the 1950s did not really reach Ploughshare; by 1960 the only difference in the stratification system was that the two families that had formerly stood out no longer did so. The stratification that did begin to emerge strongly in the 1960s was a result of the direct participation of Ploughshare villagers in the economy and in the new class system of industrializing Taiwan.

CLASS IN INDUSTRIAL TAIWAN AND STRATIFICATION IN PLOUGHSHARE, 1972-73

Since 1960, Taiwan has been a growing industrial country. This industrial growth has given rise to a system of social classes quite different from the one that existed in the agrarian society before 1950. The most recent analysis of social classes in Taiwan (Gates 1981; see also 1979) divides the population of the island into five basic classes: the business and political elite, whose access to political power and/or large-scale capital enables their decisions and behavior to influence the economy and society of the whole island; the old middle class, which owns substantial means of production and employs hired labor, but is not an important determiner of the island's economy; the new middle class, who sells its labor at expensive rates and enjoys much of the consumption style of those who own capital, including professionals and middle- and lower-level bureaucrats; the lower class, which consists of the petite bourgeoisie, with its own means of production, that does not hire labor, including farmers, shopkeepers, and cottage industrial families, as well as industrial workers; and finally, the marginal class without steady income and in disreputable occupations. Gates's analysis is neither a fully functional (class) analysis nor a fully gradational (stratification) one. It combines the petits bourgeois with the workers and uses the term "old middle class," which often refers to small shopkeepers, meaning capitalists, but capitalists of a smaller order than those in the elite. This division is justified, according to Gates, by the absence of the proletariat as a class, because most workers in industrial enterprises are the younger generation of petit-bourgeois families, young men and women who will move into the family business, or start their own small business, when they accumulate enough money from their wages or from inheritance (Gates 1979, p. 401). Also, I suspect, this kind of division is designed to reflect the realities of power and influence in the social system as a whole: small shopkeepers tend to have the same amount of power (very little), and stand in more or less the same relationship to the higher classes as industrial workers, especially since the workers are not organized into labor unions promoting working-class solidarity (Galenson 1979, pp. 431-32). So while Gates's model is eclectic, it comes from someone who knows Taiwan well, and I will adopt it as a model of the class system of Taiwan in the 1970s.

How does this class model articulate with the stratification system of Ploughshare as I observed it in 1972-73? The answer is, in retrospect, not particularly well. It appeared in the early 1970s that the families of Ploughshare, having started with nothing but labor, perhaps a little land to grow rice on, and a strong work ethic, were in a race for differentiation, a race to elevate themselves economically, not necessarily above other villagers, but to a comfortable level where they could achieve their ideal of a good fate—lots of money and no physical labor. Furthermore, it appeared that those who had been able to mobilize a large amount of family labor in proportion to the number of family members needing support, and who had saved enough to turn the product of their labor into capital investment, constituted an upper, petit-bourgeois class within the village. Their income was higher and their interests, though not yet coalesced into class interests, were different from those of their fellow villagers, who remained wage laborers. At that time, a division was forming between an upper class of families who lived off capital investments, and a lower class of families who lived off wage labor. This division, however, was within what Gates called the lower class, and only a few families were part of the "new middle class" of rather larger capitalists.

This emerging class division was reflected both in villagers' emic categories and in measures of consumption (a stratification scale) used to rank the villagers. The villagers themselves, when they speak of a family's economic circumstance, speak of *hou-kia:* (wealthy), *pho-tong* (ordinary), or *kang-kho* (poor; literally, laboring and suffering). I never did a systematic survey of how various families were ranked by their fellow villagers, but I am certain that most people, in anyone's ranking, would fit into the "ordinary" category. When I computed rough measures of stratification, based on a consumption index (modified occasionally by a family's extraordinary political power), I found that the villagers did indeed fit into three categories, each of which could be split into two levels. These three categories I will call the wealthy, the ordinary, and the poor. I initially placed families into these categories based on a subjective evaluation after knowing them for ten months. Later, I computed an actual index of stratification, and found only 4 or 5 families out of 101 who had been misplaced in the subjective evaluation.

This stratification index was based on three measures of consumption: income per family member, size and style of house, and vehicles and appliances owned. Each of these factors was rated on a scale from 0 to 3 points, according to the scale shown in table 3. Families in the wealthy category scored 7-9, those in the ordinary category scored 3-6, and the poor scored from 0-2. In the subjective evaluation, I divided the wealthy into the elite and the near-elite, primarily on the basis of their political power; the ordinary into upper- and lower-

TABLE 3

AN INDEX OF ECONOMIC STRATIFICATION, 1972-73

Points	Income per person per month (NT$)	House	Vehicles and appliances
0	0-500	Mud-brick	No motor vehicles or major appliances
1	500-1,000	Brick, dirt floor	Television or motor-cycle
2	1,000-2,000	Brick, concrete floor	Television and motor-cycle
3	over 2,000	Two-story brick or finished floor	Television, motorcycle, and refrigerator

ordinary, according to both their economic and political standing; and the poor into poor and very poor, depending on the misery of their living circumstances. These subdivisions also correlate well with the stratification index, though there was some overlap between the sub-categories within each major division. The number of families in each category, along with whether part or all of their livelihood was derived from investment or not, is shown in table 4. These stratification rank-ings also corresponded to the households' economic place in the larger

TABLE 4

SOCIAL STRATIFICATION IN PLOUGHSHARE, 1973

	Wealthy		Ordinary		Poor		
	Elite	Near elite	Upper	Lower	Poor	Very poor	Total
Capital-investing families	5	5	15	3	2	0	30
Families with no capital invested	0	0	22	29	13	7	71
Total	5	5	37	32	15	7	101

system. All ten families in the wealthy category were living off invested capital, with or without hiring labor, and they had enough money to secure their economic position, and probably to expand. There was little, it appeared, that would drive them out of business altogether. The families in the upper-ordinary category lived mostly off wage labor, but a minority had invested capital, in most cases in the form of knit-ting machines worked by family and hired labor. The families in the lower-ordinary category were almost all wage laborers, and only three of thirty-two had any capital investments. What set off the whole ordinary category from the wealthy was that they appeared to have little economic cushion. Workers would have to go on earning wages, and capital investment was precarious. Indeed, by 1928, some families with invested capital in 1972-73 had gone back to wage labor as a primary means of support. What set these people off from the poor was that, even without much cushion or security, they had no trouble making ends meet. Finally, the poor were those who were really in trouble, and their low living standard was a result of their inability to participate gainfully in the island's economic growth, usually because of little labor power in the family (money to invest was, of course, totally out of the question).

Case studies of a few families in each group will illustrate both the range of income and consumption, and the relationship between labor, capital investment, income, and placement into the wealthy, ordinary, or poor categories.

Five families of the elite and five of the near-elite made up the category of wealthy. The elite was distinguished from the near elite more by its political power, inside and outside of the village, and by its business operations on a scale wider than the village, than by differences in income or consumption patterns. The most important of the elite families was headed by Ong Cin-hieng, proprietors of the large, successful, vertically integrated knitting operation described in chapter two. Cin-hieng had once been a cart pusher, but through skillful use of opportunities and hard work, his family had risen to the top of the stratification system. Around 1961, Cin-hieng had sent his two sons, recently returned from military duty, to learn the knitting trade at a factory in Sanchong, a Taibei suburb.They earned enough to purchase a single machine, worked it nearly around the clock, and saved most of what they earned. By 1972, they had expanded to the point where they had twenty-two machines, a truck, and a retail store. Their income varied seasonally. In the summer they often contracted with larger factories to do export work, and their income was probably not over NT$80,000 per month. In the winter, however, when the domestic demand for knitted goods was high, they used not only their own machines, but subcontracted work out to other knitting families, raising their income considerably. With fifteen people in the family, they certainly needed no more than NT$25,000 per month to maintain an above-average standard of living. The rest of their substantial income could go to paying off mortgages (they bought, over the years starting in 1972, several five-story shophouses in Taibei), and to further expansion of the business. Even a substantial drop in income would not hurt their economic standing, at least in the short run. They thus had the economic cushion characteristic of the wealthy.

At the same time, the family displayed the other important charac-

A wealthy businessman and his son, 1978

teristic of this group—business connections and economic power outside the restricted village context. They not only subcontracted with families in neighboring communities, they were also active, in a small way, in the commercial life of the Wanhua section of Taibei. One or more members of the family usually lived in the Wanhua store, and others traveled back and forth. When they dealt in this outside business world, they did not, as did members of poorer families, simply take what work they could get from larger suppliers. They controlled their business independently of any pressures but those of the wholesale market in which they bought and the retail trade to which they sold. And even these pressures were lessened by the surplus of income after expenditures.

Other elite families shared the two characteristics of outside business interests and a sizable economic cushion. One of these was the family of Ong Cin-hieng's chief political rival at the time, Kou Pou-kim. The eldest of a tenant farmer's five sons, he had never worked on the land but had been in one business or another since his early teens, beginning as a peddler and working his way up to ownership of two small textile factories, neither of them located in the village or employing village labor. I do not have an accurate assessment of his income, but I know it was enough to enable him to halt his operations for a few months in 1973 without suffering politically or economically. As Cin-hieng, he had a cushion, and his business dealings were primarily outside the village context.

A third member of the elite was Ong Lou, a thirty-two-year-old scion of a family that had been miners and cart pushers for two previous generations. Like Ong Cin-hieng, he had prospered in the knitting business, first buying one machine in partnership with his sister's husband, and culminating in a one-third partnership (with men from other communities) in a business owning over thirty machines. Since his family had only four people, the income from the equivalent of ten machines (NT$12,000 per month) was enough to support them and to provide a substantial cushion. And again, his economic operations went beyond the village sphere.

The final two members of the village elite in 1972-73 were also economically comfortable and connected to wider business networks, but they were less integrated into the village society than the previous three. Tiu: Ong Lai was himself a bureaucrat, head of the construction section of the Sanxia township government. His family's prosperity, however, came from his eldest son's window-glass business in the town of Sanxia. The income from this business was substantial enough to give them the best-appointed house in the village, with a front room newly painted with gilt designs for a daughter's engagement in October

1973, and Lai's political connections were enough to make him the most respected leader in the village, carefully neutral in the rivalries between Ong Cin-hieng and the likes of Kou Pou-kim. When Lai retired from his government post, he was asked by Tan Then-su, Sanxia's wealthiest capitalist, to take the post of general manager of one of Then-su's factories in southern central Taiwan.

If Tiu: Ong Lai had started in the village and expanded outward, Po Hok-lai was in the village almost incidentally. Son of a former landlord family in Sanxia town, he came to Ploughshare in the mid-sixties to set up a workshop assembling plushly lined plastic cosmetic baskets for export. In 1972, however, he left Taiwan altogether to set up a travel agency in Hong Kong, leaving his family behind in Ploughshare. Insofar as he participated in village activities, he did so at the top, by hiring village labor. But he was, more than the other elite families, really marginal to Ploughshare economy and society.

The five families in the near-elite category in 1972-73 generally had the same, or slightly lower, level of income as the elite families, and also had some economic cushion. But they lacked either the outside economic operations or the political power of the elite family leaders, and thus were classified into this somewhat lower category. All of them, like the elite families, derived most of their income from capital investment.

One of these families was headed by Lou Kim-bi and her uxorilocally married-in husband, Lua Pieng-kui. They were among the wealthiest in the village, having one of its two color television sets and one of its handsomest houses, complete with an electrically pumped fountain in the courtyard, and only their relative lack of political power prevented them from being counted among the elite. They had achieved their current status through the establishment, by their third son, of an enormously successful electrician's business in Taibei. Two other families with clear near-elite status were the Iap brothers, general storekeepers at the upper end of the village, and Tiu: Phieng's, owner of the general store near the Blacksmith Gulch bridge. Each of these families had invested capital at, or before, the beginning of the industrial expansion, and their business had prospered because of the general increase in purchasing power during that expansion, elevating them to the near-elite. The elder Iap brother was elected village representative in late 1973.

Moving to the next broad classification of families, the upper- and lower-ordinary, we find them in a somewhat different situation. Unlike the elite, these families' place in the production process varied widely. Some had invested capital while others lived entirely off wages, although the petty capitalists among them were heavily concentrated in the upper-ordinary category. But in income and consumption, the elements of the stratification scale, these families all had something in common: they had enough to get along, enough to think of expanding, but not enough to have the economic cushion enjoyed by the wealthy families. Where they were tied into outside economic networks, it was always as dependent actors, selling their labor for wages, or taking knitting work on consignment from large factories controlling both the supply of work and the pay. This meant, in turn, that no one from this group could aspire to village leadership, although the opinions of many of them carried considerable weight in village discussions.

One family belonging to the upper-ordinary group was Huan A-cai's. It consisted of Huan, a thirty-year-old former miner, now engaged in knitting, his twenty-four-year-old wife, his aged, invalid mother, and his two daughters aged four and two. A-cai and his wife had eight knitting machines, two worked by their own labor and six by hired labor, bringing them an income of approximately NT$12,500 per month, far above their estimated consumption needs of about four or five thousand. Machines at that time cost about NT$17,000, so that the price of a machine, if bought with funds from a rotating credit society, could be paid off with two or three months's profits. It looked as if they had as much cushion as Ong Lou's, but events in the next few years proved this wrong. And they never had the outside business connections; they were on their own, a village family dealing with large factories in a relationship of subordination. They had no new house or other items of conspicuous wealth and, despite their income, their station in the stratification hierarchy was ordinary.

Other families maintained a similiar standard of living simply from wage labor, or from wage labor plus farming—farming being more equivalent to wage labor than to capital investment since it offers no opportunity for expansion. A nuclear family like Ong Kui-sieng's, a foreman in a pottery factory in Yingge, and consisting of himself, his wife, and two small children, maintained itself comfortably on a salary of around NT$4,000 per month. They had a television and a motorcycle, though no refrigerator, and their small house, newly built of bricks, was neat and sturdy. Larger families, such as Ong Po-chiu's, consisting of himself and his son, both farmers, his daughter-in-law, who also helped out on the land, and his seven grandchildren, two of them teenage girls employed in local electronics factories, also managed to support themselves at an equivalent level. They had a new brick house at the upper end of the village, a television, and a motorcycle.

When we move from the upper-ordinary to the lower-ordinary families, we see a difference in degree rather than in kind. This latter group of families was still able to support itself without trouble, but at a lower level, and had no real hope of expansion in the near future. Ong Tho's family, for example, had ten people. Tho's widowed mother, in her eighties, worked only in the vegetable garden, but his wife, in addition to doing most of the housework, also took in wash from six or seven people for NT$50 per month each. Tho and his eldest son worked together in the mines, constructing frameworks in the shafts and tunnels, and each earned around NT$2,500 per month. The second son was employed in the Xinfeng paper plant, and brought in a further NT$2,000. This gave them a monthly income of NT$7,000 or NT$7,500 for ten people, enough to live on at a modest standard, and to replace a section of their house, wiped out in a typhoon, with a new brick wing, but not enough to save or invest. When the daughter-in-law required surgery in 1971, they had to start a credit association to pay the medical costs. A family in similar circumstances was Ong Hong-ik's, younger son of the former wealthy tea processor Ong Hieng. Since the collapse of the family tea-processing business in the early 1960s, they had fallen on hard times. Their once-proud tiled house was sadly in need of repair, and had no appliances or other modern conveniences of note. Ong Hong-ik and his eldest son supported the family working in the Xinfeng paper plant, giving them a barely adequate income of about $5,000 per month. Even though the son had been a brilliant scholar in junior-middle school, he had had to go to work immediately after graduation to support the family.

We now come to the bottom two stratification categories in 1972-73, the poor and the very poor. These can be considered together, since the difference between them is one of degree and not of kind. What set them off from the ordinary families is that their incomes were insufficient to provide them with even the momentary security and small number of modern conveniences that the ordinary families enjoyed. A total of twenty-one families were placed in these categories at that time. All the poor lived in substandard, mostly mud-brick housing, owned no appliances or motorized vehicles, had family incomes of NT$500 per person per month, or less, and were of no political importance in the village or outside of it. Two of these families actually had some capital invested. Song Ka-hui's married-in son-in-law had recently purchased two knitting machines, and Hakka barber Zhong Min-hui had his shop and its equipment. Their incomes were still rather low, however, which placed them in the poor category along with nineteen families of wage earners. It is interesting that eight of these families contained mainland Chinese men, and that nearly all of them had at least one member with a severe mental or physical disability, although it is not clear which is the cause and which is effect. Were they poor because the added burden of the disabled member increased their expenses and decreased their potential earning or managerial ability, or was the disability simply more obvious to an observer of a poor family? Or was the disability the result of poverty? It is impossible to tell. What we can safely say is that these people had been least able to take advantage of the opportunities for economic mobility that had arisen with the industrialization of North Taiwan. The family headed by Huan Kim-kiet was typical of the poor. Although he was sixty years old in 1972, Kim-kiet still spent over twenty days per month in the coalpits, bringing the family an income of about NT$2,700 per month. His wife did not work, having to stay home and care for their mentally retarded eldest son, who represented a considerable drain on what resources they had. Their next four children were still in school, and one coal miner's salary could support seven people only in rather miserable style. They rented two rooms in a mud-brick compound owned by the family of former landlord Ong Cin, and had little furniture, and no modern appliances. Even poorer was Chua Li Hong, who lived with a man from Xinzhu in a ramshackle mud structure facing the Sanxia River near the upper end of the village. She was disabled and could not work, and her man, though he had a janitorial job at a Taibei market, was a heavy drinker and general troublemaker who contributed little. One of her sons had gone off to serve in the army and never returned, and the others were reaching the age when they could begin to earn wages.

To what extent was this system of stratification also connected to class differences within the village, and did any existing class differences conform to Gates's model of class in Taiwanese society? From a functional standpoint, it did appear that a class system, if it did not already exist, was emerging in Ploughshare. All the families in the wealthy category earned their living from investment, and a substantial number in the upper-ordinary group also living from investment had ambitions, and perhaps potential, of reaching the level of wealth and participation in the island-wide economy characteristic of the wealthy. Families living off wage labor, on the other hand, had farther to go: even the best-off of them would have to begin with capital investment on a very small scale, and then work up from there. And few of the wage-earning families had incomes that could allow sufficient savings for the purchase of two or three knitting machines. A family with two miners and two knitters, for example, would have a monthly income of around NT$12,800 and they might be able to save, since eight people could be supported for around six or seven thousand. But take away two of those wage earners, or replace them with factory women earning only around NT$1,000 a month, and the margin of savings diminishes, or disappears. So had the 1973 conditions persisted, the village might well have developed into a two-class community, with an upper class of small entrepreneurs and a lower class of laborers.

But the emerging class system was only partial, because the classes were not related to each other as elements in a closed system. And even the limited class structure did not conform very well with the system that Gates found in Taiwan as a whole. According to her scheme, the village elite families might well be members of the commercial-industrial middle class, but even the capital-investing families in the ordinary group, including shopkeepers as well as small knittingmill operators, would belong, with the laborers, in the lower class. They all interacted with members of the commercial-industrial middle class, be it village head Ong Cin-hieng or the manager of a parent factory in a distant city, in an assymetrical relationship of dependency.

THE DISAPPEARANCE OF INCIPIENT CLASSES IN PLOUGHSHARE, 1973-78

Like the stratification hierarchy of that time, the incipient class system of Ploughshare in the early 1970s was based on one major economic fact, the differential returns on capital investment, as opposed to the sale of labor. The relevant wage rates, costs, and returns on investment in knitting are set out in table 5.

Some kinds of labor, such as mining and masonry, brought in nearly

TABLE 5

RETURN FOR VARIOUS ACTIVITIES, 1972-73

Activity	Daily wage or profit (NT$)	Days required to purchase a new knitting machine (ca. NT$17,000)
Coal mining (male)	130	130
Xinfeng Paper Co. (male worker)	90	190
Masonry (male)	130	130
Hod carrying (female)	70	240
Agricultural labor (either sex)	120	140
Electronic or textile factory (female)	40	420
Knitting for pay on someone else's machine (either sex)	100	170
Knitting on own machine (either sex)	140	120
Profit from hiring someone to work knitting machine	40	420

as much income as knitting on one's own machine. But masonry was a skill that took a long time to learn, and mining, while unskilled, was also very undesirable; at any rate neither of these was accessible to women. And almost nobody was willing to do agricultural labor for wages. If a family was fortunate enough to have two or three able-bodied males who could mine or build houses, its labor might well produce enough surplus to purchase knitting machinery. If the majority of a family's labor force was female, on the other hand, it would be very difficult to amass enough to invest in machinery, since a female factory worker earned less than a third of a coal miner's wages. Knitting for wages, by contrast, provided the best alternative. Although it paid a man somewhat less than mining, it taught him a skill that he could later use to more profit when he got his own machine, and for a woman it was by far the most lucrative form of employment. Even the high-paying wage-earning jobs could not compete with knitting on one's own machine, especially since it took only three or four months' labor to repay the investment. But an even greater advantage was that it was not limited by family labor power. Once all able family members were working their own machines, additional ones could be purchased and worked with hired labor, which was readily available. Despite greatly diminished returns when additional machines were worked by hired labor, those returns were still there, and one could keep adding more machines. A further advantage of owning knitting machines was their low vulnerability to changes in the ratio of family labor to family consumption, which varies with the family development cycle. A family with small children and elderly retired parents, for example, may only have one employable member, especially if the mother stays home to take care of the children. Its situation is like that of family (a) in figure 2, with eight mouths to feed and only one laborer. This same family ten years later, however, will be in a very different situation. Grandmother will have died, four of the five children will be old enough to earn money, and mother, freed from full-time child-care responsibilities, can go to work as well. There will be six laborers and seven mouths to feed, giving the family good saving potential. At this stage in its cycle, the family may be able to think about invest-ing in knitting machines. If it does not, it will see its income drop considerably, relative to its neighbors, when the children grow up, marry, have children, and must support their aging parents. A family with a few knitting machines, on the other hand, is not as susceptible to this cycle. It can go on earning money with hired labor even if a daughter marries out, or a daughter-in-law quits working to have children.

Although knitting families could widen the gap between them and

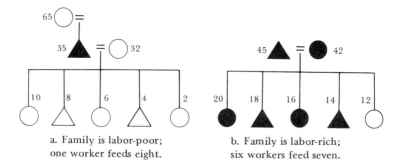

a. Family is labor-poor;   b. Family is labor-rich;
one worker feeds eight.   six workers feed seven.

Fig. 2. Labor and consumption at two stages of a hypothetical family cycle.

wage-earning families, other kinds of capital investment did not offer the same potential. Storekeeping produced a rather constant profit, but afforded little room for expansion, whereas larger-scale investment, such as Ong Cin-hieng's big knitting operation or Kou Pou-kim's textile factories, provided enough cushion to make them relatively impervious to shifts in the balance of economic forces. Such forces, however, produced a crisis for the small-scale knitting mill proprietors between 1973 and 1978, which greatly reduced the economic distance between them and the wage-laborers.

The shift in the balance of forces was a simple one: the average value of wages, as compared with investment returns in knitting, rose dramatically, as shown in table 6. The wages for knitting were no longer higher enough than factory wages to lure young workers into the physically exhausting work.

While wages and earnings generally went up (faster than the consumer price index, which increased between 1973 and 1978 by a factor of 1.8)[1], two important categories went up fastest of all: factory wages for women, and wages paid to young boys who had not yet served in the army and were not considered desirable as workers in 1973. The former actually rose more in the interval than indicated by the starting wage, because factories in 1978 tended to give larger seniority raises and pay more overtime, which by law paid one and one-third time. It was still true in 1978 that a young man or woman could earn more by knitting than by working in a factory, but the

1. Official consumer price indexes for 1978 were not available to me at the time of writing. The increase from 1973 to 1977, however, was 1.7, almost all of which occurred during the 1973-74 oil crisis. Official figures also show wage increases for the island as a whole commensurate with those I recorded for Ploughshare workers (Directorate General of Budget, Accounting and Statistics 1978, pp. 280-83).

TABLE 6

Returns for Various Activities, 1973 and 1978

Activity	Daily wages or returns 1973 (NT$)	Daily wages or returns 1978 (NT$)	Ratio 1978/73
Coal mining	130	350	2.7
Xinfeng Paper Co. (starting)	90	220	2.4
Knitting for wages	100	250	2.5
Female electronics worker (starting)	35	110	3.1
Female electronics worker (maximum)	60	220	3.7
Young boy in factory (starting)	n.a.	135	—
Earnings from knitting on own machine	140	350	2.5
Earnings from hiring a knitter	40	100	2.5

difference was not so great. And chances were the family would be less desperately in need of the young person's earnings, because earnings in general had risen faster than prices, and with them the family's savings, living standards, or both.

This shift in the relative value of labor and investment usually meant two things: small-scale knitting mills had difficulty finding laborers, and wage labor of any sort began to compare more favorably with ownership of knitting mills as a source of income for a family. The labor shortage for the knitting proprietors had to do not so much with the diminishing wage differential—even an experienced electronics worker would only make NT$150 or 160 per day, compared with the knitter's NT$250—but with the conditions of work. Knitting no longer has the advantages for a young woman that it used to have, and for a young man, whose only choice in 1973 might have been knitting, factory jobs are available at an almost commensurate scale. Pure economic rationality would still have dictated a large labor supply for knitting, but other considerations, such as time off and working conditions, influenced people to take factory jobs instead. Knitting-mill owners could not afford to soften the conditions for their hired workers, since they were required by their suppliers to do a certain amount of work in a certain time; if they did less, they would either have to decrease the workers' pay, and lose them altogether, or take a smaller profit, which would make their business efforts useless. This underscores the point that the small-scale knitting-mill proprietors, like the wage laborers, interacted with the larger economy in a position of dependence, and their choice was rapidly narrowing to a switch to automatic machines, or a return to wage labor.

At the same time, the differences between wage labor and the small-scale capital investment represented by knitting mills had diminished with the rise in the value of labor, both in relationship to the returns on investment and to consumer prices. In 1978, the stratification hierarchy of Ploughshare, as a measure of the income from these various activities, was much less dependent on the differences between labor and capital investment, and mobility within that hierarchy, except at the very top, was generally correlated with increase in the ratio of family labor to family members. Table 7 shows the point scale used to classify families in 1978. As before, the same number of points classifies people as wealthy, ordinary, or poor, but since the general standard of living has increased, so has the value of each score.

TABLE 7

AN INDEX OF ECONOMIC STRATIFICATION, 1978

Points	Income per person per month (NT$)	House	Vehicles and appliances
0	0-1,250	Mud-brick or dirt floor	No motorcycle or refrigerator
1	1,250-2,500	One- story brick, concrete floor	Motorcycle and refrigerator
2	2,500-5,000	Two-story or finished floors	Color TV or car
3	over 5,000	Three-story or unusually large	Color TV and car

According to this revised scale, and in agreement with subjective assessments, the number of families in each category in 1978 is indicated in table 8.

Comparing these data with those in table 4, we find several differences. First, there are fewer poor people, the same number of wealthy people, and a marked growth in the "ordinary" category, biased somewhat toward the upper end. Second, capital investment is still required to be wealthy, but capital investment and wage labor were much more evenly distributed over the two halves of the ordinary category. Capital investment no longer nearly guaranteed a place in at least the upper part of the ordinary category. This is because capital investment was now more nearly equivalent as a source of income to wage labor, as wage labor was more generally available and paid better than it did previously. And if we look at upward and downward mobility in the stratification hierarchy, we can see the equivalence between labor and investment all the more clearly.

TABLE 8

SOCIAL STRATIFICATION IN PLOUGHSHARE, 1978

	Wealthy		Ordinary		Poor*
	Elite	Near elite	Upper	Lower	
Families with capital investments	2	9	20	10	1
Families with no capital investments	0	0	18	22	12

*Nobody in Ploughshare is "very poor" anymore; the kind of squalor suffered by the poorest families in 1972-73 is now found only in remote mountain districts.

Table 9 shows the 101 families residing in Ploughshare in 1972-73, along with what happened to them by 1978 in the stratification hierarchy: whether they moved up, moved down, stayed in the same relative position, or moved out of the village altogether. Twenty-six families moved either up or down relative to their fellow villagers. The one elite family who appeared to have moved down was Ong Lou's, who had gotten caught in an employment squeeze with his large stock of manual knitting machines. When I was about to leave Ploughshare in August 1978, however, he was negotiating to purchase some automatic machines, and could possibly regain his position. The near-elite family who moved down was Tiu: Phieng's, who ran the store by the small suspension bridge. He died in 1974, and the decline of the business may well have been due to inefficient management by his wife and sons. Far more significant is the move from the village of the two elite families, Tiu: Ong Lai and Po Hok-lai's. The elite families were operating in a larger economic arena, and were not as tied to the village. Both Ong Cin-hieng and Kou Pou-kim, it should be noted, stayed in the village, both men having political and economic bases grounded in the kinship structure of the village itself.

The vertical mobility in the ordinary and poor categories is more interesting, because it was fundamentally of a different order, and illustrates the importance of labor power in the rise and fall of a family's fortunes. In table 10, I have taken just those families who moved up or down in the stratification hierarchy, and indicated the direction of change in the ratio of laborers to family members in each category. The relationship fits almost perfectly with our expectations, with only three anomalous cases. Two of those who decreased their labor-member ratio, and still moved up in the stratification hierarchy, were families with considerable amounts of invested capital. The other case, in which a family gained labor but still moved down, is something of a puzzle, to other villagers as well as to me. This is the family of Kou

TABLE 9

STATUS AND FAMILY MOBILITY, 1973-78

1973 Status Mobility 1973-78	Wealthy		Ordinary		Poor	
	Elite	Near elite	Upper	Lower		Total
Up	0	0	2	7	8	17
Down	1	1	4	3	0	9
Same	2	4	26	20	11	63
Moved	2	0	5	2	2	11

TABLE 10

MOBILITY AND FAMILY LABOR RESOURCES, 1973-78

	Families moving up	Families moving down
Families who gained labor relative to members	9	1
Families who lost labor relative to members	2	7
Families whose labor/member ratio stayed the same	6	1

Pou-kim's first agnatic cousin Kou Pou. She and her husband farmed land in the village, had one son working as a cab driver, and two sons and a daughter-in-law working in factories, which should have given them enough income. But their house was coming apart in 1978, and they had no expensive modern conveniences except their son's cab. Pou's husband was not a notorious gambler or philanderer, so their case must remain unexplained.

Far more typical are the great majority of cases in which an increase in labor power has brought prosperity, or a decrease in hard times, like Ong Pik-chin's family. Only daughter of a village cart pusher, she contracted an uxorilocal marriage with Fan Jinzhong, an amiable, hard-working ex-soldier from the Shanghai region. They had five children, three daughters and two sons. In 1973, Jinzhong worked as a coal miner, his wife as a hod carrier, and one daughter had just begun to work for low wages in a nearby factory. This brought them an approximate monthly income of NT$6,500, and with monthly expenses for seven people at between five and six thousand Taiwan dollars, afforded them little margin. They lived in a mud-brick house, and had only one appliance, a television set. They belonged firmly to the "lower ordinary" group of villagers. In 1978, they were building a spacious new house on the site of the old one, and people were commenting that they were doing very well, despite Jinzhong's having been partially disabled by a stroke suffered a year before. Pik-chin could still work, and did at knitting, while their son and two daughters worked in factories, for wages at least double what the eldest had drawn when she had gone to work in 1972. This gave them a monthly income of NT$15,000 or more, against expenses of NT$12,000. Even with the two smallest children in school and the father disabled, their earning power and their margin of savings had increased over what it had been in 1973.

Another family that had turned labor power to good use was Ong Chun-lai's, a miner in his late fifties. They lived in very simple style in a mud-brick house in 1973, the father mining coal, one son in a factory, and another apprenticed, not yet bringing in income. This gave them monthly earnings of around NT$4,500 for seven people, a very low amount. By 1978, things had changed dramatically: the father's mining and the four sons' wages in factories brought in a very comfortable sum of over NT$25,000 per month. They too had a new house, built with the earnings from the father and his sons, none of whom was married yet. At the time, this family had reached the height of its earning power from labor alone—the father was about to retire from the mines and the sons, in their twenties, would soon be marrying, perhaps dividing the household, and certainly having children.

A family that had already shown the detrimental effects of the development cycle is the Ong brothers', living near the upper end of Back Street. There were originally five of them, but the second never returned from army service and was presumed dead. In 1973, though they still lived in a house built partially out of mud-brick, their knitting business appeared to be prospering. Their widowed mother reeled the yarn, and three of the four brothers, and one of their wives, knitted it, allowing them to work four of their eight machines with family labor and hire only four workers. But the combination of more mouths to feed and the unfavorable labor market had taken its toll by 1978. In 1975, the brothers divided their households, and the first and third continued a reasonably successful knitting business elsewhere. But the fourth, who stayed with his mother, his wife and three daughters, and his younger brother, was not doing well. He had only one knitting machine, and neither his mother nor his wife was able to work, leaving him and his younger brother, a factory worker, to support six people in what seemed like squalor in the Ploughshare of 1978.

There has thus been a blurring, or perhaps even an elimination, between 1972-73 and 1978, of what was earlier an emergent system of two classes, the small-scale capitalists and the wage laborers, that correlated well with the existing system of social stratification. Wage labor, as a means of livelihood, had become almost equivalent to

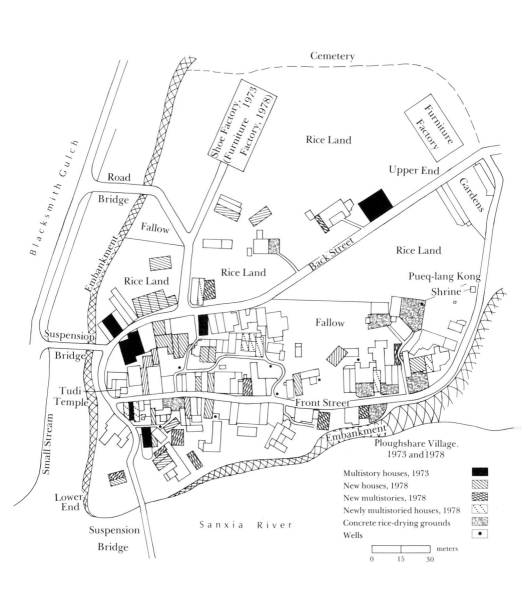

Cemetery

Shoe Factory, 1973
(Furniture 1973
Factory, 1978)

Furniture
Factory

Rice Land

Road

Bridge

Upper End

Gardens

Fallow

Embankment

Rice Land

Back Street

Rice Land

Rice Land

Rice Land

Pueq-lang Kong
Shrine

Suspension

Fallow

Bridge

Tudi
Temple

Front Street

Small Stream

Embankment

Ploughshare Village,
1973 and 1978

Lower
End

Sanxia   River

Suspension

Bridge

Multistory houses, 1973
New houses, 1978
New multistories, 1978
Newly multistoried houses, 1978
Concrete rice-drying grounds
Wells

meters

0   15   30

small-scale capital investment. And the new stratification scale reflected this, everywhere but at its upper end. These changes in the relationship of class and stratification in the village can be explained in terms of changes in Taiwan's economy as a whole. By the early 1970s, Taiwan had reached full employment, and in 1978, factory managers were almost all actively looking for additional labor. The only way they could get any was by raising wages or improving working conditions, which, apparently, most of them felt they could afford to do, since wages had gone up with respect to prices. Small knitting-mill proprietors could not afford to raise wages commensurately, and they certainly could not afford to improve working conditions, so they lost as the workers gained. But the small-scale knitting mill proprietors and the wage laborers, although they were incipient classes, had not yet become fully formed classes. A family that owned machines and hired outside labor might still hire its own labor out to a factory, and indeed many families participated in the economy both as entrepreneurs and as wage earners. Thus it is perhaps inaccurate to say that petty capitalists lost and workers gained. It is more accurate to say that capital investment lost and work gained to the point where they had become nearly equivalent, and those who engaged in them were once again a single social class.

This is, I think, what Gates (1979, pp. 397-402) means when she speaks of the self-exploitation of Taiwan's petite bourgeoisie. Younger members of petit-bourgeois families sell their labor, constituting a large part of the extremely young working class (ibid., p. 401, quotes figures showing that only about one-third of manufacturing workers in Taiwan in 1973 were over thirty). Hence the proletariat does not reproduce itself (ibid., p. 396), which Gates sees as deleterious to the long-term development of Taiwan. It is certainly deleterious to the development of a revolutionary class consciousness among a proletariat; whether that is desirable or undesirable depends on one's opinion of what might result from it. But for our purposes, it is important that this self-exploitation results from a particular set of circumstances, in which the fruits of selling labor are worth enough to petit-bourgeois families to induce them to send their young sons and daughters into the factories instead, for example, of sending them to expensive private schools (relatively easier to enter than the more prestigious public schools) during their late teen years. That it is advantageous to send the sons and daughters to work in this way is an indication of the rough equivalence between small-scale investment and selling labor. The example of knitting mills and factory work in Ploughshare is but an instance of this widespread phenomenon.

If the ordinary category of Ploughshare's stratification system

shows a rough balance between investment and wage labor as primary
sources of a family's income, neither the rich nor the poor end of
the scale shows any such balance. All the families on the rich end
have remained petty capitalists throughout the economic changes of
the 1970s. They have enough financial cushion and enough autonomy
in their operations to appear relatively impervious to the economic
changes that can affect laborers or small-scale investors. If these form a
class in Taiwan's economy and society, the larger investors definitely
form another class. Even though they both operate knitting mills,
there is a great difference between Ong Cin-hieng's family and Lou
Khieng-hun's. As we have seen, one operates with a cushion, the other
without; one acts relatively autonomously as a successful wholesale
and retail business, while the other depends for its livelihood on larger
factories who supply work. If Gates's analysis of classes in Taiwan
society did not fit Ploughshare in 1972-73, it fits it almost perfectly in
1978: there are members of the "old middle class," like Ong Cin-hieng
and Kou Pou-kim, and there are both knitting mill proprietors and
wage-earning families in the lower class. Some families are intermediate
or transitional, but then any class system has a certain amount of
upward and downward mobility (Stavenhagen 1975, pp. 24, 34;
Giddens 1973, p. 107). Wage labor is equivalent only to *small-scale*
capital investment.

Despite this equivalence, people still prefer small-scale investment
as a strategy for a family economy. First, people perceive small-scale
investment as existing on a continuum with larger-scale investment,
since there is always the hope that one machine or one store might
lead to many. More important, small-scale investment is not so vulner-
able to cycles in family labor supply, or to family calamities that
eliminate laborers. The rich end, as well as the poor end of the Ploughshare stratification scale shows an imbalance between capital and labor.
Those who are totally dependent on labor suffer most when their
family passes through labor-poor points in the developmental cycle,
or when a physically or mentally defective adult drains the family
budget. Even if labor produces equivalent returns in the short run,
investment is safer. Whether a family can afford it in the first instance
depends, of course, on the amount of savings they can amass from
their available labor power.

Such then is the nature of social inequality in Ploughshare. Villagers
ordinarily do not think in terms of exploiting each other, and indeed
the amount of exploitation that goes on within the village is relatively
small. They do think in terms of some people being better off than
others, and their picture of who is better off fits well with an outside
observer's. But to understand why some are better off than others,

we must move outside the village and look at the class system of Taiwan. Social inequality is another feature of Ploughshare society whose particular nature is explicable in terms of Ploughshare's position in Taiwan's economy and society.

Spatial economy, work, and inequality are three aspects of Ploughshare that can be explained in relatively culture-free terms: we need to know little of Chinese culture, or specifically of Chinese social structure, to understand these aspects of Ploughshare society. I will now concern myself with those aspects of social organization that cannot be explained strictly in contextual terms, but rather only as the effect of contextual variation upon cultural norms, or structural principles, that were there in basic form to begin with, but have been modified over time in accordance with the particular position of different communities in the economy and society.

Community Relations

There are two levels in the social organization of Ploughshare, the family, which is the basic budgeting and consumption unit for each villager, and the network of connections between families, which unites the village and makes it not just part of a local or regional system, but a social system in its own right. In practically any Chinese community, the family is the most fundamental unit, with boundaries drawn more clearly than those of social systems at any more inclusive level. Despite this, the model of social organization adopted in this study sees organization as a product of the interaction of structure and context. It therefore dictates that the family be considered last because the web of relationships tying families together is, from the perspective of the families themselves, an aspect of context, and must be discussed first. In describing village organization, I am talking about a network of relationships between families, not between individuals independent of their families. Families are linked to each other through various ties between their individual members, but it is always the families, not simply the individuals, who are thus linked. It is the pattern of cooperation and conflict between this network of families that this chapter attempts to explain.

PATTERNS OF COOPERATION

The Chinese Structure

In preindustrial China, as in other agrarian societies, family members worked primarily to ensure and, if possible, better the livelihood of their own families (E. Wolf 1967, pp. 76-80). In this world of "every family for itself" no family approaches self-sufficiency, however, and every family must depend at times on help from other families for its survival and well-being. As Wolf (ibid.) has pointed out, there are a variety of solutions to this problem of self-interest without self-sufficiency. Competition can be explicitly discouraged by economic leveling mechanisms, such as periodic redistribution of land or wealth, as in the Russian *mir* or the highland Maya *cargo* system. At the opposite extreme, families can adopt a hostile attitude to others and cooperate, unwillingly and with much suspicion, only when absolutely necessary, as appears to have been the case in parts of southern Italy (Banfield 1958, Silverman 1968). Chinese communities seem to fall somewhere in between. While there is no legal requirement for exchange of resources or redistribution of goods across family lines (Smith 1970, p. 251), both moral pressure and good practical sense compel families to adopt, at least on the surface, a cooperative attitude toward one another. Moral pressure comes from the all-pervading Chinese emphasis on harmony within social and cosmic systems as the key to peace and prosperity, and it manifests itself on the social level in codes of proper conduct between people who stand in particular relationships to one another. Practical sense derives from the observation that help extended to others is likely to be reciprocated in times of need. If Chinese social structure is at bottom familism, it is not amoral, and families, who know they have to cooperate to survive, enshrine this necessity in terms of high morality and the desirability of a general harmony.

At the same time, if Chinese social structure shuns forced redistribution mechanisms, families are in explicit competition for wealth and other resources. In my experience (some authorities differ with me—for examples, see Freedman 1979b, p. 329, and Stover 1974, p. 105), this idea of competition does not encompass the idea of limited good, that families within a community are competing for different proportions of a fixed pie. Instead, it is quite possible, at the community level, that one family's gain may also be another's gain. This is so because Chinese communities have rarely been closed social and economic systems. Rather it has usually been possible for family members to seek fame and fortune outside their local communities, and, if successful, to bring back the benefits of their quest to enrich either their own families or wider social groups, such as village or lineages, to which they belong (Skinner 1976, 1978). Closed village communities, though not unknown, have been rare in Chinese history, and important relationships between families extend to families outside the village. All through its history, and especially since 1960, Ploughshare has embodied this characteristic of the Chinese village community.

What is it then that has made the Chinese village a community? For an answer, we need to turn again to Eric Wolf's discussion of peasant social organization, this time to his typology of relationships between peasant families, which is constructed along three dimensions—dyadic/polyadic, single-stranded/many-stranded, and vertical/horizontal (E. Wolf 1967, pp. 81-89). What has made Chinese villages into communities is the contrast between ties within the village, which have tended to be many-stranded and usually horizontal, and those reaching outside the village, which have tended to be single-stranded and usually vertical. There are numerous exceptions to this generalization, but, as a rule, families who are kin and neighbors within a village community, even if greatly unequal in status and power, have relationships that are diffuse and at least maintain a fiction of equality. This is the case, for example, when members of a patrilineage have equal rights to participate in ritual banquets or have their names entered into genealogies (Freedman 1958, p. 70; Baker 1968, pp. 27-28), or when locally resident landlords assume an attitude of patronage, rather than a purely business one with their tenants.

If there is a general tendency toward multistranded and horizontal relationships within the local community, and single-stranded and vertical ones outside, where does Wolf's dyadic/polyadic dimension come in? Here there is no structural norm in Chinese culture, but a wide range of variation. The emphasis in most studies of Chinese community organization has been on polyadic relationships. Maurice Freedman, and before him D. H. Kulp and Hu Hsien-chin, stressed the patrilineage and its segmentary structure as the basic building block of Chinese society in Fukien and Kwangtung. Even though ecological or historical variation meant differential ability to build large, wealthy, and complex patrilineal organizations, it was assumed that Chinese would build such impressive organizations whenever possible (Freedman 1966, p. 8; Kulp 1924; Hu 1948). It has been known for a long time, however, that, especially on the North China Plain, agnatic organization is less common and less highly developed. An interesting study by Gamble (1963, pp. 32-38) has shown us how a large number of different principles could be used for the internal organization of Chinese villages, including patrilineages, genealogical segments of patrilineages, and residential proximity. From Fei's earlier ethnography

(1939, pp. 172-73) we can deduce a fourth principle, the cultivation of land irrigated from the same source. Villages thus might be divided into lineages, lineage segments, neighborhoods, or watersheds, much like villages in Bali described by Geertz (1959). Pasternak (1972a, b) took us a step further by positing that lineages on the one hand, and cross-kin associations, formed for specific purposes such as irrigation or military defense, on the other, could be expected to be distributed in a complementary fashion. Where it was necessary to cooperate with nonagnates, cross-kin associations would be strong and preclude the formation of lineages, and where the need for cooperation was absent, lineages would be free to form.

The literature thus presents us with a range of variation in Chinese local organization, and with at least a preliminary idea for explaining this variation. But this idea is somewhat misleading in its assumption that Chinese villages will be somehow segmentary, divided into discrete or nearly discrete polyadic groups. One might even infer that the social structural principles entail the existence of polyadic groups within rural communities. A closer look at the ethnography and, specifically, Ploughshare in comparison with other communities in the Sanxia area, reveals that there is no necessity, indeed no structural pattern, requiring such polyadic relationships to be important in Chinese village organization. Ploughshare is organized almost entirely in a network of dyadic relationships, with polyadic groups playing a very minor part.

The Ploughshare Case

The Unimportance of Corporate Groups

No lineages. In Chinese society, a patrilineage (the only kind of lineage known to exist in China) is a group of male agnates, together with their wives and unmarried daughters, tracing descent to a known common ancestor. For patrilineages to form, two conditions must be fulfilled: there must be a group of agnates living in reasonable proximity to each other (depending on what sort of activities they are organized for), and they must have one or more common activity that makes it worthwhile for them to organize, to cooperate, even to recognize each other as members of a corporate group. These conditions quite naturally restrict the situations in which lineages can form. In fact, a famous early study of a Chinese village portrayed a community in which the only trace of agnatic organization was a recognition of mourning grades,[1] and there was otherwise no lineage or organization (Fei 1939). But since Freedman's analysis of patrilineage as an

1. The length of mourning and the type of mourning clothes depended on the kinship distance between the mourner and the deceased.

important aspect of the social organization of rural southeastern China (1958, 1966), ethnographers have tended to describe lineage organization as a variable in nearly all village studies. Gallin (1966a) and Cohen (1968) describe situations in which agnatic organization reaches beyond the patrilocal family, although there are no large lineages. Diamond (1969), in a telling case, even found groups calling themselves lineages, but not organized according to strict agnatic principles. Jordan (1972) describes a situation without "corporate lineages," but where groups were nevertheless organized on the basis of fictive agnation (clans, perhaps, in Freedman's terminology [1966, pp. 21-24], although Jordan does not use the term), and were important enough to wage wars with each other. Other studies, such as those by Ahern (1973), Baker (1968), Potter (1968), and Watson (1974), describe unambiguous lineage communities. Against this background, I think it is important to treat carefully the absence of agnatic groups in Ploughshare, and to see this in terms of its particular history and socioeconomic context.

Two reasons have been advanced for the existence of corporate lineages in Chinese communities, corporate landholding and military organization. Corporate land, first proposed as an explanatory variable by Freedman (1958, pp. 128 ff.), was land held in common by the lineage as a corporation, and used for the benefit (theoretically, at least) of all lineage members. Specific uses for the income from such property might include direct share payments to member families (Potter 1968, p. 108), building of ancestral halls and support of common ritual observances (Freedman 1958, p. 85; Baker 1968, pp. 64-70), sending bright young lineage boys to school or to take the imperial civil service examinations, and many others. But Pasternak has rightly pointed out (1972a, p. 150) that even in the absence of corporate property lineages might be organized as corporate groups, especially when they could be effective units of military organization in local feuds and vendettas. Where lineages proper did not exist, clans, or groups of people with a common surname but no demonstrable common ancestry, might take their place as military units (Jordan 1972, p. 17). In Ploughshare, there are no lineages because there are only small numbers of agnates living in reasonable proximity to each other, and because even these small groups have historically had no reason to cooperate. Let us consider the detailed evidence for this assertion.

First the numbers. Both in 1973 and in 1978, there were twenty-six families in the village with the surname Ong, but those who cannot demonstrate common ancestry consider themselves unrelated. Their common surname means that they cannot intermarry and that they kill big pigs in the same year (see pp. 185–87), but carries no other rights or obligations whatsoever. Among these Ongs, there is one group that contains altogether eight families. While recognizing their relationship to one another, each family has its own house, its own ancestral altar, its own economy. They do not do anything as a group. The same is true of the eight Tiu: families. They recognize their kinship, they get together, along with others, for important occasions, but there is nothing they do as a group, excluding outsiders. There is also a group of seven Kou families, which similarly never acts in a corporate manner. The same can be said for smaller groups of Ongs, Chius, Huans, Iaps, Lous, Tiu:s, and others.

It is easy to see why there are no lineages in Ploughshare. First, there are no very large groups of agnates. This is hardly surprising when we remember that only about 140 years have passed since the first ancestor of any current resident came to Ploughshare Point, and that most of them came considerably later than that. Under the very unlikely circumstances that each male descendant of the original settler had two sons, and that both sons remained in the village to reproduce, there would be a maximum of twenty-four agnatically related males, or approximately sixteen families, after a 100-year span of four generations. Under the less than optimal conditions that prevailed in Ploughshare, the results are even more modest than that. In addition, the economic logic of poor people makes it improbable that all the descendants of a settler would remain in his village after 100 years. One of the most important characteristics of the *than-chiaq-lang* and poor tenant farmers of Ploughshare is that, with no binding attachments to land or other real property, they are very mobile. If nearly half the current residents are descendants of original settlers who came after 1905, about half the descendants of the earlier settlers have left the village.

It could be argued that even the small clusters of agnates who do reside in Ploughshare could organize corporate activities if they were so inclined. But, lacking a reason, they have not done so. The villagers have never held corporate property because they have never, with only two exceptions until recently, held significant income-producing property at all. No aspect of their economic livelihood has ever been tied to membership in a group of agnates. There has been no other reason, such as warfare, to tie groups of agnates together either, and if nothing else, such tiny groups would be quite ineffective as a military organization.

Today, with Ploughshare families competing for economic wealth and social status, they need to shift resources of capital and labor around quickly to take advantage of new opportunities and avoid new hazards. Thus they need to operate with a measure of economic independence that precludes agnatic groups acting in a corporate fashion even more than did the old economic structures. It seems clear, then, that agnatic groups, never important and perhaps never even present in Ploughshare, are even less likely to arise now.

I have spent so long discussing the absence of lineages in Plough-share because it is often assumed that patrilineal organization must play some role, if not necessarily a predominant one, in Chinese village society, and because the absence of agnatic groups, and a consequent de-emphasis on agnation as a principle of social organization, has important implications for other aspects of Ploughshare's family and religious organizations. It should also be noted that the absence of agnatic groups does not imply the absence of agnatic ties; while less important here perhaps than in other villages where patrilineages do exist, agnation is still a frequent basis for the formation of dyadic relationships, and will be treated below.

Few cross-kin associations. According to Pasternak's formulation, villages without lineages might be expected to have strong voluntary associations, or cross-kin corporate groups, either single-stranded groups organized for a function such as crop-watching, irrigation, military training, or recreation (Pasternak 1972a, p. 108; Gamble 1954, p. 139), or many-stranded groups that arose out of single-stranded ones. We might thus expect to find voluntary associations important in Ploughshare. But as a matter of fact, they are not—only rotating credit societies would qualify as such associations, and these societies are only in a very broad sense corporate groups. Although Pasternak has attributed the absence of lineages in certain communities to the strength of cross-kin associations, the absence of lineages in Ploughshare is explained simply by the occupation and geographical mobility of its population. Cross-kin associations in Ploughshare have also been unimportant for similar reasons, because there are few functions for them to serve. To understand why other kinds of associations are unimportant, and why the rotating credit society is a special case that does not really possess the characteristics of a corporate group, we must look at the contextual requirements that have given rise to associations in other Chinese villages, and at the reasons why these requirements are not present in Ploughshare.

In Pasternak's account of two villages in southern central Taiwan, he stresses that the village that has always been organized primarily according to voluntary associations has been so because it "required extensive cooperation for defense and environmental exploitation among unrelated family and lineage fragments" (1972a, p. 146). Specifically, irrigation and protection from raids by aborigines required the cooperation of every resident in the village, and associations not based on kinship developed as the primary modes of organization. Similarly, in the Canton Delta village of Nanching in the 1940s, important associations existed primarily for defense against banditry and theft of crops (C. K. Yang 1958, pp. 109-12). The crop-watching associations in many northern villages described by Gamble (1963, pp. 32-44) had the same functions. Examples from yet other parts of China could be multiplied, but the point is clear: associations arise in response to specific contextual needs, generally for irrigation or defense. In Ploughshare, neither of these needs has been important since the Japanese takeover of Taiwan. Aborigine raids were quickly stopped at that time (Wolf and Huang 1980, p. 44), so local military organizations, although they extended beyond the individual village (Ahern 1973, p. 13), quickly went out of existence after the "pacification." And with very little of Ploughshare's land under wet-rice cultivation from the beginning, irrigation has been important to only a few families. It is significant in this regard that the family of Kou A-kim, who were tenant farmers from the time they moved to Ploughshare in 1918, were members of a corporate irrigation association, along with five other families from Shisantian. This association not only kept its waterworks in order, it also had a shrine to the earth god, Tho-te Kong, which later developed into a temple visited by many of the villagers, including those not members of the irrigation association.[2] It is thus definitely not the case that there is something innately opposed to associations in the social structure in which Ploughshare villagers operate. They will form and have formed associations when the need has arisen, which has been rare.

The need for cooperation in the current socioeconomic context is somewhat different. Aside from ritual events such as weddings, funerals, and big-pig sacrifices, where bilateral kin are mobilized to help out, the primary needs are employment for potential workers and employees for potential entrepreneurs (both may be gotten either inside or outside the village), and credit for commercial and domestic expansion. Jobs and employees are best gotten on a purely dyadic basis (it is difficult to imagine an association either hiring itself out or investing in a small knitting mill). This leaves credit as the economic need that leads people to form corporate groups in the form of rotating credit societies.

These societies seem to be common to Chinese social organization

2. It should also be recalled that much of the land in and near the village was owned, before the land reform program by two cross-kin temple associations based in Sanxia.

everywhere, but they flourish especially in today's rural Taiwan. Practically everyone needs credit in today's expanding economy. Those starting or expanding businesses need credit, and so do families whose primary desire is to raise their standard of living by building a new house or adding onto an old one. Commercial sources of credit, such as banks, require collateral that almost no villager has, so people must turn to each other for loans. Since it is extremely unlikely that one family will have enough cash to float a business or home loan to another, almost all borrowing is done through rotating societies. They work as follows. Old Ciu's family was once extremely poor—one son was sold when he was young, and another was mentally retarded and unable to work. The youngest son, however, got a good job in a lumber mill in Taibei around 1970, and a few years after that began to earn fairly decent money as a cab driver, though he could still not afford his own car. By 1975, the family had managed to save around NT$100,000, about a third of what they would need for a new house to replace the run-down mud structure they had lived in for the past twenty-five years. To raise the extra NT$200,000, they began a credit society. They found twenty families of friends, neighbors, and relatives who were willing to contribute NT$10,000 each, which at that time was around one-and-a-half to two months' earnings for a well-paid worker. The first time the society met, the Cius took NT$10,000 from each of the society members. This enabled them to pay for their house. They met again in another month, and all the other members who wished to borrow money bid a certain amount of discount. I do not have the complete records of this or any other individual credit society, but I know that a discount of around 5 percent usually takes the bid. Say the Ongs were the highest bidders at 5 percent discount. Each of the other families in the society, excepting the Cius who organized it, would give the Ongs NT$9,500, while the Cius, having already taken out the principal, would pay them the full amount of NT$10,000. The next month if, say, the Tans won the bidding at 4 1/2 percent, the Cius and Ongs would each give the Tans NT$10,000, while the other families would give them the discounted amount, NT$9,550. And so on until the Cius had paid back the entire amount and stood even again. In effect, this means that early bidders, like the Ongs and Tans in this example, would receive a low interest loan early in the life of the society; they could use the money in the same way the Cius did. Those who left their money in until the final rounds of bidding would have been paying discounted amounts all along, but would receive the full amount from most of the families when they finally did take the money out, and would thus be earning interest on the society. The Cius, as organizers, were getting an interest-free loan, but they would have to make up the balance if anyone else defaulted or absconded with the money.

This was a real risk. When butcher Kou Hieng left the village secretly in July 1978, he owed over NT$700,000 (approximately US$19,000) to various credit societies, including NT$50,000 to another society that the Cius had organized to pay for their son's new taxicab after the house loan had been paid off.

Rotating credit societies fuel a lot of economic expansion, and they also provide small additional incomes for those who are willing to leave their money in the pool. My landlady, for example, belonged to eight societies in the summer of 1978, five organized by Ploughshare people, and three by people from surrounding communities. By manipulating her bids and payments to various societies, she managed to earn enough extra income that she was planning to replace her outmoded black-and-white television set with a color one.

In spite of their importance in the village economy, I would argue that rotating credit societies are not very corporate as groups. They exist only for the lifetime of the particular loan, and do not act together except when the villagers meet to bid for the next month's pool. They are better seen, I think, as agglomerations of dyadic ties brought together by the organizer—ties that are basic to the organization of Ploughshare in the absence of significant corporate groups. To emphasize that the unimportance of such groups in Ploughshare can be attributed to context rather than to structure, let us look briefly at the nature of corporate organizations in some neighboring communities.

The near-absence of corporate groups. The community of Xi'nan described by Ahern (1973, 1976) provides an instructive contrast with Ploughshare. Located just below the foothills of the Central Mountain Range, Xi'nan was settled in the eighteenth century by Anxi folk, who cleared the area and have been cultivating rice there ever since. They have grown some tea on the nearby hillsides, and in the twentieth century many of them have taken wage-labor jobs, but even in the 1970s a great majority of households still grew rice. Because of this, population has been stable, settlements have been islands surrounded by rice fields, and patrilineal descendants of four original settlers still compose over 80 percent of the population of the village, which is divided into four hamlets, each of which is dominated politically and demographically by a single patrilineage. And it is these four lineages that see themselves as the basic building blocks of the community and that organize for ritual, for minor dispute settlement, occasionally for local development projects, and in conflicts with one another or with outsiders. They also own some corporate land (Ahern 1973, pp. 75-88). Other nearby communities also display lineage organization, though not perhaps of as corporate a nature. For example, Xiaxizhou is a single-lineage village, again a community of rice farmers, located on the plains near the Danshui River (Wolf and Huang 1980, p. 56). In Shitouxi, on the plains between the Sanxia and Tohokam rivers, housing is dispersed, and most families live in large, U-shaped compounds with from one to ten other agnatically related households. Lineages there are less corporate or solidary than in Xi'nan or Xiaxizhou, probably because they are not localized, but agnatic corporations still organize for ritual and still keep written genealogies (see Harrell 1981c). Ploughshare contains no lineages, not because there is something in its peculiar social structure that precludes their formation, but because the context made it difficult for large groups of agnatically connected families to form and gave such small groups as did form little incentive to organize as corporations. I do not have comparative data on cross-kin associations for other communities in the southern Taibei Basin area, but my guess is it would show a similar pattern: we would find cross-kin associations where there was a need for them, but the need, and thus the occurrence of such associations, would vary widely from one community to another.

The importance of dyadic relationships

That Ploughshare villagers do not form many corporate groups does not mean that the village is a Hobbesian world of unbridled competition between families. Even though the ultimate relationship between two families is a competitive one, leading a decent existence still requires that families turn to others for help or cooperation on many occasions. They need cooperation in times of life crises, especially those involving elaborate rituals; they need labor to exchange at busy seasons if they are farmers; many of them need either employment or employees; and they need credit to finance the expansion both of their business ventures and of their homes and living standards, and sometimes to tide them over, as in medical emergencies. And to establish cooperative relationships with other families in a competitive world they need to rely on a particularistic tie, something that the parties have in common besides the functional aspect of the relationship itself. Kinship is one basic tie that can be used to insure this brake on one-sided manipulation of a relationship, as is fictive kinship. In addition, various other ties, such as common native place, common surname, or common anything, can be used to the same effect, and have been by groups as diverse as overseas Chinese businessmen (Skinner 1957, p. 167) and officials recruiting officers for their personal armies (Kuhn 1970, p. 184). We have already looked at what the social organization of Ploughshare is not; to see what it is, we now examine the various dyadic relationships important to villagers.

Agnatic ties. For all practical purposes, these are ties between brothers, first degree agnatic cousins, or father's brother and brother's son.

No family heads in the village are related to other family heads by agnatic ties of wider span than this, and the relationships between brothers vary greatly.

At one extreme, we have the Tiu: brothers, a set of six men who divided their land and households about 1965. The eldest, Sui, is a former coal miner now working in a factory, the second is a miner and farmer, as is the third, who recently moved across the bridge to Blacksmith Gulch, the fourth is a mason, and the fifth and sixth each own enough knitting machines to hire a few laborers. The sixth had purchased three automatic machines by 1978. The mother was still alive in 1973 (she died in 1976) and resided with her youngest son. The Tiu: brothers, despite their inability to cooperate as a single household, still rely on each other in many ways. The two youngest often exchange work between their separate knitting operations. When their youngest sibling, a sister, was married in March 1973, they all contributed generous amounts to the largest dowry for a Ploughshare woman probably in the village's history up to that time. At the same time, however, there was visible strain between the two eldest brothers, and although they were civil to each other and cooperated when necessary, they seemed to avoid each other's company whenever possible. For Tiu: Sui, the eldest, an influential man in village affairs, his brothers clearly were an important part of his support.

The same is true of Kou Pou-Kim, a well-off businessman, who was the village representative to the *zhen* council until 1974. He is the eldest of five brothers, and the younger ones are all his political supporters. When he got into a feud with the village head, Ong Cin-hieng, it was his third brother, Kou He-tho, who assaulted and severely injured Ong. The Kou brothers were often in each other's company, and I never saw any signs of animosity between them. Their female agnatic cousin, Kou Pou, while no constant companion of theirs, was also a political supporter.

Both sets of brothers described here were recently divided. It is probably the case that recently divided brothers, especially when one or both of their parents are still alive, feel stronger obligations toward each other than do either brothers who divided long ago or agnatic cousins. In ritual matters in particular, they tend to cooperate as a matter of course, helping out, for example, at engagements and weddings in each others' families.

In some cases, agnates do not get along so well. This is illustrated by the case of the two sets of Li brothers who live in the houses adjacent to the Tho-te Biou at the lower end of the village. One set of brothers, Kim-hieng and Kim-hok, though they had divided their household economies (there was no property, since both were landless miners), were almost constant companions, something unusual for brothers even when they are on quite cooperative terms. Their close relationship stood in stark contrast to their relations with their cousins, both Li Cieng who lives with his mother on the other side of the temple, and Cieng's adopted sister Hong, who lived with (but is not married to) a man named Peq in a rented house. There had been, several decades ago, a dispute between the father of Cieng and Hong and his elder brother, the father of Kim-hieng and Kim-hok, over the inheritance of a vegetable garden. In 1972-73, they were not speaking to each other. I only saw them interact once, as I was sitting talking to Kim-hieng just inside his doorway. Hong suddenly appeared at the door, looking for her children. Kim-hieng's response was swift and polite: he offered her a chair with the utmost solicitude, a signal that relations between them were of the stiffest possible nature, despite their being agnatic cousins.

Such animosity between close relatives often endures for decades, but in some cases it can be ameliorated in times of need, as in the case of two brothers named Tiu:. The elder of the two, Tiu: Pun-a, is a blind bone setter. For a number of years before 1973, he had not been on good terms with his next younger brother, the well-to-do and successful Tiu: Ong Lai, a section head in the Sanxia zhen government. So when Pun-a's granddaughter was overcome by an acute psychosis (see Harrell 1974a for a fuller account of this incident), I was surprised to see Ong Lai's wife taking a major part in her care, and thus interacting frequently with her brother-in-law.

What emerges from these case studies is that agnatic relationships are a perfectly good basis upon which to build dyadic ties, and would seem to entail absolute obligations, at least in time of severe crises. But agnatic relations do not preclude the possibility of serious disagreements, and in no way imply membership in, or activity with, agnatically organized groups.

Affinal ties. By affinal ties, I mean ties between families that involve a woman, once a member of one of the families, having married into the other.[3] On the whole, affinal ties are as important, or perhaps more important, than agnatic ties as a basis for forming dyadic relationships. This is made possible by the large number of village-endogamous marriages in Ploughshare: of 101 families in the village in 1972, 56 had some affinal relatives living in the village. Of these, 30 had wife-giving affines, 18 had wife-taking affines, and 8 had both wife-giving

---

3. There is no conceptual distinction between affinal and matrilateral ties. The affinal ties of one generation become the matrilateral (or "amitalateral") ties of the next.

and wife-taking affines. Between 1973 and 1978, there were four intravillage marriages, creating affinal ties in the village for five families who had not had them before. Slightly more could call on agnatic ties, but the importance of affines is in some ways greater, because a powerful man is unlikely to have powerful brothers, but much more likely to have powerful brothers-in-law or coparents-in-law. It is through affinal ties, then, that the politically important men of the village are linked to each other. Some examples will illustrate how ties of affinity, like those of agnation, can be important means of linking families, but can also fall into disuse or even active animosity.

The closeness of affinity is illustrated by the case of Lua Hok-ke, a thirty-five-year-old son of the Lou-Lua house (see pp. 98-99). His wife, though not from Ploughshare itself, came from a farming compound just across the river in Blacksmith Gulch. Her family had recently gone into the knitting business, and when Hok-ke, who had been injured, finally decided to quit the mines and take up something more promising, he began to knit at his wife's natal house. He was there every day during late 1972 and early 1973, and he even asked me to dinner at their house for a festival, saying *"Lai ho gwun chia:"*—"Come and be our guest," using the term *our* in a context usually restricted to one's own family. Similarly, when the youngest sister of the six Tiu: brothers married out in the spring of 1973, she nevertheless returned to her natal home to work as a knitter for wages. And one of the two wealthiest knitters in the village, Ong Lou, got his start by going into partnership with his sister's husband from Shisantian—they managed to scrape together enough cash to buy a single knitting machine, which one worked in the daytime and the other at night. Part of Ong Lou's extensive business is still held in common with his sister's husband.

Ties through women are also important for the women themselves and for their children. Lou Hok-ke's mother, Lou Kim-be, is a robust woman, a former cart pusher, who was sixty-five years old in 1973. Two of her daughters married within Ploughshare—the eldest into Ong Hieng's family, and the second into Ciu Hon-ik's family. The elder daughter is handicapped by a heart ailment, and the younger often assists her mason husband as a hod carrier, so that Lin ends up doing a lot of the child care. In addition, her daughters visit frequently because she is their mother and lives close by. But the relationship extends beyond child care and mother-daughter closeness: when there was a minor drought in the fall of 1972, and many wells went dry, including the Ongs', Lou Lin and her husband allowed the Ongs to haul water for cooking, bathing, and watering their vegetable garden from her well, which still had water in it.

Brother-sister relationships can also be important in the lives of older men and women. There were only two brother-sister pairs over sixty in the village in 1973 (both members of one pair had died by 1978), but both were almost constant companions. Ong Hui-chin, a sixty-year-old woman, was the village's only active tea grower. She was rather poor and had always worked hard and experienced considerable misery. She left her first husband after a quarrel, was an opium addict for a while, saw an adopted daughter, her only descendant, go mad (though she later recovered), and suffered the ignominy of having to marry this daughter to the mainland Chinese policeman, Zhang Xiaoyi. Her only close companion through all this was her brother, Ong Chiu-tik, himself a rather difficult retired coalminer. The two were nearly always together, sitting and talking, despite the fact that Chiu-tik was literate and had a lively interest in geomancy and charm-writing, while his sister was illiterate and professed no interest whatsoever in religious or magical matters. Similarly, old So A-bieng and his sister So Hong are nearly constant companions, although each is married and has a perfectly agreeable spouse.

The most striking case of active hostility between affines is the continuing animosity that exists between Li Ong and his near-neighbor Tan Cin-thuan. Ong's wife is Cin-thuan's sister, so the relationship should be a cooperative one. It seems that during the early part of their marriage Ong beat his wife frequently, a reason many villagers give for her retiring behavior; though not a mute, she never speaks to anyone. Even though husband-wife violence is usually regarded as something to "shut the door and listen to," Ong's behavior reputedly became too much for Cin-thuan, who one day about twenty years ago broke in, stopped Ong from beating his sister, and fought with him. The outcome was inconclusive, but the two remain on nonspeaking terms to this day.

Sworn brotherhoods and sisterhoods. Agnatic and affinal ties, though probably the most important bases upon which Ploughshare villagers form dyadic relationships, are sometimes not enough. For the typical villagers, affines and agnates are few, and in many cases the people one really needs to cooperate with are not relatives. But it is difficult for Chinese to trust others with whom they have no formal connection (Silin 1972, pp. 336-40; DeGlopper 1972, pp. 301-4). After all, we must keep in mind that cooperative relationships are basically entered into for one's own benefit and the benefit of one's own family. The temptation to cheat or exploit, as well as to suspect the other party of cheating or exploiting, is extreme. But if there is a formal connection, especially of kinship, between the parties to a dyadic, cooperative relationship, then the parties have some obligation not to exploit the relationship too blatantly to their own advantage. So if someone needs to cooperate with a nonrelative, it is best to establish a relationship resembling one of kinship. To do this, Ploughshare villagers, like all Chinese traditionally, swear brotherhood or sisterhood.

To swear brotherhood (sisterhoods are much less common) is a fairly simple process. A group of friends, upon deciding they want to "exchange invitations" *(wa: thiap)*, agree to hold a feast at one "brother's" house, and to hold similar celebrations each year on the same day in the house of a different brother. Many sworn brotherhoods also swear fealty to a supernatural patron, usually Guan Di (H, Kuan Kong), one of the most popular Taiwanese deities and hero of the Three Kingdoms period, who was a sworn brother of the Han pretender Liu Bei and the hero Zhang Fei. If the brotherhood does have a patron, an image is purchased on the occasion of the original ceremony, and each year the image rests on the ancestral altar of the brother who will hold the annual feast the following year.

The formal obligations of sworn brotherhood are slight. Younger sworn brothers address their elder brothers by kinship terms, as would real or adopted brothers, and this usage is usually extended to other members of the brothers' families. Sworn brothers must mourn for each other and for their respective parents. Otherwise, the only regular obligations are to attend the annual feast. But no one goes to the trouble of swearing brotherhood just to eat a good meal once a year, or to have more mourners at his funeral. People swear brotherhood so that they may enter into cooperative relationships similar to the ones they establish with agnatic kin and affines. In this sense, sworn brotherhood, although a polyadic relationship like agnation and affinity, is a basis for dyadic relationships. Some examples will illustrate how sworn brotherhoods are important.

I have already mentioned the case of Ong A-bi, the young girl who lived with her blind grandfather Tiu: Pun-a and went mad in February 1973. The old man was not on the best of terms with any of his three brothers in the village, and although his third brother's wife, with whom he had previously feuded, did come to the girl's aid, this was not enough. His agnates were insufficient and he had no affines in the village, so he turned to his brotherhood. Although his two sworn brothers—one was the father of Li Kim-hieng and Li Kim-hok, and the other the husband of Iap Ka-bi—were dead, he found help in their families. When it was decided that the cause of the girl's illness needed to be determined more precisely by consulting a god through a spirit medium, it was Li Kim-hok who rode his bicycle twice to the temple in Sanxia town to procure the most efficacious image of the local deity Cieng-cui Co-su. And Iap Ka-bi helped out by running errands, comforting the girl, and offering general solicitude.

Another very clear example of sworn brotherhood at work occurred in the middle sixties, when Tiu: Chin-ong killed two men in self-defense and was sent to serve a twelve-year prison term. Chin-ong had not been married for very long at the time of his crime, and his wife was threatening to run home to her natal family. Chin-ong's mother and eldest brother did not want this to happen and decided to induce her to remain, and to solve the difficult problem of providing descendants for a man in his own physical absence, by adopting a daughter for Chin-ong's wife to raise while he was away serving his time. They turned to Huan Pak-ti, a sworn brother of Chin-ong's eldest natural brother Sui. His wife gave Chin-ong's wife her sixth daughter (she also had one son) to raise, although she continued to play a significant part in her care since she was still nursing and lived only four houses away. This relationship continued, with the girl (who was ten years old in 1973) making frequent visits to her natal family, which was considerably better off than her adoptive one, to have dinner, bathe her three younger sisters, born after Chin-ong was released on parole, in the Huans' comparatively spacious bathtub, and to visit with her older brother and sisters. Chin-ong's wife, having accepted a daughter, technically eligible to marry a son of hers, from her natural mother, continued to call her *a-so,* or elder brother's wife, in deference to the relationship of sworn brotherhood between her husband's elder brother and the natural mother's husband, although she was entitled to call her *chi: -m,* or comother-in-law.

Like other relationships, sworn brotherhoods sometimes become dormant or even degenerate into hostility. The brotherhood that included Tiu: Sui and Huan Pak-ti also contained several other men, including village head Ong Cin-hieng and Li Ong. They swore brotherhood when they were in their late teens, and all of them are now over fifty. But Li Ong has become isolated in village life in recent years; people are polite to him, but he has few friends, and spends most of his time working his quite extensive rice fields. He has also become closely associated with a sworn brother of his from another brotherhood, the former village representative Kou Pou-kim, the chief rival of Ong Cin-hieng. With his shift in loyalties, he has also informally withdrawn from the first brotherhood and no longer takes part in their annual feasts. As a matter of fact, he is on bad terms with nearly every one of them. Even sworn brotherhood, which is after all a voluntary relationship, is subject to the same uncertainties as agnation and affinity.

Relationships without pre-existing ties. All these cases demonstrate that the easiest, most reliable way to enter into a cooperative relationship is through a pre-existing particularistic tie, in the village context usually one of kinship or fictive kinship. But, as De Glopper (1972, pp. 303-14), Silin (1972, p. 339), and others point out, such a tie is not absolutely necessary. It takes longer, and people are warier of nonkin, but eventually the relationships can become as solidary, or more so, as those between actual or sworn relatives. People eventually build up the trust that Fried (1953) calls (M) *ganqing,* though I have not heard Taiwanese use the equivalent of that term. In fact, many ties involving employment begin this way: one villager simply goes to work for another, and after a while a patron-client relationship evolves, with the employment constituting the particularistic tie. This was the case with village head Ong Cin-hieng and some of his most fervent political supporters. Iu: Ong-iong, for example, can claim no direct kinship link with Cin-hieng, but his wife has worked for Cin-hieng for a long time. When Cin-hieng's feud with Kou Pou-kim came out into the open, Iu: Ong-iong was fervent in denouncing Pou-kim and backing up Cin-hieng's claims. The same is true for Tan Cin-thuan, whose only connection with the village head is that he lives across the street from him. For other people, ties that are originally ones of employment can result in other concrete benefits. People feel obligated to their employers, and will usually become their political supporters, as well as helping out at times of crisis. There are no formal kinship or fictive kinship ties between them, but employees are beholden to employers, and this creates obligations in both directions outside the realm of purely economic transactions. For example, wealthy knitting entrepreneur Ong Lou, who owned about twelve machines in 1973, employed two young men from the village, one of them his eldest brother's son. The other was Ciu Hok-kok. Hok-kok was married in the spring of 1973, and Lou drove his truck all the way to central Taiwan to help carry back the dowry goods that came with the bride. *The general nature of dyadic relationships.* From this discussion of the various ties people use to form dyadic relationships, certain general points emerge. First, dyadic interactions are by far the most important basis for interpersonal cooperation. There are very few activities in this community that are undertaken by members of a group as a group. Even where help is recruited on the basis of group membership, as in the case of sworn brotherhoods, it is recruited on an essentially dyadic basis: other members of the brotherhood, if asked to join in, do so as individuals. In most cases, a cooperative undertaking with one sworn brother implies nothing about cooperation with any other sworn brother.

Second, forming relationships involves picking and choosing. Every

family, except those very new to the village, is related to other families
by agnation, affinity, sworn brotherhood, previous employment, or
whatever, whom it can enlist in various cooperative relationships. But
very few families mobilize all these ties at the same time. In a sense,
kinship, affinity, and other ties are primarily of a potential nature.
Except for common participation in ritual affairs, there is very little
that related families need to do together in the ordinary run of life,
but when a need arises, the ties can be called upon for help.

Third, these relationships are essentially equivalent to each other.
There is something special between brothers, but aside from that, it
does not matter what specific relationship one has with the people one
calls upon. There is no special help that might be rendered, for example, by an agnatic cousin but not a sister's husband, by an employer
but not a sworn brother. The various ties are bases for establishing
relationships, but no particular tie implies a particular relationship,
at least not in the sphere of economic cooperation and mutual help.

Fourth, if one does not have ties to call upon, one can create them.
To swear brotherhood or sisterhood, to enter someone's employ when
that person needs workers, or simply to begin thinking and talking of
someone as a friend, are all ways of creating ties that can then be
mobilized.

Finally, it should be emphasized that Ploughshare is a local community with a significant community consciousness. It is by no means
rare to hear people talk about "we of Ploughshare," even attributing to
all villagers common characteristics, such as poverty, hard work, knitting, or honesty. Everyone knows everyone else, with the exception of
children and some recently married daughters-in-law, and everyone
keeps up through gossip networks with what everyone else is doing.
There are, after all, only a little over a hundred families in the village,
all packed into less than one-eighth of a square kilometer. And there are
no clear cleavages that internally split the community into discrete
groups, in strong contrast with lineage villages such as the one Ahern
(1973) described. In Ploughshare, villagers have ties with practically all
other villagers, and the network of dyadic links is much thicker within
the village than outside of it. For major things, it is best to rely on kin,
affines, or sworn kin. But for little everyday matters, people cooperate
with anyone toward whom they have no active animosity. For example,
I remember a village woman whose husband was ill, and who was told
by a folk practitioner that he ought to eat the meat of a *tho-ke,* a
chicken that had been allowed to forage and not been given any commercial chicken feed. She simply asked around the village until she
found one.

Even for a cooperative loan society, just about any villager will do.
The organizer can ask anyone considered reliable, and for most villagers

A bridal couple in 1973 in front of their mud-brick house and the bride in 1978 in front of her new house with neighbors and children, including her three.

that means most other residents of Ploughshare. Some people, who are known to be better off, are asked more often than others, but people do not restrict membership in such societies to their own kin, or to others with whom they have close relationships. This is, in a real sense, what defines Ploughshare as a community. Others, outside the village, are clearly important members of many people's kin and affinal networks. But within the village, no one, by definition, is a stranger: common residence in Ploughshare is in itself a particularistic tie.

Why should this remain so in today's industrial Taiwan? I can only speculate, but I would like to guess at what might hold the community together despite the great economic changes of the last two decades. I think the continued solidarity is primarily due to Ploughshare's location in the industrial core zone of northern Taiwan, allowing people both to participate in the modern economy and stay in the village. They can commute easily to factory jobs, or they can become small-scale entrepreneurs (in a few cases, even middle-sized businessmen) without leaving the village. It may not be long before neighboring Shisantian is turned into an industrial district, taken up entirely by factories. People prefer to remain in the village, if it gives them the same economic benefits the city does, because the people there are trustworthy. They know that because they have been cooperating with them, living side by side with them and their families, in some cases for decades. Not only are neighbors willing to share child care, they are also better risks for sharing capital, becoming business partners, or serving as employees. Since there are advantages to working and living in a familiar environment, there has been only a small drain of population from the village. For those who stayed there, relationships with other villagers have remained as important as they have always been, except that they are now part of an industrial, rather than a purely agricultural, economy. Village solidarity and the industrial economy, at least at this stage of development, tend to reinforce each other.

PATTERNS OF CONFLICT

Relationships between Ploughshare families are not solely ones of potential cooperation; they are also relationships of potential conflict. And just as we see cultural norms about the formation and content of relationships organized within a particular social context to produce patterns of cooperation, so we can see conflict as arising out of cultural norms about the process of disagreement and its resolution. Whom people fight with is part of the social organization, and the way it is organized in Ploughshare often differs from the way it is organized in other socioeconomic contexts. How they fight with one another is part of the culture, and is the same in Ploughshare as in any Chinese community. This section first examines Chinese ideas about fighting, then relates these to the organization of Ploughshare, and finally shows how these cultural principles are worked out in behavior.

The Chinese Model

Cooperation and the avoidance of conflict

That people should get along, that they should cooperate, is not only a necessity in China as elsewhere, but also an ideal applying to all defined relationships, with the precise nature of the cooperation often depending on the relative statuses of the parties to the relationship. The end product of cooperation in any social unit, be it family, village, or nation, is harmony, from which flow the comforts and security of the good life. But harmony in social relations is difficult to achieve and to maintain—the interests of different persons, or groups of persons, conflict at some point. In a situation like Ploughshare, where families are often in competition with each other for resources such as labor, wealth, and especially political power, the tension between the ideal of cooperation and the reality of conflict is particularly manifest on an everyday basis. The people with whom one should cooperate, those with whom one shares labor, exchanges loans, or consults in political and economic decisions, have interests that sometimes coincide with one's own and sometimes do not. When they do not, the possibility of conflict arises.

But it is only the possibility that arises every time the interests of cooperating parties do not concur. For several reasons, competition between interests usually does not lead to overt conflict. First, there is the cultural ideal of harmony. Anyone who, for trivial reasons, violates this ideal and initiates conflict, has committed a wrong simply by doing so.[4] This wrong may be overshadowed by the hurt or insult suffered by the initiator of conflict, and in this case to initiate conflict may be seen as the only way out, but it cannot be done lightly. Second, there is the cultural ideal of face. Face is perhaps best defined as respect gained from behavior appropriate to one's social position, and in any social position, the appropriate behavior is, except in extreme cases, to avoid conflict with those with whom one should be cooperating. To initiate conflict over petty causes, or when there is another way out, is to behave inappropriately to one's station, and to risk losing face. We will see later that the process of conflict and its resolu-

---

4. This principle is graphically illustrated by Qing court procedure, which required that someone be punished in every case of litigation. If the accused were found not guilty, the plaintiff was guilty of bringing false suit, a crime of disturbance of harmony and order (Van der Sprenkel 1962, p. 69).

tion, as well as its avoidance, are shaped by considerations of face. Third, there is the real possibility that, even though one feels antagonistic toward another for some real or imagined wrong, one will still have to cooperate with that person in the future. So in cases of venial slights, it is not only culturally sanctioned but also more prudent to avoid open conflict, as it closes future options.

In addition, there are cultural ideals of personal interaction that stress behavior appropriate to relationships rather than to emotions or personal feelings, and along with these go mechanisms for suppressing negative feelings. Even the basic pattern of personal interactions in everyday life promotes social solidarity and works against the open expression of conflict. In any situation involving two or more people, there is culturally defined, appropriate behavior. Such things as greetings, invitations, and polite "small talk" are all prescribed and enable people to act properly without revealing much of their feelings. For example, let us take the case of leaving someone's house where one has been a casual guest. When it is time to leave, one announces "I am leaving now," and the host responds "Stay a while." If the guest continues on his or her way, the host says "Come back," the guest says "Good, I will" and leaves. In this simple situation, we can see prescribed behaviors acting to conceal or allowing concealment of the actual facts of the social situation. The host tells the guest to stay, not because he necessarily wants him to stay, but because that is the right thing to say. The same with the summons to come back— one can hear this even if the two have been arguing and the guest is leaving out of barely concealed anger. In a case like this, both the host and the guest know that there is a possibility of conflict, but courteous behavior, observed by all, can deny the conflict and thus preserve the possibility of good relations between the two people. And as a general rule, the more hostility there is between two people, the more they will observe the courtesies of socially proper behavior to paper over the real possibility of conflict between them.

The process of conflict[5]

Although a few conflicts, usually very serious ones, take place in secret because of the great loss of face that would result from public knowledge, the great majority of arguments and fights occur in the open, purposefully under public scrutiny. This makes perfect sense given the principles of harmony and face. Since it is wrong to initiate

---

5. It is difficult to find other accounts of the process of conflict that would corroborate that this is indeed the Chinese model. Arthur Smith's account of "Social Typhoons" (1894, pp. 217-25) mentions, if rather unsystematically, many of the same points brought up here.

conflict, or often even to become involved, one should think seriously before getting into a fight. But since anyone who does is either emotionally overwrought, or has calculated that there is less to lose from fighting than from idly standing by, the argument or fight already entails a certain loss of face and respect. And usually there are witnesses to any fight, despite attempts to hide it, in a place like Ploughshare, or for that matter any Chinese village, where there is little space and less isolation between dwellings. Since the village knows about the argument in any case, it is better to present one's own side of the argument to the community: people will understand why you are fighting, and if the community supports you, your opponent may be persuaded to give up the battle or seek a compromise.

The initial or lowest stage of conflict, then, is the *public* argument *(siou: ma),* in which the parties tell what they think of each other, and point out to the audience what a scoundrel the opponent is to have gotten them into this situation. Since public arguments tended to occur in front of the house where I lived in 1972-73, I got a good idea of how they are structured. One party confronts the other in the street, begins to yell, and to attract a crowd. Typically, the two parties stand fifteen or twenty feet apart and yell at each other, making frequent asides to the bystanders arrayed behind their respective principals, including many neutral observers present out of curiosity, or because of the gossip value. It is unusual for both parties to yell at the same time or to interrupt each other; rather they seem to play a verbal tennis game according to prescribed rules, with each party having a say and then waiting for the other to answer. A monologue on either side may last several minutes, but a more usual time for a single barrage is thirty seconds or so. Occasionally one combatant will threaten to escalate the conflict by grabbing a handy weapon such as a bamboo laundry pole, but most often this is but a threat and no blows are exchanged.

The next stage of conflict is physical fighting *(siou: -pha).* I have never actually seen adult men fighting in this way, but from what I observed with women and children, an argument suddenly gets out of hand for one of the parties who, displaying facial and other signs of extreme rage, assaults the other. Bystanders usually try to pull the combatants apart, sometimes succeeding before any injury is sustained and sometimes not.

The final stage of conflict is killing *(siou: -thai),* and it is mostly a distant threat. As far as I can tell from one killing in the 1960s, one purported attempt while I was there, and several offhand remarks, it is usually attempted with a knife, secretly at night, as mere possession of firearms is a serious crime in Taiwan. A killer usually feels himself so wronged and threatened that saving face is no longer important, anger and vengeance are all, and there is no real hope of reconciliation, mediation, or other settlement.

The amelioration of conflict

Except perhaps in the most serious cases involving actual killing, parties to a conflict have every reason to try to settle. The term *conflict resolution* seems inappropriate here, for it is almost impossible for an overt conflict in a Chinese village to be resolved. But conflicts are settled, or at least ameliorated. The more important the parties to the conflict, the more likely they are to try to reach a settlement, for the more they have to lose by letting the conflict remain open. The same forces that prevent and shape conflict also shape its settlement. No conflict would have occurred had there not been some real or imagined breach of a cooperative relationship, undertaken because it promised some advantage for the parties. There is little hope of real cooperation once serious conflict has broken out, but there is still incentive to settle—or at least to paper over the conflict, so the parties do not actively hinder one another's aims. The values of face and harmony are also important here. Particularly anyone aspiring to leadership must be able to cooperate, and will lose support if his actions are seen as divisive or a hindrance to others.

Less important conflicts, those between women and children, generally are left to run their course, often rearing up at intervals. Some women married into the village have acquired reputations for not getting along with people, and seem to be in constant quarrels with one neighbor or another. But because their quarreling affects mostly themselves, no strenuous efforts are usually made to settle or impose the appearance of a settlement.

Settlements are usually achieved through the services of a mediator, since two people involved in a serious conflict are unlikely to sit down and talk to each other directly, at least not at first. But eventually, if there is some progress on the mediator's part, there will be direct talks. After a certain amount of negotiations a settlement will be reached, one that preserves interest and face for both the parties, and that will probably be formalized by a banquet or religious ritual. For example, in a case where one of a widow's lovers tried to either kill or scare the other, they worshipped together at a local temple.

The settlement and formalization mark an official end to the overt conflict, allow both parties to save a certain amount of face and perhaps to cooperate minimally. They do not, however, resolve the conflict: the mere fact of past conflict becomes an issue in itself. Like minor conflicts, which are seldom formally settled, major conflicts continue to simmer beneath the formal reconciliation.

The Organization of Conflict in Ploughshare

The causes of conflict

If the forces shaping the avoidance, process, and amelioration of conflict are cultural, the organization of conflict—who fights with whom over what—is primarily determined by context. Because of the different consequences of conflict for people, one's position in the social organization to some extent determines the ability of the cultural values to prevent conflict. For some people, particularly women and children, the effects will be less severe, because their conflicts will disrupt only their own lives or those of their families, and because their reputations are not as demanding of proper behavior as those of important adult men. So women and children tend to fight more often, and over seemingly more trivial things, than do adult men. In Ploughshare, probably three causes account for the great majority of incidents of overt conflict between adult men: property, local politics, and sexual jealousy. These are the things worth fighting for. No matter how angry a man may get over a slight of another kind, he will probably lose more face by fighting. But where property is involved, a man is risking his own livelihood and that of his family by doing nothing, and this tends to provoke open conflict rather easily. For example, a generation ago, the father of Li Cieng and Li Hieng quarreled with his brother, the father of Li Kim-hieng and Li Kim-hok, over the ownership of a small plot of land now used as a vegetable garden. Their children are still on bad terms with one another.

The same is true of disputes over political power. Those who play the power game seem to be nearly consumed by it. Maneuvering for position, for allies, or simply for prestige, takes up much of the lives of men such as those involved in the beating case described below. To be threatened with loss of one's position, or to see another eroding one's position, is extremely dangerous, and can be cause for fighting, especially if property is involved as well.

And finally there is sexual jealousy. This can involve complex configurations of men and women accusing and counteraccusing, and it is an issue over which adult men will come to blows or at least sharp words. For example, in a case alluded to briefly, a widow in the village had a lover for several years, and he supported her in addition to his own family. When his payments diminished after he suffered a mine accident, she took another lover, a recent widower from outside the village. When the first lover heard of the second, he attempted to sneak into her house at night and kill, or perhaps only scare away, the other with a large butcher knife.

Notable for their absence are conflicts over irrigation water (Pasternak 1972b, p. 197), often found in Chinese communities where access to water is competitive. Ahern (1973, pp. 11-12) reports no conflicts over irrigation in Xi'nan, where water is plentiful and rainfall well-distributed through the year, and in Ploughshare, where only a few families have had irrigated fields, people quarrel over other things.

The organization of conflict

Just as cooperation and the causes of conflict have special characteristics in Ploughshare, so does the organization of conflict. In many Chinese communities, made up of corporate groups, conflict between members of corporate groups leads to conflict between the groups themselves. Ahern, for example, provides a case study from the four-lineage community of Xi'nan. Here we find disputes both between lineages and the genealogical branches of a particular lineage. In one instance, the Lou and Ui lineages had a long-standing antagonism. It began with a dispute over land in the Qing period, continued when the Lous aided, and the Uis resisted, the Japanese police forces during the colonial period, and endured into the postwar period (Ahern 1973, pp. 71-74). In another case, two branches of the Ong lineage, known as *thau* and *be,* or head and tail, were reported to be chronically at odds over many different issues. In a classical segmentary model, they were, however, able to unite against an outsider who attempted to build a river embankment that would have eroded the rice land belonging to both branches (ibid., pp. 21-36). M. C. Yang (1945, pp. 157-72) reports similar conflicts between Christians and non-Christians, and between lineages, in a Shandong village, and Jordan (1972, pp. 23-26) speaks of disputes between common-surname groups that escalated after a minor offense to one person by a member of the other group.

There is also another model for the organization of conflict in Chinese society, the factional model. Gallin, in one of the first analytical studies of such factionalism, shows how the breakdown of the traditional lineage-based social order of a rural township in central Taiwan led to the formation of township-wide political factions, based on personal loyalties to patron-leaders (Gallin 1966b). These factions contested elections to political office and engaged in other disputes, reaching into and dividing individual villages. Similar factions permeate the political life of Yingge township, close to Sanxia. Indeed one cannot talk to a man from Yingge for more than a few minutes without hearing stories of the factions, their disputes, and their relative success in the latest elections. But for reasons not entirely clear to me, *zhen*-level politics in Sanxia are different. Individual leaders have their own followings, but these have not crystallized into factions.

So when we look for the organization of major conflicts in Plough-share, we cannot easily explain them in terms of either corporate groups or the penetration of higher-level factions into the village, as seems to be common in other parts of Taiwan. Rather we need to look at the networks of dyadic relationships upon which cooperation in Ploughshare is based, and at the incipient formation of personal factions at the village level. In particular, Ong Cin-hieng, although elected to two terms as village head, and able to pass on the office to his eldest son when his own health began to fail seriously in spring 1978, has only partial support within the village. He maintains a close network of clients, including his brothers, several families of affines, neighbors, and employees, but people outside this network often view him as partial to his own people, and neglectful of the needs of other villagers. The major conflict during my 1972-73 stay in Ploughshare took place between him and his opponents.

The organization of conflict in Ploughshare thus reflects the special characteristics of the village, themselves derived from its socioeconomic context, when the parties of the conflict are important enough that the conflict affects more than their own immediate families. Conflicts between women and children, or between unimportant men, on the other hand, show no characteristics peculiar to Ploughshare. Three examples of actual disputes, involving progressively more important disputants, will illustrate both the process of conflict and its amelioration, and the way conflict involving important people is organized.

Examples of conflict
An unstable woman and a young boy fight over a game. Huan Thuan-hok was about twelve years old when he lost his father in a motorcycle accident in November 1972. At the funeral, he had to play the role of principal mourner, and perform a demanding series of rituals usually falling upon a mature man. He seemed to hold up quite well, but later it was understandable to all that he was disturbed. His mother's small salary now had to pay all the family's expenses and, with three younger siblings at home, it seemed doubtful that he could finish his remaining year-and-a-half of junior middle school before he would have to start supporting the family.

One day in February 1973, Thuan-hok was running a small-scale gambling enterprise often indulged in by village children. He bought the game from one of the stores in town, and sold chances to village children for one *kho,* a Taiwan-dollar coin. The children then picked one square on a sheet ruled off into squares, and removed the sticky-paper cover of that square. If they hit a lucky square, they got a piece of candy; otherwise, they lost their coin. On that day Cng Lei-pi, married daughter of Cng Pun-lai, was visiting her father with her small daughter. Lei-pi was rather a querulous sort, a fat, sloppy young woman who would not speak to her mother (even though she visited her reasonably frequently with the grandchild) and who was fond of ridiculing foreigners to their faces. Her little girl wanted to try a chance at Thuan-hok's gambling game, and won a candy on her first try, but neglected to pay the requisite *kho*. I don't know exactly how this led to an argument, but when I emerged from my house onto Front Street, Thuan-hok and Lei-pi were shouting at each other. This went on for a while, and they both appeared quite angry, with red faces and tears in their eyes. Finally, the boy could stand it no longer and began lunging at either Lei-pi or the child, probably at the child, since people kept telling him "You can't hit a child like that." Thuan-hok eventually grabbed the little girl by the hair and threw her to a sitting position. He and Lei-pi then went after each other, struggling and scratching, with Ong Tho and his wife trying to pull them apart, and Ong Tho's eighty-two-year-old mother pounding one of them on the back. Finally they were separated, and stood a distance apart but continued to yell at each other, while people kept telling the boy to go home and the woman to desist. Finally, Thuan-hok disappeared into his house, with bloody fingernail scratches on his cheeks. Lei-pi showed no sign of injury.

Things were quiet for a while, and then suddenly a large crowd headed for the boy's home, as it seemed there was something wrong with his ear and his hand. After some discussion, the people decided that Lei-pi had inflicted these injuries, and decided to send someone to fetch Thuan-hok's mother from her job at a nearby sawmill. When she returned, she was crying bitterly, and began yelling nearly incomprehensibly at her son. When she had recovered somewhat, she came out of her house again and headed for Lei-pi's parents' house, and began to engage in an argument with the woman herself. Lei-pi was rather conciliatory by this time, saying that she and the boy had both been wrong, but that he shouldn't have hit her child like that. Meanwhile Thuan-hok's mother accused Lei-pi both of interfering in other people's affairs ("adults shouldn't hit children unless they are their own") and of taking advantage of the boy's not having a father to defend him. She also said that Lei-pi should have given Thuan-hok his *kho* in the first place, which both she and her father professed willingness to do. Finally Thuan-hok's mother drifted into her house, but an hour later Lei-pi was still sitting on a stool in front of her father's house, looking belligerent.

Although it escalated to a minor physical skirmish, this fight illustrates the least important hostilities that take place in Ploughshare. Neither of the opponents—a young boy and a daughter already married out of the community—was an important person, and people who matter entered the fray only to try to bring the opponents to their senses. The issues involved were trivial, and responsible people certainly could have settled them without resorting to the least threat of violence, or even ignored them without losing anything significant. Only unstable, immature, or unimportant people would be foolish enough to get into such a fight, and anyone who would not avoid such a conflict would be destined to remain unimportant.

The pattern of the fight was typical, and as for resolution, it really needed none. In the end, little harm was done to the parties, to them physically or to their reputations, because neither one had much of a reputation to begin with. Such a conflict would merely go away. Even if it were to continue, it would not make much difference.

Suspicion of adultery between a married man and a widow. Li Hieng and his wife Tan A-hong were having a hard time. They had quarreled bitterly with Li Cieng, Hieng's brother, and his neurotic wife two years before, and had built themselves a new house at the upper end of the village, far away from the impossible sister-in-law. They struggled to make ends meet, and were doing better, but still had no furniture in their house. I am not sure what their domestic life was like, but it certainly got worse when Li Hieng was seen in the house of Lou Tiu: A-bi, an attractive widow. His wife accused him of adultery, and a public quarrel ensued, in contrast to the usual pattern of private husband-wife conflicts. According to informants, this had happened around six in the evening, when I was out of the village. When I returned around nine or ten, I found A-bi standing in the street, in a shouting match with Peq, the alcoholic living with Hieng's sister Li Hong. Peq was drunk, as usual, and was accusing A-bi of taking NT$1,000 from Li Hieng for her sexual services. He kept asking her, with a grin, where her NT$1,000 were, and she became angrier and angrier. First she invited Peq to sit in her house and see if anything happened, but when he continued baiting her, she picked up a large wooden stick and started threatening him with it. Lou Kim-bi's eldest daughter, usually a placid woman, was encouraging A-bi to hit Peq with the stick, and she looked almost as if she might use it, but in the end he retreated back to his house and his bottle.

About the same time, Big Fat Suat, a forty-year-old widow, who always got involved whenever anything scandalous was going on, was leading Tan A-hong home, though A-hong was in tears and looked as if she might break loose. She kept saying to her companion "But Fatty, don't you know. . . ." Later on, after A-bi and Peq had both disappeared, Li Hong was still trying to lead Tan A-hong back to her house, but she resisted, and the last I saw they were struggling inconclusively in one of the back alleys at the lower end of the village. Subsequently, A-hong ran away from the village for three or four days, but she missed the children she had not taken with her, and, having no job, was in no position to support herself, let alone five little ones. So she came back to her husband, however grudgingly.

This is a complicated case. The original parties were the triangle of Li Hieng, his wife, and his supposed lover, but the real conflict was between Hieng and his wife A-hong. It was Hieng she was avoiding by running away, and him she would have to answer to, while her behavior, especially not wanting to return home, was directed at her husband and not at A-bi, who lived several houses down the street. In such circumstances, many people would resort to direct conflict, and nobody could be blamed for irresponsibility for acting like A-hong, though running away might seem a little extreme. A husband is expected to have his nights out at the whorehouse every once in a while, but consorting with a neighbor without his wife's tacit permission is going too far. In the end, however, A-hong had to reconcile: she had no place to go, no way to support herself, and five children belonging by right of descent to her husband's family. People said afterward that she continued to feel bitterness toward her husband, but what was she to do? Like so many other parties to conflicts, she had more to lose by continuing the battle than by settling. Even though the settlement might be almost exclusively on her husband's terms, she had to settle nonetheless.

The other participants were more or less trying to help A-hong, except for her sister-in-law's man, Peq. He was simply being querulous and drunk, interfering in other people's affairs. Of all the adults in Ploughshare, he was by far the least respected, precisely because he gets involved in conflicts for no reason at all. Sometimes, when one has much to lose by being silent and acquiescent, there is enough justification for violating the cultural ideals of cooperation and harmony. But to make trouble for its own sake is totally inexcusable: there is enough trouble around without a person like Peq getting involved for the fun of it.

Village head Ong Cin-hieng is beaten up. In 1972, Ong Cin-hieng, the poor cart pusher turned knitting entrepreneur, was in the fifth year of his first six-year term as *lizhang* (village head) of Jiatian li (the rural district consisting of Ploughshare, Blacksmith Gulch, and Baiji), a position he owed primarily to a network of affinal and patronage relationships he had built up with a large number of Ploughshare households. His two brothers are his only agnates in the village, but he is affinally related to the six Tiu: brothers, to So A-bieng and to A-bieng's sister So Hong, as well as having two sisters' husbands in the village. These are but his direct affinal connections, and other people claim relationship with him through these intermediaries.

In addition, the people he has long employed in his knitting mill will give him further support.

But Cin-hieng is neither alone nor without opposition in his role of village leader. Many people feel that he treats people unfairly, dispensing favors to "his relatives" (mostly affines), and being short with others whose connections to him are not so close. There is no one leader or focus of the anti-Cin-hieng forces, but in 1972, the person with the most following was Kou Pou-kim, who represented Jiatian and three other *li* on the *zhen* council. Pou-kim was the eldest and most successful of the Kou brothers, and was counted a close cousin by the interior Ongs and their relatives on Back Street. People speaking about the village leadership would often contrast the generosity and good-heartedness of one of these men with the calculating, scheming stupidity of the other. The factions around these men were loose and rather small, and most families in the village managed to maintain reasonably good relationships with both leaders. Political power alliances in Ploughshare, like other social relations, are networks rather than aggregations of discrete groups.

Against this background of political competition, we can look at why the village head got beaten up in August 1972. He had, several months earlier and before we moved into Ploughshare, assumed the leadership of a government-sponsored local construction scheme called a *shequ*. This is a program in which the country government, through its constituent townships, gives money for construction of public facilities to various local communities. They must decide what improvements to make, make them within a specified time, then enter a contest judged by various notables in the county government. Ploughshare had become a *shequ,* and the *lizhang's* task was to oversee the use of the money. When I first arrived in Ploughshare, I often noticed heated meetings going on in Cin-hieng's house. At that time I did not really know enough to listen, or understand enough Hokkien, but I learned later that the discussions concerned the use of the construction money.

Naturally, there was considerable disagreement since even public works benefit some families more than others. For example, Ong Lou, Cin-hieng's rival in wealth and a political supporter of Kou Pou-kim, told me he had to threaten the *lizhang* with loss of face, by offering to pave the path in front of his house himself, to get the *lizhang* to include that improvement in the *shequ* plans. Many other such small disputes were going on at the same time. But everyone agreed on one project: they would pave Front Street and widen its north end so that motorcars could drive its entire length. The fact that everyone agreed certainly had something to do with three cars in the village being owned by Ong Cin-hieng, Ong Lou, and Po Hok-lai, all of whose houses faced Front Street. But to widen and improve the road, the community would have to purchase a small plot of land, amounting to approximately two *pieng,* an area of about eight square meters altogether. This land was part of the rice fields at the upper end of the village owned and worked by Kou Pou-kim's third brother, Kou He-tho. He-tho was promised the money as soon as the *zhen* government got back on its feet after having most of its officers jailed for corruption a few weeks before.

The road paving and other work on the *shequ* proceeded for the next few weeks, as the day of inspection by county officials approached. The village was prettied as never before: vacant lots were neatly graveled and adorned with signs indicating they were parking lots; potted plants, normally kept on roofs, decorated various crumbling walls; laundry was no longer to be hung in visible places in front of, or on top of houses (which created a problem, because there is more laundry than can be hung in back of all the houses); everybody's bathing facilities, no matter how primitive, were fitted with toothbrush holders and toothbrushes, mostly on loan from local stores, one for each member of the family.

On the eve of the inspection, there was a banquet at the Xinfeng Paper Company, attended by all the important men of the village. Like all banquets, this one involved a considerable amount of alcohol, and nearly everybody was inebriated when, on the way back to the village, Kou He-tho accosted village head Ong Cin-hieng and asked him when he would be paid for the two *pieng* of land he had sold to the community. Cin-hieng answered that it wasn't his business but that of the *zhen* government, whereupon hostilities ensued.

There were as many versions of the incident as observers, but two will serve our purposes here. A fervent supporter of the *lizhang* told me that it was Kou Pou-kim, mid-fortyish and plump, who came up behind the sixty-one-year-old, fat village head and wrapped his arms around him, pinning the *lizhang's* arms to his sides, while muscular He-tho reduced the defenseless old man to a pulp. Ong Lou, on the other hand, suggested that the village head had struck first, and it was only in self-defense that He-tho beat the old man senseless. Neither version seems likely, since Ong Cin-hieng and Kou Pou-kim are too politically astute to start something like that. It seems far more plausible that He-tho struck first, but without his elder brother's aid. The end result was that Cin-hieng was knocked unconscious, and spent the next three weeks in a Sanxia hospital bed recuperating.

While he was there, a stream of supporters and neutrals went to see him—when I paid a visit, one more visitor could not fit in the hospital room. He returned to the village, rather dramatically leaning on a cane, on the afternoon of the Mid-autumn festival (M, *Zhongqiu jie*), one of the biggest holidays and the birthday of Tho-te Kong, tutelary deity of the local community. He had, of course, been absent at the *shequ* inspection, effectively eliminating any chance Ploughshare had of winning the contest.

Kou He-tho was jailed briefly, booked, and released on bail on charges of assault, and in the next few weeks the village policeman was busy going from one house to another collecting evidence and depositions. The local edition of one of the Taipei newspapers picked up the story, and featured headlines like "61-year old *lizhang* beaten because of extreme enthusiasm for *shequ.*" It was certainly more complicated than that.

As an outsider unfamiliar with the ways of Chinese conflict and conflict settlement, I assumed the case should go to trial like any other; people were, after all, talking that way. But behind the scenes, efforts at amelioration of the conflict were going on. Through intermediaries, the *lizhang* made known to the representative and his brothers the terms for a deal: he would drop the charge against He-tho if they would reimburse him for all his hospital costs, and present him with a large pot of pigs' feet and long noodles *(ti-kha mi:-sua:)*, ritual foods that are offered on occasions of union, such as weddings. When the terms became known, the representative himself visited the *lizhang's* house, and after all the details were worked out, he presented the pigs' feet and noodles, which the *lizhang* offered to his ancestors and then used for a dinner to which Pou-kim and He-tho were invited as guests of honor.

The feud was thus officially over, and cooperation would follow. The same man who intimated to me earlier that the representative was "number one bad egg around here" now said that "Well, after all, we're all neighbors here and we have to cooperate." But the two families were still at odds with each other, and there was another overt incident in which the *lizhang* claimed that one of Pou-kim's brothers had earlier violated a building safety regulation, and supporters of one leader still went on making derogatory comments about the other. The situation stood about where it did before Ong Cin-hieng was beaten up. The two families tolerated each other, but warily.

This serious case of conflict nevertheless illustrates the same principles as the two preceding ones. The two families were at odds, essentially, because the village was too small a political arena for the two of them. Neither had the support, connections, or money necessary to make a serious run for higher office (though rumors went around about Kou Pou-kim before the beating incident), and their political ambitions had to be satisfied in the village context, at least for the moment. There was enough dissatisfaction with Ong Cin-hieng's leadership and patronage that Kou Pou-kim had an opening, but he was never able to challenge the *lizhang's* political majority. There was latent conflict as long as the two of them were playing the same political power game, but, as in most situations, the conflict would probably have remained at that level had it not been for the drunken state of all the participants in the *shequ* banquet. The emotions of hatred and mistrust were definitely there on both sides, but rational people would keep them repressed. It is noteworthy that Pou-kim's second brother, when discussing the incident with me afterward, said that Pou-kim had not been present at the time of the attack and that, as a matter of fact, his first act had been to scold his younger brother for doing such a foolish thing. Not that the *lizhang* didn't deserve it, he hastened to add, but people should not act like that with neighbors.

The ideal of cooperative relationships should have been upheld then, from either side's perspective, no matter how despicable the conduct of the other. And this explains why He-tho did not go to trial. Both sides were, in the end, anxious to settle, if a settlement could be reached that retained face for both. The Kous were concerned that their brother did not end up in jail, with the loss of labor and the smirch on the family record that would entail. Ong Cin-hieng's reasons for wanting to settle, if less obvious, were just as compelling. If he persisted in charges against Kou He-tho, to the point where he were tried and sentenced, there would be no hope of even a cosmetic settlement to the conflict. The Kous would have lost so much face that they would have no choice but to fight back. And Cin-hieng did not need a fight. His support in the village was actually based only on the solid allegiance of twenty or so families, and the wavering support of many of the rest, but he was, after all, the village head. And despite his denials, he seemed to enjoy that position, and he ran for, and won, re-election in 1974—Kou Pou-kim's wife's threatened campaign apparently never happened. To be village head in reality as well as in name, he had to head a village that could at least unite when the occasion required it, despite real internal divisions. In this situation of reconciliation, both sides held cards that they were eager to play. Ong Cin-hieng could get Kou He-tho off the hook, and the Kous, by assenting, could prevent unhealable factional conflict from emerging. Kou Pou-kim may have ended up the loser; he did not run for re-election in 1974, and when I talked to him in 1978, he told me he was out of politics for good, concentrating his energies on making money. But he would have lost more if his brother had actually gone to jail or even to trial.

There is one final reason for the settlement. The publicity was making Ploughshare look like a place where people were feuding, and, in a sense, the whole village was losing face. At least the semblance of cooperation would make the village look, and function, better. But a semblance of reconciliation was all we could expect as the outcome of a quarrel like this one, since the political interests of Ong Cin-hieng and Kou Pou-kim were still diametrically opposed.

In these three cases of conflict, then, we see essentially the same principles at work. Despite the ideals of cooperation and harmony, people experience direct conflicts of interest. They generally hold these in check, but at times their emotions get the better of them, and overt conflict ensues. If the participants are but minor figures in the community, and the dispute does not hinder their lives greatly, it may simply be allowed to simmer. Once begun, it is difficult to actually end a conflict. But in the case of important people like Ong Cin-hieng and Kou Pou-kim, the simmering dispute has to be cooled somewhat if it cannot be ended, for both parties have more to lose from fighting than from compromising. Compromising, though, is just that; in no way does it signal an end to the hostilities.

From these examples, we can see that the organization of conflict in Ploughshare parallels the organization of cooperation. Both are based on networks of dyadic ties between families, and do not involve corporate groups. Conflict between unimportant people generates few hostilities among anyone but the principals. Conflict between important people, on the other hand, does mobilize the loyalties of their followers. But their followers are recruited through dyadic ties rather than group membership. This is true because Ploughshare's social context has neither supplied the human material for the formation of lineages, nor indeed given people reason to form corporate groups based on principles other than agnation. The only real corporate group above the individual family is the village of Ploughshare itself. That it has maintained at least the degree of village solidarity that makes people worry when the village is getting bad notices in the newspapers is perhaps partly a reflection of the absence of internal corporate groups. Bad publicity reflects on everybody; a nucleated village without internal corporate groups is nevertheless a village community.

Family Organization

The developmental cycle of Ploughshare families and the relation-ships among individual family members are aspects of social organiza-tion that can be explained by the application of Chinese social-structural rules to the socioeconomic context of Ploughshare and its inhabitants. In this chapter, I consider two aspects of the developmental cycle— the growth and division of joint families and the types of marriage—and the corresponding aspects of relationships within the family, between generations and between the sexes. In each case, I attempt to show that Ploughshare family organization is a species of Chinese family organization, but that there are considerable differences between Ploughshare families and those in other communities, between Plough-share families at different times in the history of the village, and among families within the village at any particular time.

THE GENERATIONS: DEVELOPMENTAL CYCLE

The Chinese Model

Family structure, everywhere in China, follows certain basic rules, including patrilocal postmarital residence and equal inheritance of property among sons. The people drawn together to share resources in this system constitute a *jia* (H, *ke*). If the members of the *jia* reside in the same vicinity, they share a common budget and living quarters, and eat food cooked on the same stove. Hence an alternate term for *ke* in Hokkien is *cau*, or stove—each family has its own, and no two families can eat food cooked from the same stove, except as each others' guests. In addition, in many places each *jia* establishes its identity as part of a community by contributing *ding* money to the support of annual community religious celebrations, one *ding* for each member of the *jia*. *Jia* members need not be coresident, however, and often one or more members, or even one or more nuclear family units within an extended *jia*, sojourn away from home to earn a living. The sojourners are still members of the *jia* if they have the right to share a domicile, a table, and a budget with the members residing in the village should they return either temporarily or permanently. Once members of the same *jia* have established totally separate family budgets and built separate brick stoves, they will contribute separately to the *ding* collection, if there is one, and no longer be members of the same *jia*. Families who own property will express the separation by a formal process known as *fenjia* (dividing the *jia*), in which the parties to the division (usually brothers) state, often in a written document, their intent to divide household and property and to terminate the connections that had made them members of the same *jia*. In Ploughshare families without property, however, there is not always a formal *fenjia* but simply an agreement to separate, and one must rely on such factors as common budget and stove, as well as on the people's own statements, to determine who is a member of a *jia* and who is not.

In fact, it is usually much easier than this to identify the members of a *jia;* people know and there is seldom any dispute. The membership of a *jia* ordinarily follows basic principles of Chinese family structure. Wives marry into their husbands' *jia*, sons remain with their parents, and daughters marry out. Eventually, if there is more than one son in a family, the brothers will divide, either through a formal process or a gradual attrition, and form separate *jia*. The family thus proceeds through a developmental cycle, beginning with a husband and wife, newly separated from the husband's brothers, and with no parents attached. The couple will have children (if they do not bear children, they can adopt them) and the *jia* will consist of a nuclear or conjugal family (Lang 1946, p. 14). If they have at least one son, he will take in a wife and the *jia* will consist of a stem family: married parent or parents, one son and his wife, and their children.

If there is more than one son, when they each take in a wife the

family will assume the joint form, consisting of married brothers and
their wives and children, with or without their surviving parents. If
the family reaches the joint[1] stage (and in any given generation, many
families do not), the brothers will eventually divide their household
and property, each forming, with his wife and children, independent
jia, most often of the nuclear family type. There are many variations
on this pattern: some families have no sons, natural or adopted, and
must bring in husbands for their daughters; some have only one son,
with no brothers to divide from; and families divide at different times.
All variation in family organization at a given time must be analyzed
in terms of this developmental cycle and its variations. The latter
are influenced, in turn, by several aspects of the socioeconomic context, namely, the vagaries of demography and reproduction, as well as
the family economy, since division makes sense for some families
and not for others.

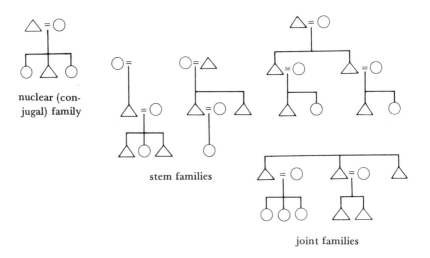

Fig. 3. Stages in the Chinese family developmental cycle

Myron Cohen (1969, 1976) has provided us with an analysis of
the variations in Chinese family organization, with particular reference
to a southern Taiwan Hakka village. Cohen shows that the timing of
family division is heavily dependent on the family economy. When

1. Wolf and Huang (1980) following Freedman, prefer the term "grand" to
"joint" for this stage of the developmental cycle. While I have no opinion in particular on the relative descriptive or connotative accuracy of these terms, I have
retained "joint" because it is conventional.

brothers are not yet married they usually tend to stay together, if only because any *jia* must have a source of domestic labor to wash the clothes and cook the food, and this is best provided by a wife. Once brothers are married, there develops within the *jia* a unit called the *fang,* consisting of one man, his wife, and children, but excluding his brothers and their wives and children. The history and eventual timing of family division is dependent, according to Cohen's analysis, on the balance between the interests brothers hold in their own *fang* and in the *jia* as a whole. In general, as they get older, their *fang* interests become more and more paramount, and always seem to the brothers' wives to be the most pertinent. Eventually, the *fang* interests outweigh the *jia's* and brothers begin to consider family division, a process that occurs within a few years. But the timing of the shift in interest from *jia* to *fang* (and the *fang* is, of course, a prospective *jia*) rests on the nature of the family economy. Two situations in particular tend to hold brothers together for a longer time than otherwise. First, some families are heavily dependent on women for productive labor. If they remain together, one woman can handle the domestic responsibilities for the entire family, freeing the others to work in the fields. If, however, they divide, then one woman will have to perform the domestic chores for each of the *jia,* since by definition no two *jia* can share the same stove or domestic economy. Thus labor that would have been available from family members must now be hired, an extra expense for the family.

The other situation in which Cohen shows that brothers tend to remain together occurs in families with diversified economies. If a family, for example, owns a store, some rice land, and a small hauling business, it is not only difficult to sort out who owns what (even if each sector of the family economy is managed by a certain *fang*), but it is also advantageous for all these enterprises to pool capital as a cushion against possible losses and to provide liquid assets for further investment and expansion. Even women who see their sisters-in-law as monopolizing all the *jia* resources will be loath to push too hard for division of a family in which everyone benefits from several sectors of a diversified economy.

What this amounts to is a demonstration that families will remain together longer when it is of clear economic advantage for them to do so. The two cases presented by Cohen, those of diversification and of efficient pooling of female labor resources, are but two examples, albeit extremely important ones, of this more general condition. The model also has another side—families will divide sooner if it is to their economic advantage. The oft-imagined case in which a family is so poor that it can support only one son on its meager land (Freedman

1958, p. 29) is an example in which families must divide early, with the other brothers going off to seek their fortunes with no hope of ever returning again. Although such sojourners will retain membership in their natal *jia* for a while, eventually they will begin to be seen as separate, and no longer hold rights in their former *jia*.

So when we apply this model of economic advantage to family organization in any particular Chinese community, we must consider specific types of family economy found there, together with the pressures for early or late division that the local economy may produce. Thus we can see the interrelationship between family organization and work: depending on what work family members do, their families will tend to divide earlier or later in the developmental cycle, and thus be larger or smaller on the average in any given census sample. And reciprocally, it may not be possible for families with limited labor power or capital (and accumulating capital depends partly on staying together) to pursue certain occupations, particularly those involving intensive labor or investment. To understand Chinese family organization in a particular community, we must examine both the basic principles of family structure and its socioeconomic context, the family economy. We can illustrate this by examining changes in the organization of Ploughshare families during the past seventy years.

Historical Changes in Ploughshare Family Organization

In 1910, five years after the Japanese began keeping detailed household registration records, there were 54 families in Ploughshare. Thirty-two, or 59 percent, were nuclear families, 13, or 24 percent, were stem families, and 9, or 16 percent, were joint families. The mean family size was 5.39 persons, and the median, 5 (see table 11).

Looking at the data another way to make them directly comparable to those reported by Wolf and Huang for nine districts in the Haishan area, including Jiatian, of which Ploughshare is a part (1980, p. 69), we find that of 59 married couples living in Ploughshare in 1910, 17, or 29 percent, lived in nuclear families, 24, or 42 percent lived in stem families, and 18, or 31 percent, lived in joint families. These figures contrast with 24 percent nuclear, 26 percent stem, and 49 percent joint in Haishan as a whole in 1906 (see table 12). Ploughshare at that time was a village consisting primarily of poor laborers and upland farmers, many of them recent immigrants or transients renting houses in the village. Several families had moved out as a consequence of the disruption at the beginning of the Japanese occupation. There were few families with any material means, and only Ong Cin owned any rice land. In a poor community like this, and

TABLE 11

Size and Composition of Ploughshare Families, 1910-78

Date	Number of Families	Mean Size	Number of Nuclear	Number of Stem	Number of Joint
1910	54	5.39	32 (59%)	13 (24%)	9 (17%)
1935	50	8.66	18 (36%)	18 (36%)	14 (28%)
1973	102	7.08	65 (64%)	29 (28%)	8 (8%)
1978	107	7.72	59 (55%)	37 (35%)	11 (10%)

TABLE 12

Couples Living in Various Family Types,
Ploughshare, 1910; Haishan Districts, 1906
(By number and percentages)

Family Type	Ploughshare, 1910		Nine Haishan Districts, 1906	
	No.	%	No.	%
Nuclear	17	29	250	24.4
Stem	24	41	269	26.3
Joint	18	31	505	49.3

especially when people are migrating into and out of the village, we can expect a low proportion of joint families. When families move into the village, they are unlikely to enter as fully formed joint families, but rather as nuclear family units, either newly divided from the husband's brothers, or formally still part of their *jia* in their old community, but sojourning in Ploughshare.[2] And when people migrate out of the village, they rarely go as fully formed joint or stem families. Either males go alone, in which case family organization is not affected (unless they go as uxorilocal husbands or as apprentices who will eventually take over their masters' businesses), or they migrate as nuclear families. Some of these nuclear families will have been independent *jia* for years before their departure, but others will be newly separated from, or still formally part of, joint families based in the home village. When such nuclear family units split off and migrate, usually because there is insufficient opportunity for all brothers to make their living at home, this leaves nuclear and stem families behind. So migration both into and

2. Unfortunately, the household registration records do not record *jia* membership, an economic fact, only household (M, *hu*) membership, a legal fact. Thus it is impossible to determine which of the transient nuclear families in Ploughshare at this time might in fact be parts of larger *jia* based elsewhere. I count each as an independent *jia*.

out of the village tends to increase the proportion of nuclear family *jia* and decrease the proportion of joint families. In fact, eight of the thirty-two nuclear family *jia* living in Ploughshare in 1910 had arrived in the village since 1900.

Although available figures for nearby communities are fragmentary, the difference between the migratory population of Ploughshare and the relatively stable population of Xi'nan, a nearby rice-growing community, strongly suggests that the difference in size and complexity between the families of Ploughshare and those of the nine Haishan districts, consisting primarily of rice-growing communities on the floor of the Taibei Basin or on the edges of the lower foothills, can be accounted for in large measure by the unstable nature of Ploughshare's population. This assertion is given some further support by the fact that, of the families residing in Ploughshare in 1910, those growing tea or lowland crops, and probably less likely to migrate because of access to land, had a mean *jia* size of 5.8, while families in occupations with no access to land, such as day laborers and tea pickers, had a mean family size of 4.9. It should be remembered, however, that even the farming families of Ploughshare had, on the average, smaller and less complex families than those in lowland, primarily rice-growing communities.

By 1935, the picture of family organization had changed. There were but fifty families in Ploughshare then, but they tended to be both larger and more complex than in 1910. There were eighteen, or 36 percent, nuclear family *jia,* eighteen, or 36 percent, stem, and fourteen, or 28 percent, joint families. The mean family size had grown to 8.66 persons, with a median of 7. Some of the joint families had grown quite large: one family had thirty members, another twenty-seven, and two more eighteen each. One of the largest, for example, was the farming family headed by Kou A-kim, who had recently come to the village from Shisantian, and whose descendants now form seven families still residing in Ploughshare. The composition of this family is shown in figure 4. When the four sons of the family head divided their property and households in 1936, the eldest *fang* itself became a four-generation stem family, and three other nuclear family *jia* resulted from the division.

The statistical growth of Ploughshare families between 1910 and 1935 can be attributed to two factors, stability of residence and timing of division. While still poor, Ploughshare's economy appears to have become more stable in the years between the opening of the mines, in the tens and twenties, and the beginning of the Pacific war in 1937. Only five families had moved into Ploughshare between 1925 and 1935,

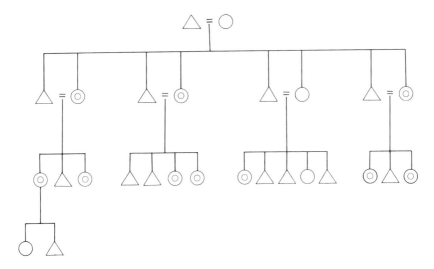

⊙, △ indicate *adopted* daughters and sons, respectively. Adopted daughters are eligible to marry their adoptive brothers (A. Wolf 1966, 1968).

Fig. 4. Kou A-kim's family, 1935

and the rest were longer-term residents who had time to grow from the nuclear to the stem or joint stage. Also, the large number of joint families in 1935 is related to the fact that many of them had been nuclear families when they entered the village between 1900 and 1910, and were just reaching the maximal developmental phase, immediately prior to division. This, combined with the economic reverses that many people began to feel as a result of the world war, meant that while only one family divided between 1925 and 1934, no less than twelve divided between 1935 and 1944. That so many joint families were capable of dividing underscores the main point: if they are not forced to migrate, families will often grow to the joint stage.

We have no figures available for the period between the end of the Pacific war and my field research in 1972-73, but by then the situation had changed again. In 1973, there were 102 families in the village, with 65, or 63 percent, nuclear, 29, or 28 percent, stem, and only 8, or 8 percent, joint. The frequencies of various family compositions resemble those found in 1910 more than those found in 1935, except that the proportion of joint families was even smaller in 1973 than it had been 63 years before. The mean family size in 1973 was 7.08, somewhere between the figures for 1910 and 1935. Even though families were less complex in 1973, they contained a larger number of members, because of the declining infant mortality rates in Taiwan (Barclay 1954, p. 161). That there was a greater proportion of nuclear families than ever before is clearly associated with economic factors, particularly migration.

Ploughshare in 1973 was part of an expanding industrial economy, one in which both work and educational opportunities were found more in the urban areas than in the villages. The young men and women who go to Taibei or other cities to avail themselves of these opportunities often retain ties with their natal *jia,* forming what I call dispersed joint families. This is particularly true in families with a little capital, where such out-migrants can send back significant remittances. But there are a considerable number of brothers who left the village with few resources, and many of these have changed residence permanently, no longer retaining rights or membership in their natal *jia.* These account in large part for the great proportion of nuclear families in the village population today. Living in Ploughshare in 1973 were representatives of thirty-two sets of two or more married brothers. Of these, only eight were living together in joint families of either the compact or dispersed type, and the other twenty-four were living separately. This contrasts with eleven of fifteen sets of married brothers living together in 1935 and six of seven sets living together in 1910.[3] But of the twenty-four sets of brothers living apart in 1973, thirteen sets had only one brother living in the village, with all the others having migrated out, set up permanent residence elsewhere, and severed connection with their natal *jia.* This leaves eleven sets of brothers living in separate nuclear families in the village, while eight sets of married brothers lived as joint families.

The predominance of nuclear families in the village was, as before, increased by the factor of in-migration. In 1973, there were twelve families who had moved into the village in the past fifteen years, with nine of these being nuclear and three stem, with no joint families among them. Thus we see that in-migrating families, as well as families who have some members move out, increased the proportion of nuclear family *jia* in the village population.

In 1978, the situation was similar: fifty-nine, or 55 percent, were nuclear families, 37, or 35 percent, stem, and eleven, or 10 percent, joint. The mean family size had grown again, to 7.72 persons. Thus the primary changes observable between 1973 and 1978 were an

---

3. It is quite possible that married men living in the village in 1910 or 1935 had married brothers living elsewhere who do not appear on the household registration records. If they did, this would decrease the difference between the proportions of sets of married brothers living jointly at the different times.

increase in the proportion of stem families, with a complementary decrease in the number of nuclear families, and an increase in the average family size. Both of these changes can be accounted for in strictly demographic terms. In the five years between the two counts, 110 people were born in Ploughshare, while only 17 died, an imbalance that reduced only five families from the stem to the nuclear type through the deaths of parents, while thirteen families grew from the nuclear to the stem type through the marriage of a son and the birth of offspring. In addition, of eleven families who migrated into the village during these years and remained there until 1978, a high proportion (5) were of the stem type. The natural increase of population, in the absence of a large number of family divisions (there were but three during this period), also accounts for the increase in the average size of households, without much increase in complexity. Thus we can see that there was no significant change in the way the domestic cycle was operating from the early to the late 1970s. This will become even clearer when we look at the relationship between the timing of family division and the type of family economy.

There are four possibilities for grown brothers. They can remain in the village undivided; they can remain in the village, but divide eventually; some of them may migrate, but retain rights in the home *jia;* or some of them may migrate, and divide from each other and from those who stayed at home. Naturally all brothers will divide sometime. It is almost unheard of in Taiwan for agnatic first cousins to remain together in a *jia* after their fathers are dead. But the time when brothers divide will greatly influence the number of joint families in any sample, and the family economy will influence the time when brothers divide. If we look at the proportion of nuclear, stem, dispersed joint, and concentrated joint families in Ploughshare in 1973 and again in 1978, plotted against type of family economy, the relationship will be clear (see table 13).

Brothers who remain together until their families reach the joint stage are brothers who are engaged in an enterprise that requires investment of capital. Of the eight joint families in the village in 1973, all had family economies that were somehow dependent on capital investment. No family of wage earners or of mixed wage earners and farmers had survived to the joint stage at that time. In 1978, there were but two out of a total of sixty-five wage-earning families. There had been more in the past, but in the modern economy it appears to be only those with good economic reasons for staying together that remain in a joint family very long after the younger brothers are married. Others, whether spread out by migration or not, divide almost as soon as possible. The relationship also appears to work the other

TABLE 13

COMPLEXITY OF HOUSEHOLDS BY OCCUPATION

Source of Income	Number of Households		Nuclear		Stem		Dispersed Joint		Concentrated Joint	
	1973	1978	1973	1978	1973	1978	1973	1978	1973	1978
Wage work only	61	50	45	33	16	16	0	1	0	0
Wage work and farming	16	15	11	9	5	5	0	1	0	0
Capital investment	25	42	9	17	8	16	4	5	4	4
Total	102	107	65	59	29	37	4	7	4	4

way, though our evidence is based on very small numbers. Of the five families that grew to the joint stage between 1973 and 1978, two were already dependent on capital, two changed from wage work to capital investment, and only one began as and remained a family of wage workers and farmers. This suggests that not only is growth to the joint stage virtually dependent on capital investment, but that joint families with large amounts of available labor are more likely to have capital to invest. Some examples of family histories will illustrate how some families break up and others remain together.

Developmental Cycles of Particular Families

Ciu A-bi, at eighty-seven the oldest mentally competent person in Ploughshare in 1978, came into the village as an adopted daughter-in-law when she was a few months old. After she grew up and married her foster brother, a coal miner with no land, they had four sons, which would seemingly give them the opportunity to form a joint family. In fact, they never did. The eldest son was not married long before he died, and his own son and daughter now live in Taibei City, and see their grandmother and uncles only infrequently. The second son died before he was ever married, which his mother attributes to the lack of money for medicine when he got sick in the hard years following the end of the Pacific war. The third son, rather than taking in a wife, followed a course common to many poorer people in this area: he married into his wife's family, across the river in Dapu, where he still lives. In marrying out, he also ceased to be a member of his mother's *jia*. There was no property, no advantage to either the eldest son's descendants or the third son in staying with their natal family. Opportunities were elsewhere and they took advantage of them. But the fourth son, Ong Tho, remained home with his mother after his father's death in the 1940s, and their family in 1973 was of the stem type, containing Tho and his wife, the old lady A-bi, Tho's six sons, and a young daughter. They lived in a house that was still mostly mud-brick, though they had replaced one wing, demolished in a typhoon in 1970, with a handsome, if small, brick structure. In 1973, their household income depended entirely on wages. Tho worked in the coal mines building and repairing scaffolding in the tunnels, assisted until recently by his eldest son, who during my first visit to Ploughshare went to work in a neighboring knitting mill. The second son, who had not yet done his military service, worked in the paper mill in Shisantian, while the third, showing the most scholastic ability, was allowed to attend junior middle school instead of going to work immediately after primary school. The fourth son, who graduated from primary school in 1972, showed no such promise, and his parents sent him to be apprenticed to an electrician in Taoyuan, where he would remain for several years, returning home only for holidays. Thus the process of dispersal through migration had already begun in the next generation. The two youngest sons and the little daughter were too young to work, but their mother also supplemented the household income by taking in washing from families whose women were all either fully employed or disabled, and could not find the time to do their own laundry. Together, the family made about NT$6,000 per month, which made them rather poor, considering there were ten mouths to feed. By 1978, increased labor power and higher wages had enabled them to do a little better. The oldest son was back in the mines with his father; he had married and purchased a knitting machine that his wife, who came from a large knitting household in Ploughshare, worked during the day while her mother-in-law tended their children. The fourth son, after an unsuccessful apprenticeship, also worked in the mines, and the fifth and sixth sons in nearby factories. They had replaced most of the rest of their house with a two-story brick structure—one of the first things the old lady did when I visited her in 1978 was to take me up to the roof to see the view. Considering the higher living standard they now have, along with the possibility of all the sons finding good, permanent jobs in the vicinity, the family may well go through a joint phase in the next generation, one that was effectively precluded for Tho and his brothers. But unless they change from a wage-earning to a capital-investing family economy, there will be no compulsion for them to remain for long in this joint phase.

Another family broken up by migration undertaken out of economic necessity was Peq Cin's. His father originally had a little mountain land, but when his three sons grew up, it became clear that the small amount of income from tea growing would not support them all. Thus the eldest was sent in the early 1940s to be apprenticed to a storekeeper in Xinzhu City. He now has his own store there and is fairly prosperous, and still sends a little money to his mother occasionally (his father died over twenty-five years ago). The second brother, like Ciu A-bi's second son, was married uxorilocally and became a member of his wife's household. Only Cin, the third brother, remained at home; his is now a stem family consisting of his mother, himself and his wife, and their six small children. Cin is a coal miner, and the sole support of his family. With less income than Ong Tho's household, their standard of living in 1973 was about the same, because Cin's family had only seven members, and neither the old lady nor the small children ate very much. In 1978, none of the children was yet old enough to earn money, and the family, unchanged in form, remained rather poor.

In both these cases, economic opportunities elsewhere precluded brothers from remaining together as joint families. Neither of these was a case of absolute necessity or possible starvation, for there were always jobs available in the coal mines and on the pushcart railway when the brothers were growing up, and it would have been perfectly feasible for them all to take such jobs, remain in the village, and form joint families. But the point is that there was no particular advantage in their staying. As long as the youngest brother was available to provide eventual support for the parents when they grew old (in both cases, this turned out to be the mother only), the elder brothers found it feasible to take jobs elsewhere or marry into their wives' families. Thus joint families never arose, because only one brother remained in the village and those who left cut off their ties with their families.

But migration out of the village, important as it is in paring down potentially joint families, is not the only cause of early family division. Even when married brothers all remain in the village, often there is no particular incentive for them to remain together, and they divide also. A case in point are the four sons of Iu: A-po and his wife Ong A-khim. A-po (his name means old lady or great-aunt) married into the village uxorilocally, and he and his wife had five sons, four of whom survived to adulthood. In 1965, the eldest two had married and produced children, and both worked in the coal mines. The third brother was married in the late 1960s and the youngest in 1971, and they too earned wages in the coal pits. The eldest son died, apparently of lung disease incurred in coal mining, in 1968, and his father followed in 1970. The youngest son's marriage in 1971 was a sign that the brothers should divide, and by 1972, though they had undergone no formal ceremony, their households all had separate budgets, with the responsibility for the support of their mother rotating among them. This was the case even though the youngest brother, Ong-iong, had no house of his own and was forced, with his wife and baby daughter, to occupy only a kitchen and a miniscule bedroom in the house belonging to the third brother. The son and daughter of the eldest brother, who had died in 1968, still remained with their second uncle because they were not old enough to form a household on their own. They were both apprenticed in Taibei and visited but seldom. Again we see the dispersal principle beginning to operate. Their household was still technically joint, but only in the sense that a man and his mother cared for his niece and nephew, her grandchildren, who were orphans. And by 1978 they, along with their grandmother A-Khim, had formed a separate household in Taibei City. As for the two younger brothers, they separated as soon as it was possible. When I asked them if their property had been divided also, they answered, rather incredulously, that there was none. They had nothing in common, no advantage in maintaining a common budget, and so they had split, even though they all continued to occupy the same two adjoining houses, and were on perfectly good terms with one another.

Another case of early division is provided by Li Cieng and Li Hieng, both coal miners. They also had a younger brother, Li Khun, but he married uxorilocally into a nearby mountain community in the 1960s. Cieng and Hieng lived with their wives, their mother, two of Cieng's children, and five of Hieng's children until 1971. At that time, Cieng's wife, always an unstable person, simply became intolerable to her hard-working and somewhat downtrodden sister-in-law, whereupon they divided not only their budget and stove but their residence as well. Hieng and his family built a new house at the upper end of the village and moved out of the one at the lower corner occupied by Cieng. A few months before I came to Ploughshare the first time, Cieng's wife left altogether and was officially divorced from him, returning only once while I lived in the village. Dressed in fashionable urban style, she made her way down the village street, demanding to see her children, and when she found neither her ex-husband nor her mother-in-law at home, she smashed a window of their house and took off for parts unknown. But even with the neurotic sister-in-law gone, Hieng and his family made no move to reunite their *jia* with Hieng's older brother's. They had faced considerable economic hardship in building the new house, but by 1973 the debt was gradually being paid off, there was furniture in the house, and with both brothers earning income only from the mines, there was no particular reason to cooperate. The old mother, no longer too stable on her feet, still trekked the length of the village several times a day: the households were separate and that was that. After the mother's death in 1974, there was even less reason to get back together, and in 1978 there was not much daily contact between the two families.

In all four examples cited so far, brothers, all laborers, have either

found their families split by migration before there was any chance
for them to assume the joint form, or have divided early in the developmental cycle despite their remaining in the village. But this is not the
course always followed. In other families, brothers, sometimes dispersed and sometimes residing together, have maintained their households in joint form. As we shall see, they have had good economic
reasons to do so, since all have household economies involving investment and management of capital.

As an example, we may look at the Tiu:s who run the general store
by the bridge to Blacksmith Gulch. The father of the family, Tiu:
Pun-iek, came to Ploughshare just after the Pacific war and established
the store, which is the oldest in the village. They had five boys and
three girls, and in 1973 the oldest son, already married, was serving
his army time, while his wife tended their child and his parents ran
the store, the father mainly busying himself with butchering and
selling meat while the mother ran the dry goods business. The second
son, too young for army duty, ran their rice mill, the only one in the
village. A few months after I left Ploughshare the first time, Tiu:
Pun-iek died suddenly, leaving his wife and children to tend the family
business. In 1978, they had grown to a true joint family, with fourteen
people sharing a common budget. The mother and the first daughter-in-
law took care of most of the retail business, while the first son ran the
rice mill. The second son and his wife both worked in factories. The
third and fourth sons were both in the army, but the fourth was already
married, and his wife lived in their house and took factory work as
well. Their two younger daughters, not yet married, also worked in
factories. It would have been conceivable for this family to divide.
The mother, the eldest son, and the eldest son's wife could share
with the younger children the income from the store and rice mill,
while the second, third, and fourth sons all went their separate ways.
But the nature of the family economy argued against this solution.
The store was not going particularly well in 1978, so it would have
been difficult to persuade the first brother to accept a division. At the
same time, the second and fourth daughters-in-law would be expecting
children soon, and if the family divided would either have to depend
on their mother and eldest sister-in-law for child care while they
worked in the factories or quit their jobs, leaving each of their separate
nuclear families dependent on the income of a single wage earner. In
this family, both diversification of holdings and the possibility of
gaining extra income from female labor prevented division, even several
years after the father's death.

Even stronger pressures operate to keep together the wealthy family
headed by village head Ong Cin-hieng. Each of Cin-hieng's sons and

daughters-in-law has a vital role to play in the operation of their large knitting business, the management of family finances, the transportation of materials and finished goods, and the tending of their Wanhua store, as well as in the operation of the complex household numbering nineteen persons in 1978. If the brothers were to divide, they would have to sort out these roles somehow, but it is doubtful whether any of them would be able to earn as much money or manage their affairs as efficiently with four budgets, four separate household economies, and four smaller businesses. It seems safe to say that they will stay as a joint family for years to come.

While it is easy to see how economic considerations have held these households together in the joint form, it is also important to realize that, in every joint family, there are pressures working for division, and that no set of brothers stays together throughout their lives. We can see this from the example of the Iap brothers, who ran what in 1973 was the largest of the village stores. Their parents, originally proprietors of a noodle shop that served the railway pushers, had eight daughters and three sons, but the eldest son was killed in a mining accident when he was only fifteen. The two younger brothers, however, married and established the arrangement of elder brother Bu-kiet selling fresh produce and younger brother Tiek-iek dealing in miscellaneous dry goods. By 1973 their father had been dead several years, Bu-kiet had five children and Tiek-iek three, and either brother by himself could have easily supported their seventy-one-year-old mother. But the nature of the business encouraged cooperation. If one brother and his wife were to get away at all from the daily grind of storekeeping, the other couple would have to cover for them; if one or the other suffered any business or financial reversal, the funds would be available from their common holdings to cushion the loss and keep both businesses going. But in 1974 or 1975 the tensions between the *fang* of the respective brothers apparently reached a breaking point, for they divided in 1975. After all, each store could exist independently, and each couple could manage with the labor they had, even if it meant more difficulty. Then in early 1976, Iap Tiek-iek was killed in a motorcycle accident, leaving his wife with five children and a dry goods store to manage. Since division had already been accomplished, there was no question of going back, and she had to bring her own natal grandmother to live with her and help with the store and the children. It is probably a safe bet, however, that if her husband had died before the households were divided, they would have remained together to this day: it would have made no economic sense whatsoever to divide. But as in all such situations, division finally did come, and when it did come it was final.

In all these cases, economic pressures kept families together, at least for several years of the developmental cycle, and being together meant living in the same house and sharing a common budget. In other cases, however, joint family organization takes a different form: some members of a joint family live apart from the others, typically in a higher-level central place such as Banqiao, Taibei, or Jilong, but do not separate totally from their original family. Rather they retain part of their income for daily expenses and contribute the rest to a general fund, usually controlled by the senior male or the senior couple of the joint family. Since many temporary or permanent migrants to urban areas simply separate from their natal *jia*, as did Ong Tho and Peq Cin's brothers, we must look for reasons why other migrants remain part of dispersed joint families. We find the answer, not surprisingly, in diversified economies and capital investment, as illustrated by the following examples.

One such family is headed jointly by Lou Kim-bi, the fourth of seven sisters, and her uxorilocally married-in husband, Lua Pieng-kui. The couple had four sons. The eldest was a coal miner, and was killed in a mining accident in the late sixties. His widow, considered mentally disturbed by the local people, though seemingly perfectly normal to an outsider, did not get along with her sisters-in-law, and her father-in-law built a separate house for her and her two children near the main family dwelling. They cook and eat separately, but are not formally divided from the Lou *jia;* they have no ancestral tablets of their own, nor are they registered separately on the temple records. I believe they also get a share of the family rice harvest. The other three sons remain unambiguously part of a dispersed joint household with their parents. The second son, formerly a coal miner, quit his job after an injury in late 1972. He raised a large brood of ducks and sold them, and then went to work knitting for wages at his wife's natal home in nearby Blacksmith Gulch. In 1978 he had become a partner in a small factory in the Taibei industrial suburb of Sanchong, though he continued to live at home, which by that time was a separate house across the street from the family compound. His wife and eldest daughter worked knitting machines there, and there was much coming and going between the two houses. The third brother resides most of the time in Taibei, where he and his family operate a highly successful electrician's business. He was able in 1973 to purchase a four-story building in Wanhua and rent out three floors while living and operating his business out of the fourth, thus increasing his income even more. The electrician's business profits were not shared equally among all members of the *jia*, but he did contribute substantial money to his parents' support and to the upkeep of the house in Ploughshare, which even in 1973 boasted such luxuries as a color television set and the only linoleum floor in the village. At the same time, the father works the family land, which he managed to buy from the landlord, a religious association, in 1964, partly from surplus profits generated by the electrician's business, successful even then. The electrician and his wife always return to help with the harvest, allowing the family to avoid ever having to hire agricultural labor. The grandchildren in the Taibei branch of the family frequently stay in Ploughshare for long periods and the family is united at all holidays and listed as a single *jia* in the temple records. The youngest son was still in the army in 1973. By 1978 he was married with a child and drove his own taxicab, while still living in the old house together with his parents and, when they visited, his third brother's branch of the family. In general, there was a gradual dispersal process going on in this family over the years, but even in 1978 it was not complete: there was the land, which still fed all of them, and there were the parents, who provided a focus. Even with independent businesses, there were advantages to remaining at least somewhat together as a dispersed joint family.

Another family with a diversified economy is headed by So A-bieng, a retired cart pusher who came to Ploughshare during the bombing attacks at the end of the Pacific war. A-bieng and his wife had five sons, but two did not survive to adulthood. The three who did all lived outside Ploughshare in 1973, but they still remained a dispersed joint family. The eldest son worked as manager of a dancing hall in Taibei, the second ran a noodle shop in the port city of Jilong, and the third ran a similar noodle shop in the same town, but in partnership with A-bieng's sister's son. Although none of A-bieng's sons resided in the village except for a few weeks after New Year's, the second son's wife and some of each son's children did, including the third son's only child, a one-year-old adopted daughter, who could be seen at any hour of day or night riding around the village on her devoted grandfather's back. *Jia* finances in this case were complicated; basically each brother supported his own *fang* and contributed from 500 to 1,000 Taiwan dollars per month to the upkeep of the retired parents. I am not sure whether any of the brothers actively contributed capital to the others' businesses, but for people in business, even the residual possibility of such help in time of need would be something of an incentive to keep the family undivided. Also, cooperation in child care, with one wife and the still-active parents at home, clearly helped to solve the domestic labor needs of the various branches. And the support of the parents was more easily managed in a joint arrangement such as this, for the amounts each brother could contribute sometimes varied from month to month.

While parents are at work, grandmothers care for little ones.

In the ensuing years, So A-bieng's successful economic strategy—he began acquiring houses—acted as further impetus to keep the family undivided. The ramshackle mud-brick structure that was their home in 1973 was torn down and replaced by a two-story modern house that was given to the eldest brother and his family, who then moved back to the village from Taibei when he quit the dance hall to take a local job. At about the same time, A-bieng, using accumulated *jia* funds and some money borrowed from a rotating credit society, purchased another house in Blacksmith Gulch for his third son's family. They stay there when they return to the village, but while they are busy with their noodle shop the old couple occupies the house, along with the third son's two adopted children, cared for by their grandparents. Finally, when butcher Kou Hieng went deeply into debt in 1977, A-bieng bought his house and, after Hieng and his family fled the village, was making plans to offer that house to the second son. After their father dies, I assume the sons will fully divide, but the combination of their diverse economic holdings and their father's strategy kept them together for several years as a dispersed joint family.

This case is similar to the preceding one: allocation of capital, and domestic and productive labor work out better in each case if the family remains a single *jia,* even though the various *fang* reside separately and keep their own budgets, at least for everyday expenses. It is noteworthy that the same principles worked for the Lou-Lua family, affluent through the whole period, as for the Sos who were relatively poor until very recently. It is not the amount of income but the structure of income that is similar for the two families and that keeps each of them together despite their physical dispersal.

From these examples we can see much more clearly that the variations in family organization found in Ploughshare are a result of particular courses taken by sets of brothers as they grow up, marry, and beget children. Those who are divided by economic necessity at an early age, and have little to contribute to each other's income or the support of their parents, never reach the joint-family stage of the developmental cycle at all; this was the case with the families of Ong Tho and Peq Cin. Others, who do go through a brief joint phase with several brothers remaining in the village, nevertheless break up quickly in the absence of any economic incentive holding them together; examples of this type were the Ong-Iu: brothers and the two Lis. On the other hand, some sets of brothers, those whose income can be enhanced or made more secure by pooling labor or capital resources, tend to remain in the joint stage of family organization longer. This is true whether all brothers remain physically coresident, as in the case of the Tiu: storekeepers and the Ong knitters, or whether their economic diversification carries them apart, as is true with the Lou-Lua family and the sons of So A-bieng.

The case of Ploughshare thus reinforces the point made by Cohen (1970, 1976) about variations in the Chinese developmental cycle: brothers remain together longer, despite the inevitable tensions between *fang* within a *jia*, as long as it remains economically advantageous for them to do so. What Cohen's data show for primarily agricultural Hakka families in southern Taiwan, my data confirm for primarily laboring and petty-capitalist Hokkien families in the northern part of the island. In this connection, there is basically no difference between agriculture, commerce, and industry. The difference, rather, is between those types of family economy, such as rice growing or coal mining, that can support people just as easily in a series of independent nuclear family *jia* as in a complex joint family, and those other types of economy, such as tobacco growing (Cohen 1969, pp. 165-ff.), sweater knitting, or a whole range of economically diversified types, in which there is clear benefit in staying together.

THE GENERATIONS: FATHER-SON RELATIONSHIPS

The Chinese Model

In Confucian social philosophy, human society was built on the five relationships: those between minister and ruler, father and son, husband and wife, elder and younger brother, and friend and friend. Of these, the one between father and son was usually considered the most important (Mote 1971, p. 45). The proper content of this relationship, and by extension of all those between parents and children, was *xiao*, or filial obedience (often translated as "filial piety," but I fail to see what is pious about it). It is this obedience, total and unconditional, that a son owes to his parents. It is expressed in ritual deference, in unquestioned compliance with the parents' wishes, and in ancestral worship after the parents' death. Ideally, the parents should prompt this filial obedience by being nurturing *(zi)*, but filial obedience remains an absolute imperative regardless of the nature of the parents' conduct.

Between mother and children, filial obedience in China seems to consist of a mixture of harsh discipline and warm, emotional bonding (M. Wolf 1972, p. 79). Between father and son, by contrast, the relationship often becomes more difficult. There is enormous tension between the two, for two reasons. First, the father feels that ensuring the son's filial obedience is so important that he cannot afford to be nice to the son and thereby appear soft. Second, the father and son are both aware that, at least when there is productive property in the family, the son is the one who will eventually take control and make the father an old man (Harrell 1981b), while the father is the one keeping the son from full control of the property. All this adds up to a situation described, as an example, in a farming community in Shandong:

> The relationship between father and son has none of the warmth and freedom existing between mother and child. The father's attitude is dignified, even remote; his authority is unquestioned and he expects submissiveness from his sons. When the son is an infant, the father may on rare occasions play with him or take him out. When the boy is old enough to help in the fields, father and son walk together and work together quite often. But by the time the boy reaches the age of fifteen, the father assumes a more dignified attitude toward him and is frequently severe. . . . When father and sons do work together, they have nothing to say, and even at home they speak only if they have business to discuss. [M. C. Yang 1945, pp. 57-58]

Closer to home, in the rice-farming community of Xi'nan, Ahern reports that:

> . . . When a boy reaches six or seven years of age, a formal distance springs up between him and his father. They seem to avoid interacting whenever possible; what verbal contact they have deals with pressing household or business matters. This lack of interaction . . . is especially apparent when groups of people sit around chatting. In this sort of casual situation, fathers and sons seldom, if ever, speak directly to each other, and indeed do not even respond to one another's general remarks. [Ahern 1973, p. 216]

I have also witnessed a similar sort of father-son interaction in the farming community of Xiyuan on the floor of the Taibei Basin (Harrell 1981c). Fathers and sons are polite to each other, and no more. When business comes up, they speak; otherwise, they avoid each other as much as possible.

Ploughshare in Comparison

In Ploughshare, however, things are somewhat different. I knew several older men who used to sit and discuss whatever went on with their adult sons, in a casual way. Noticeable among these was old Ong Chiu-tik, a retired coal miner and lay religious specialist who died in 1975. He and his eldest son, domiciled in Yingge, had both studied the arts of geomancy, horoscopy, and charm writing, and often used to sit in Chiu-tik's front room and compare knowledge, as well as exchange innuendoes about the neighbors, some of whom did not get along with them very well. Similarly, such senior men as So A-bieng and Ong Tho would often talk with their sons, and village head Ong Cin-hieng, who managed his knitting business jointly with his two eldest sons, also used to spend lots of time with them talking business and politics in an informal manner. This is a difficult subject to quantify,

A young storekeeper and two of his children, 1973

and the difference between my impressions and Ahern's or Yang's may be one of viewpoint. But I think not, as I noticed the differences between Xiyuan and Ploughshare.

The father-son relationship, then, is looser in Ploughshare. The difference from Shandong might be one of regional cultures if there were not such a striking similarity between Yang's description of Shandong in the 1930s and Ahern's description of Xi'nan in the 1970s And the difference between Xi'nan or Xiyuang and Ploughshare would be difficult to attribute to regional cultures. We must thus seek an explanation in the socioeconomic context of the different Sanxia communities, and we find this explanation again in the nature of the family economy. If it is correct that one of the primary causes of coldness between father and son is implicit resentment over the son's eventual ousting of the father from the position of power and authority in managing the family estate, such resentment should be considerably less where the son's income does not derive from family property that he will someday control. In the laboring families of Ploughshare, fathers and sons have each contributed to family income by earning wages; one's income does not depend on the other or, more important, on the other's being subordinate. The income is, of course, generally controlled by the father, but the son has a lever—he, after all, brings in part of that income, sometimes the major part, totally independently of anything the father does. And with respect to the employer, father and son are equal; each is simply another wage earner.

So the tension over the estate, one of the two causes that have generally been seen as bringing about father-son distance, is absent in most Ploughshare families. And even in exceptional families like those of Ong Cin-hieng, the estate is often as dependent on the sons' managerial skills as on their father's.

In sum, we can see how the Chinese model of the family developmental cycle and the relationships between generations, while operating in Ploughshare, takes on particular forms because of the socioeconomic context of Ploughshare. In particular, the specific patterns families assume at certain phases of the life cycles of their members are explained in the main by the types of economic activities those families are engaged in. In addition, the perceptible weakening of generational authority can be seen in the context of the lack of dependence on a family estate.

TYPES OF MARRIAGE AND THE ROLES OF THE SEXES

The Chinese Model

There are many different forms of marriage in premodern Chinese society, but almost all first marriages fall into three categories, termed by Arthur Wolf (1974b) the major, minor, and uxorilocal. Major marriage is the nominally preferred form, the cultural ideal, and the statistical norm in most parts of China. In this form, a young adult woman is transferred from her natal family to that of her young adult husband, accompanied by an ostentatious and expensive ceremony as well as the exchange of direct and indirect dowry payments. She then lives as a wife and, most important, a daughter-in-law in her husband's family. In the minor form of marriage, a daughter-in-law is brought into her husband's family as a young child, often as a baby, and brought up there. When she and her intended husband reach maturity they change from being "brother and sister" to being husband and wife. In the third form of marriage, the uxorilocal, an adult man marries into his wife's family. Neither the minor nor the uxorilocal form demands an expensive ceremony or a lavish dowry.

For reasons not entirely clear as yet, the entire area of northern Taiwan seems to have had one of the highest (if not the highest) rates of minor marriage anywhere in China in the early part of this century. In fact, Wolf and Huang (1980, pp. 124, 281) have argued that Chinese in this part of Taiwan preferred to marry their children in the minor fashion if at all possible. And in the early years of this century at least, before what Wolf and Huang call the "Revolt of the Young" (ibid., pp. 193-201) led to the refusal of young people to marry in the minor fashion, the relative frequencies of major and minor marriages of Ploughshare were about what they were in the rest of the nine districts surveyed by Wolf and Huang, approximately equal, with slightly more major than minor marriages. But when we look at the relative frequency of uxorilocal marriages in Ploughshare and in the nine districts taken as a whole, we find a consistent difference. Where the percentages of uxorilocal marriages in the nine districts remain relatively constant from 1905-45 at about 10 to 12 percent for men and 13 to 15 percent for women, the corresponding figures for Ploughshare are 18.4 percent for men and 16.8 percent for women, consistently higher rates. In addition, the rate of uxorilocal marriage in Ploughshare remained high in the postwar period. Although there are no comparable figures for other districts, I am sure that Ploughshare's rate of 16 percent uxorilocality among currently complete marriages (spouses living together) is unusually high. At the same time, it should be pointed out that the relative numbers of men and women marrying uxorilocally in the nine districts and in Ploughshare are reversed. In the former, women are more likely to take in husbands than are their brothers to marry out, while in the latter more men than women married uxorilocally.

Both these differences can be traced to Ploughshare's position as a poor, peripheral village within the southwestern Taibei Basin. Uxorilocal marriage in this area was primarily a means of assuring a line of descent for a family with no natural sons, and secondarily of increasing the supply of male labor in a family whose sons were too young to work. Both these needs, however, can be met by one or another form of male adoption without resort to uxorilocal marriage. A family can adopt a son from an agnate, in which case he is called a *ke-pang kia:* (a son who crosses from one room, or agnatic segment, to another), or it can buy a boy from a nonrelative. In many parts of China, especially where lineage organization was strong, adoption of an agnate was the preferred, or even prescribed, method of obtaining an heir when there was no natural son. In Zhejiang, for example, genealogies usually stipulate that children of uxorilocal unions are not to be recognized as lineage members, and that lineage men who marry uxorilocally are to be excluded from the lineage genealogies.[4] In the Taibei Basin, however, uxorilocal marriage always seems to have been the preferred alternative (Wolf and Huang 1980, p. 212). And in Ploughshare, with no agnatic organization and indeed few agnates available for anyone to adopt from, uxorilocal marriage was practically the only alternative. I know of only one agnatic adoption in the village before 1945, and adoptions by purchase were similarly rare, because the price was so high (ibid., 1980, p. 205)—again, I know of only one before

---

4. Based on my unpublished survey of several genealogies from Xiaoshan County, Shaoxing Prefecture (see Harrell, n.d.).

1945, and two since then. So Ploughshare villagers took in sons-in-law, rather than adopting sons, when they needed heirs of when their heirs were too young to contribute labor. What does not seem to have happened in Ploughshare, however, is for families with living, laboring sons nevertheless to take in additional sons uxorilocally, as was the case in the southern Taiwan rainfall-irrigated rice farming village of Zhongshe, as described by Pasternak (n.d.). In this area, peak-season labor requirements were unusually intense, even for wet-rice farmers, so that even families with adult sons often required extra laborers. And in this village, until the construction of a large-scale irrigation project relaxed demands for peak-season labor, the percentage of uxorilocal marriages for both men and women was about twenty-five (ibid., n.d.), considerably higher even than in Ploughshare, where I know of no family with adult sons that ever took in a son-in-law, though some families with several daughters married more than one of them uxorilocally.

If the lack of other alternatives for assuring continuity of descent and minimum male labor seems to account for the high rates of uxorilocal marriage in Ploughshare generally, we still have to explain the higher rate of uxorilocal marriages in Ploughshare for men than for women. Wolf and Huang (1980, pp. 125-26) provide us with the explanation when they state that, in their nine districts lying mostly in the lowland core of the North Taiwan system, more women than men married uxorilocally because uxorilocal marriages tend to be hypogamous: the men marry up. The relatively prosperous farmers of the valley floor tended to attract men from poorer communities around the periphery, and Ploughshare was one of those peripheral communities that was likely to give away more men to richer villages than it took in from even poorer, more remote communities.

SEX ROLES IN FAMILY AND COMMUNITY

The Chinese Model

Inequality of the sexes has been a fundamental tenet of Chinese moral philosophy and a basic part of Chinese behavior patterns since earliest times. For the last thousand years at least this has meant inferior treatment for daughters, as compared to sons, compounded from the twelfth through the nineteenth centuries by foot-binding; inequality of husband and wife, both jurally and in practice; and only a gradual emergence of a woman into a position of relative equality with her husband and authority over her adult sons, when she grows old. In many communities, official heads of households are always male, with even baby boys taking at least ritual precedence over their mothers

(Wang Sung-hsing 1971). Nearly everywhere, men were usually the actual heads of households, exercising authority over the family budget and all other important decisions. And what was true in the family was true in the community as well, with women ordinarily excluded from positions of official political power or ritual responsibility. The obverse of male domination in the public sphere, Margery Wolf has argued, is the formation of a "women's community," a female society with a female subculture, in which the washing place by the river becomes the counterpart of the male gathering place in a store or restaurant, and in which female solidarity is maintained through an effective gossip network and the inculcation of matrifocal "uterine family" values on younger women by their mothers-in-law (Wolf 1972, p. 41). In such a context, most activities, leisure as well as work, are segregated by sex. In the nearby farming community of Xi'nan, for example, Ahern (personal communication) reports that men sit around and talk in some places, women in others. A similar pattern even seems to hold in the Chinese People's Republic province of Guangdong, where women now participate fully in agricultural labor. Parish and Whyte (1978, p. 242) relate that in the 1970s, "the most important informal groupings in the village are male: the older men who sit around in the evenings and chat about village affairs. Insofar as village opinion is formed and altered in these discussions, women are not included." The general pattern, nearly everywhere, is thus one of male dominance and female subordination in the household and in the community at large.

Ploughshare

There are several aspects of the relationships between the sexes that suggest that, while there is nothing resembling actual equality of the sexes in Ploughshare, many of the extremes of the relationship of dominance and subordination are mitigated by the peculiarities of Ploughshare's socioeconomic context. For one thing, there are several households where married women with living husbands are both official and actual heads of family. Some of these are the households of uxori-locally married couples. While no uxorilocal marriage involves the actual reversal of the roles of husband and wife, the nature of the marital residence does have considerable influence on the relationship. For in ordinary virilocal marriage, of all the factors contributing to the woman's oppression, among the most important is her being an outsider, usually coming into her husband's family from another community. It is her husband who has the relatives and the contacts in the community, who knows who is who and what skeletons they have in their closets, and who knows his way around generally. Besides, as Margery Wolf has aptly pointed out, the new daughter-in-law is seen as a threat by her husband's mother, which contributes to the strain in the already tense relationship between the two women. But in an uxorilocal marriage, the woman, at least, is not a stranger. According to Wolf, this is offset by an uxorilocal marriage being a shameful business for both the woman and her husband (1972, p. 192), but as a matter of fact, it does not carry the same stigma in Ploughshare that Wolf attributes to it in neighboring "Peihotien." This may be because uxorilocal marriage is relatively common in Ploughshare, or it may be because agnatic groups are unimportant in the community, and a man who marries uxorilocally is violating a principle much less strongly than in a basically lineage community such as Wolf's "Peihotien." Be that as it may, a woman who marries uxorilocally typically has a different relationship with her husband and a different status in the community than one who marries virilocally. The example of Lou Kim-bi has been mentioned before. She is considered coequal with her husband as head of their large and successful extended family. This is certainly because she was born and raised in the village and has a large number of both agnates and affines there. Her own agnatic cousin Lou Ong Cim is an even clearer case. Adopted into her family as a daughter and potential daughter-in-law of a childless couple, she later contracted an uxorilocal marriage with Lou Phieng, a poor man from up in the mountains. There is no question that Cim is head of this household. She is officially listed as such in both the name plaque that villagers hang in their doorways and in the roster of citizens posted in the Tho-te Biou, or village temple. When outsiders have any business with the family, they approach her and not her husband; she takes charge and he retires into the background. This sort of relationship is not the only one observable in cases of uxorilocal marriage, but it is common enough to be considered one possible pattern: a wife with reasonable abilities and strong personality can often control a family, and be its representative in village affairs.

A greater percentage of uxorilocally married couples in a community will mean more families in which the wife is potentially dominant over, or equal to, her husband, but the relatively small difference between the number of uxorilocally married couples in Ploughshare and the number in other communities does not, in itself, have great implications for the status of women in the community at large. I would argue, however, that it is nevertheless significant, and in two ways. First, it shows that the people of Ploughshare, either forced to make more uxorilocal marriages because there were no alternatives available, or willing to because they had fewer property rights to defend against invading sons-in-law, in practice accepted this form of marriage more readily than did their neighbors. This is in concert with my finding that uxorilocal marriage was not particularly stigmatized in this community. Second and more important, it argues that the people of Ploughshare, faced regularly with a large percentage of rather ad hoc family arrangements, had in their midst more examples of couples in which the wife was dominant or at least on a par with her husband, and perhaps would tend to be less critical of marriages that worked out that way.

This perhaps partially explains the number of virilocally married couples in which the wife is the dominant figure. For example, So Hong is married to Tiu: Kun-ong, a rather meek and ineffectual farmer. He is the official head of household and appears on the temple records, but people usually refer informally to the family by the name of its real leader, the astute and confident So Hong. Another case involves Kou Tieng and his wife Kou Pou. Tieng is a farmer. He was the third son of the second Lou brother who came from Liucuopu, but was adopted into the Kou family as a child. His wife was also adopted around the same time, and they were married in due course. Pou is loquacious, assertive, and fat, a combination found in many middle aged Taiwanese women who have managed to get themselves into positions of authority. Sometimes people refer to them as Tieng's family and sometimes as Pou's family, but again it is clear who is in charge: Pou is the politician and the plotter, and usually speaks for the family as she is recognized as quite articulate, if a little untrustworthy. Thus we see that, while uxorilocal marriage gives a woman a certain advantage in domestic sexual politics, it is not the only situation in which a woman can gain control of a family.

Women's participation in ritual is another subtle indicator of the weakness of sex differences in Ploughshare. For example, Ahern states that in Xi'nan, a lineage community, it is nearly always the men who remember the ancestral deathdays and perform the yearly ceremonies (Ahern 1973, p. 99). But in Ploughshare, it was generally the women who both remembered the days and performed the sacrifices. Wang Sung-hsing, writing of the fishing village of Guishan dao (Kueishan tao), states that, even when a woman is legal head of household, a situation that occurs only when there are no adult males in the family, she cannot serve as household head for ritual purposes or be listed as family head on the temple rolls; hence the temple lists contain the names of even baby boys as household heads (Wang 1971). But in Ploughshare, there were several women household heads, many of them with husbands, who were listed as such on the temple rolls. Among these were Lou Kim-bi, her cousin Lou Ong Cim, and Huan Mien, all of whom married uxorilocally, and my landlady Chua Ciu Kiok, a widow with teen-age children. Whether a woman could actually serve as *lo-cu* (master of the incense pot), the yearly organizer of community rituals, was a matter of dispute. Everyone of whom I asked this hypothetical question answered in the affirmative, and when the divining blocks where thrown to pick next year's master, the names of female household heads were included. But Big Fat Suat, a widow with teen-age children, disputed this. She told me that she had once been chosen according to the fall of the divining blocks, and that the runner-up was the octogenarian woman, So Bi. But, Suat asserted, the village leaders *(thau-lang),* all of them male, had refused to let either her or So Bi serve, because they were women. But this case may well not prove much, for Suat is a notorious ne'er-do-well, idle gossip, and spendthrift, who would surely fritter away all the village funds entrusted to her, and So Bi was a senile crone who was forever accusing her relatives of stealing. Whether a competent female would be allowed to serve if chosen, or whether an incompetent man would be prevented from serving, I don't know.

There is also another aspect to the relative damping down of sex role differences, and this is the amount of casual interaction that goes on between the sexes in village life. My comments on this subject are impressionistic, since this variable cannot be measured easily. Nevertheless, the impressions presented here are suggestive and as such might form the basis of more systematic research. While the women's viewpoint described by Margery Wolf certainly exists in Ploughshare, I would venture that it is neither so clearly distinguished from the man's viewpoint nor so strongly articulated as elsewhere. When one walks along Ploughshare's Front Street in the mid-afternoon, after the miners have returned from work and before it is time to start dinner, or if one goes out on a warm evening, one will find mixed groups of people everywhere, sitting and talking, discussing the latest events and gossip. There are, of course, places that are more segregated by sex: in particular, women can talk out of range of male ears at the springs and creeks where they wash clothes. But a lot of interaction goes on in mixed groups, and men and women seem to assert themselves equally strongly in these gatherings.

One obvious factor in promoting a breakdown of some of the rigidity of sex roles in Ploughshare is the absence of agnation as an organizing principle for community groups. Agnatic organization, in and of itself, does not constitute male dominance, but it does mean male solidarity: the patrilineage is a group of related males and their wives who share a common interest, usually either in land and its management or in military organization. Both farming and fighting have traditionally been all-male activities. The whole structure of the ancestral hall cult (Freedman 1966, p. 91; Ahern 1973, p. 99) is one of a male solidarity group. But agnatic group organization, as opposed to agnation as a basis for dyadic ties, is absent in Ploughshare, and this may be one reason for the weakening of sex role differences.

Another reason, which seems the more important to me, is the nature of work. Traditionally in this community, women worked. They did not mine coal, plow fields, or transplant rice, but they did grow and pick tea and oranges, harvest rice, and push carts on the railway. The early success of the cottage knitting industry was based on a mixed labor force as well: I never took a census of knitters, but my impression is that they are about half male and half female. And the factory work force is still at least half female. There are two aspects to women working that might influence the nature of sex role differences. First, a woman who works has an economic lever in the family because she produces some of the income. And second, men and women have, traditionally as well as today, worked together. The weakening of sexual segregation already takes place in the context of work, and thus is not surprising when carried over to the context of leisure.

This is not to suggest that the villagers of Ploughshare have departed from Chinese ideas about sexual politics or have achieved anything remotely resembling the equality of the sexes. They have not; women as a category are less powerful and considered inferior, here as elsewhere. But the differences and the separation are weaker than in other communities, and insofar as this is true it can, I believe, be attributed to the socioeconomic context in which Ploughshare exists. Male solidarity of the usual Chinese type was not promoted either by the development of agnatic lineages or by sexual segregation in the workplace. And both the lack of agnatic groups and the mixing of men and women at work resulted from the way Ploughshare villagers made their living and from the village's position in the larger socioeconomic context. An economy of cash cropping and particularly wage labor meant both work that could be done by either men or women, and the necessity, in poor families, for women to work. It led to frequent migration and impermanence of residence, thereby precluding the emergence of agnatic group organization. And both these things led to a loosening of the rigid Chinese definition of sex roles.

CONCLUSION

It is evident from this discussion that family organization in Ploughshare, while following the Chinese model, displays a particular variant of that model, which might be characterized as a looser organization, with the formal hierarchies of sex and generation less rigidly adhered to than elsewhere. It is also evident that this loosening of family hierarchies is partly due to the imperatives of a wage labor and cash crop economy and its concomitant mobility. At the same time, however, we must remember that Ploughshare family organization is still recognizably Chinese in every respect. If families at certain times were smaller and more typically nuclear than in neighboring communities, joint families still existed, as a result of the same residence rules and developmental processes. If fathers have less authority over their sons, and are less stern in their dealings with them, there is no question who is in charge, and even a retired old man is shown more deference, for example, than his Japanese counterpart (Nakane 1967, p. 21). Uxorilocal marriage is more frequent in Ploughshare than elsewhere but virilocal marriage is still overwhelmingly the norm, and even male adoption is often practiced where possible. Uxorilocal marriage is not the norm but simply a less desirable alternative that people have had to resort to more often. Finally, if women are less stigmatized and less segregated in Ploughshare than elsewhere, they have nothing resembling equality with men. It would be difficult to explain these resemblances between family organization in Ploughshare and other Chinese communities simply by resort to environmental conditions or even the socioeconomic context as a whole. Chinese settled Ploughshare with Chinese family structure as a model for their behavior. They have adapted and modified that model to fit the context in which they live. As Chinese, they have not abandoned the model or formulated a different one.

The Organization
of Religion

It is commonplace among anthropologists that religion mirrors social organization in a general sense, and we need not venture into socio-functionalism (Evans-Pritchard 1965, pp. 48 ff.) when we note that ancestor worship, for example, tends both to illustrate and reinforce descent and inheritance, or that the worship of tutelary deities is shaped by the social structure of the communities worshipping them. For Chinese society, some of the most sophisticated analyses of the relationship between religion and social structure are those by Freed-man (1958, pp. 81-91; 1966, pp. 118-43), Brim (1974) and A. Wolf (1974a). While none of these authors maintains that religion itself is somehow caused by, or a reflex of, social organization, each shows how religious practices in a particular Chinese context are congruent with and supportive of the social units in which they exist. This chapter will show how the particular features of Ploughshare's social organiza-tion are expressed in particular aspects of its organization of religion.

 The religion of the people of Ploughshare is in many ways identical to that of surrounding Hokkien-speaking villages, as described by Wolf (1974a), Ahern (1973), Harrell (1974a, b), and others. The types of supernatural beings and forces believed to exist, the kinds of offerings presented, the occasions on which they are offered, all are perfectly familiar to one who has observed religion in any nearby place. All of these villages partake in a similar variant of Chinese folk religion. But because the basic beliefs and practices are so similar, because the cultural tradition is common to all these communities, in the study of Ploughshare we are in a better position to observe the effects of social organization on the organization of religion. If we find differences (and we do) in ancestor worship between Ploughshare and a neighboring community, for example, it would be difficult to attribute them to differing cultural traditions—the people's origins are all in the same county of mainland China and, in addition, there is extensive intermarriage and even daily contact between them. It would seem much more appropriate to attribute these differences to variations in social organization, especially when they are congruent.

The organization of two aspects of Ploughshare religion is explored here: the worship of gods and the worship of ancestors. The organization of the worship of gods reflects both Ploughshare's place in the greater socioeconomic systems and its internal organization. The organization of ancestor worship reflects the relative unimportance of property as a means of livelihood and the lack of emphasis on agnation as a principle of village organization. I will first consider the content of Hokkien Taiwanese folk religious beliefs about the supernatural beings that they worship (gods or ancestors), and then describe the particular way the worship is organized in Ploughshare. God worship leads me to describe Ploughshare's place in the total ritual system of which it is a part, as well as its internal organization in contrast with nearby communities. I will also describe the way the organization of ancestor worship in Ploughshare contrasts with its organization elsewhere.

GODS

The gods are the most important focus of community ritual nearly everywhere else in China (C. K. Yang 1961, pp. 58-80; Shryock 1931; Wolf 1974a). These gods, perhaps more accurately referred to as saints, are mostly the souls of people who were so powerful or meritorious in life that they have been rewarded posthumously by the Jade Emperor, ruler of the gods, with supernatural bureaucratic positions, or have assumed other statuses of great power and importance in the next existence. Worship of the gods ordinarily takes two forms: individual worship, in which people approach the gods as potentially powerful helpers who can aid them in certain crises or can afford them protection in exchange for devotion; and community worship, in which all members of a local social system participate in a festival, usually annually, to celebrate the god's birthday and ask protection, in a very general way, for the community as a whole. It is this community aspect of god worship that I am concerned with here since it reflects, quite naturally, differences in community organization.

The people of Ploughshare, like all the Anxi inhabitants of the southern Taibei Basin, participate in three major religious festivals each year: the birthday of Tho-te Kong, the local earth god, celebrated in the eighth lunar month; the birthday of Ang Kong, the collective name of the two gods who once saved the Anxi people from disaster at the hands of either aborigines or Zhangzhou people, depending on whose story one believes, celebrated in the ninth month; and, most important, the birthday of Cieng-cui Co-su, colloquially known as Co-su Kong, which comes just after the lunar new year during the rest period in the first month of the Chinese calendar. The ritual system as a reflection of the socioeconomic system is best illustrated by a detailed consideration of the organization of this last festival.

The festival is organized on four levels. The highest of these includes all the inhabitants of the southern Taibei Basin who are of Anxi origin: everyone in Sanxia township; people living in those parts of Shulin township that are closest to, and formally part of, the economic as well as the ritual hinterland of Sanxia, including all of Shitouxi, Shanzijiao, and Pengcuo; all of Yingge township; and that area known as Zhongzhuang, which is actually located in Taoyuan County, but was settled by residents of the Sanxia and Yingge areas. The ritual center for this level of organization is the Tiong-hok Giam, an imposing temple in the heart of Sanxia town that houses fifty or sixty carved wooden images of the black-faced deity Co-su Kong. This temple was still not completed in 1978, having been under construction for about thirty years up to that time. If it is ever finished (and the people who work there estimated in 1978 that it would take another ten years), it will be one of the finest examples of popular temple architecture found anywhere in Taiwan, or perhaps in all of China. Every one of its stone pillars and wall panels is intricately carved; the roofs and eaves are of carved, gilded, and painted wood; and the tile roofs bear ceramic decorations of the utmost intricacy. In addition to front, inner, and back pavilions, there are plans to ring the structure with a colonnade of like workmanship, and to build a bridge across the Sanxia River to a proposed park on the other side.

The important thing about Cieng-cui Co-su is that he is an Anxi god, and indeed seems to be a feature of Anxi communities all over Taiwan (Hsieh 1964, p. 150; Diamond 1969, p. 85). Like most gods of the Taiwanese version of Chinese popular religion, he is thought to be a competent military leader, and there are stories of his saving Anxi people from certain defeat at the hands of various enemies. But this official-turned-Buddhist monk, who reportedly served in Anxi sometime during the Song dynasty, is primarily known as a doctor, a healing deity. This one temple is a center for all the Anxi people in the southern Taibei Basin, except those at Mazutian and Dingpu, and as such is the location and focus of a great celebration on the sixth day of the first lunar month, the traditional birthday of the god.

This celebration is organized according to seven surnames and surname groups, each of which kills large pigs and sacrifices them to the god once in seven years. Thus the Lous sacrifice the first year, miscellaneous surnames *(tua-cap-si:)* the second, followed by the Ongs, Lis, mixed surnames from Zhongzhuang (H, *Tiong-cng cap-si:*), Tiu:s, and Peqs. In 1973, it was the Tiu:s' turn, and every Tiu: household in the area, except those who were recent migrants from other parts of Taiwan (Ahern 1973, p. 8), or had experienced a death in the family during the previous year, raised and sacrificed a pig to the god. There was also a contest to see who could raise the largest pig. The winner, a man from Yingge, managed to force feed an animal to the weight of 912 *jin* (553 kilograms). When the animal was weighed several days before the slaughter and offering, word got around that there was a record-sized pig that year, and hundreds of people went to Yingge, where they were rewarded after a short wait in line by a view of the swine and an explanation by the proud owner. This and the next eleven pigs in order of size were brought to the temple in Sanxia, where a large crowd watched them displayed in gaudily decorated frames atop motorcyle-driven carts. Those Tiu:s who were not lucky or ambitious enough to raise such monstrous pigs slaughtered theirs at home, offered them to Co-su Kong in the village itself, and used the meat as the basis for a banquet of about 150 guests, held on the fifth, sixth, or seventh, so that not too many feasts would be held on the same day. There were eleven Tiu: families in Ploughshare itself who killed pigs that year, and everybody in the village attended a minimum of two feasts, each consisting of a ten-course meal and, for the adult males, enormous amounts of rice wine. By 1978, most people were no longer raising pigs, and planned to buy from commercial hog farmers. But there were no plans to stop offering them as part of the festival.

With the exception of Zhongzhuang, no distinctions of local residence are made in the pig-killing festival. This part of the annual celebration serves only to distinguish people of Anxi provenance from their neighbors who came from other parts of southern Fujian. This is brought out clearly by another pig-killing festival in Sanxia, organized around a temple for the goddess Ma-co (M, Mazu), by people

The twin gods Ang Kong and the earth god Tho-te Kong are carried around Shisantian in their birthday procession, 1972.

The procession ends at the *lo-cu*'s house, where they rest on a table before his altar. The twin gods known as Ang Kong are in front row, with a stone image of Tho-te Kong between them.

whose ancestors came not from Anxi xian but from (M) Yongchun ting, a nearby subprefecture belonging neither to Zhangzhou nor to Quanzhou. The Yongchun festival takes place on the goddess's birthday in the third lunar month, and as with the larger celebration in honor of Co-su Kong, the responsibility for slaughter rotates among seven surnames, but not the same seven that worship Co-su Kong. That some people originally from Yongchun now participate in the Co-su Kong festival as well is testimony that mainland origins are becoming less important than current domicile in determining ritual community membership (Wang Shih-ch'ing 1974, pp. 89-90). As a matter of fact, that the seven-surname rotations still exist, and that there are still separate rotations for people whose ancestors came from Anxi or Yongchun, points out some of the limits of using ritual organization as a guide to understanding social organization in general. The Anxi/ Yongchun cleavage, like other such ethnic differences, was important in the nineteenth century; otherwise such ritual organization never would have come about. But the salience of such ethnic distinctions was gone by the mid-twentieth century, and by the 1970s few young people had much idea where their ancestors came from on the Chinese mainland, or even where Anxi, or Yongchun, or even Quanzhou was. And yet the ritual organization, reflective of an earlier social reality, remained by force of custom. We would be amiss, then, if we tried to understand the socioeconomic system by looking at the ritual system because the latter reflects some features of the socioeconomic system and not others, and also tends to remain unchanged long after the social units that gave rise to it have changed their shape and relationship to each other.[1]

The lower levels of the ritual systems' hierarchy are reflected in the organization of another phase of Co-su Kong's birthday celebration. In addition to the pig killing, every family in the area participates in a community festival, in which an image of the god, rented from the Tiong-hok Giam temple in Sanxia, tours each local community. At the same time, each family prepares offerings of a chicken or duck, a fish, and a large hunk of cooked pork, and sets these on a table in the parlor, facing outward toward the street where the god's image will pass by. The god, brought from Sanxia by young village men, then comes through in a colorful and noisy procession, and villagers meet him in the street to exchange incense from the burners on their offering tables with incense carried by the bearers of the god's sedan chair. After the tour is finished, the god is treated to a Taiwanese opera,

1. I am grateful to Arthur Wolf for information concerning the Yongchun temple and festival.

presented by a traveling company, and the people of the community invite relatives and friends from other communities to share dinner and wine with them. It is this last aspect of the celebration that is most important to the villagers, since it presents an opportunity to cement social ties with people living outside their own community. To allow for this, different communities must worship on different days, and it is the organization of the timing of worship that illustrates the next two levels in the local systems' ritual hierarchy.

The second level, immediately below that of the Anxi inhabitants generally, is expressed in the noncoordination of dates of worship between Sanxia and Yingge. Each group of local communities in Sanxia worships on a different day, Hengxi on the fourth, Jiaoxi on the fifth, Shitouxi on the tenth, Ploughshare and its immediate neighbors on the sixteenth, and so forth. There is no duplication between communities around Sanxia or among those surrounding Yingge. But no attempt is made to coordinate the schedules of communities in Sanxia with those in Yingge, and there are two entirely separate rotations. The second level of ritual organization is also manifested in Yingge's having a separate festival for the birthday of a different god on the fifteenth of the third lunar month, while the Sanxia area celebrates the birthday of the twin gods Ang Kong in the ninth month (these gods are not worshipped on a community basis in Yingge). It is noteworthy that some communities that are administratively part of Shulin township, but that have long marketed at Sanxia, remain part of the Sanxia temple community at this level. Other Anxi communities closer to Shulin, whose inhabitants ordinarily do their marketing there, have retained only a residual relationship with the Sanxia Tiong-hok Giam, and no longer take part in either the pig-killing contest or the rotation of community festivals. Another point, somewhat contrary to that observed from looking at the pig-killing festival, emerges: whereas the pig-killing festival remains relatively unchanged as a reflection of nineteenth-century social organization, that the ritual hinterlands of Sanxia, Yingge, and Shulin for the procession and opera organization have changed during the past century shows that ritual organization, while perhaps more conservative than social organization, is not immutable. At one level, then, ritual organization reflects a change in social organization; at another level, ritual organization ignores such change. The lesson is the same. Although we can always, in light of the facts, determine that a relationship exists between ritual organization and social organization, we can never use the former to determine or predict the nature of the latter. Neither can we, knowing the social organization, predict exactly in what manner this social organization will be reflected in the organization of ritual.

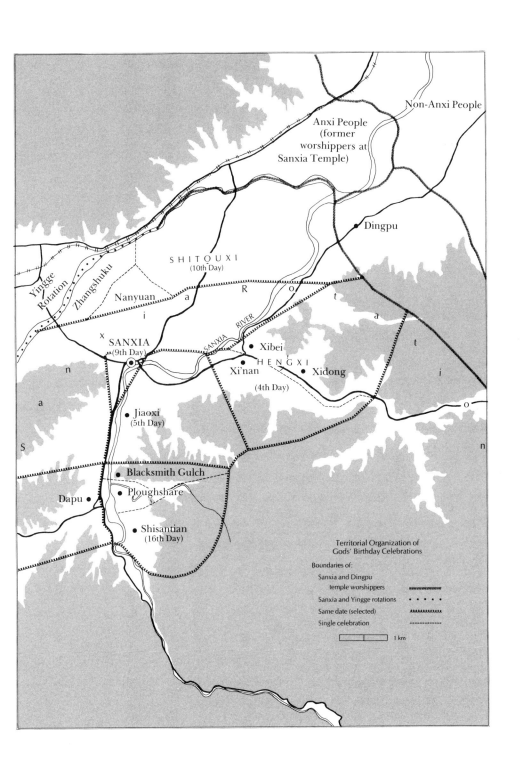

Non-Anxi People

Anxi People
(former
worshippers at
Sanxia Temple)

Dingpu

SHITOUXI
(10th Day)

Yingge
Rotation

Zhangshuku

Nanyuan

SANXIA
(9th Day)

Xibei

HENGXI

Xi'nan

Xidong

(4th Day)

Jiaoxi
(5th Day)

Blacksmith Gulch

Dapu

Ploughshare

Shisantian
(16th Day)

Territorial Organization of
Gods' Birthday Celebrations

Boundaries of:

Sanxia and Dingpu
temple worshippers

Sanxia and Yingge rotations

Same date (selected)

Single celebration

1 km

The next level down in the ritual hierarchy consists of a group of villages within the larger area centered on Sanxia or Yingge. These groups seem to correspond in size, though not in function, to the "village alliances" described by Brim (1974). Communities at this level are defined by their celebrating Co-su Kong's birthday on the same day. Ploughshare worships on the sixteenth of the first lunar month, the same day as the farming community of Shisantian immediately to the south, and the small community of farmers and laborers in Blacksmith Gulch, which begins just across the small stream from Ploughshare and extends a few hundred meters upstream. These three communities do not cooperate in their celebration of Co-su Kong's birthday. There are no joint activities, and each has its own procession and its own opera. But in worshipping on the same day, the three communities express at least a modicum of unity. It is perhaps noteworthy that unity of a group of villages at this level is more manifest in the nearby district of Hengxi (Ahern 1973, p. 9) and in the farming district of Shitouxi (Harrell 1981c) located on the flood plain of the Dakekan River, between Sanxia, Yingge, and Shulin. In both these places, the named group of communities celebrates Co-su Kong's birthday on the same day. But in the area around Ploughshare, this level of ritual organization exists almost by default. Instead of reflecting an old aspect of social organization, as does the pig-killing festival, or a current feature of social organization, as do the separate opera rotations for Sanxia and Yingge, it reflects geographical proximity and not much else.

The same is not true for the fourth and lowest level of ritual organization, which centers around a single Tho-te Biou, or earth god shrine. In each case, when Co-su Kong is brought from his temple in Sanxia and taken to a particular local community, Tho-te Kong, the earth god, as the supernatural village head, is responsible for escorting his bureaucratic superior around the bounds of his own village. Typically, where there are discrete, nucleated villages, each has its own Tho-te Biou, and in nearly all cases it is the ritual focus of a significant level of local social organization. Such is the case with Ploughshare, which has its own Tho-te Biou, located at the lower end of the village, and it is from this temple that Tho-te Kong emerges to lead Co-su Kong on his inspection tour. It is also in this temple that the *lo-cu,* or incense master, who will take responsibility for the organization of the celebration in the following year, is chosen by lot from all the family heads in the village. Ploughshare not only has its own procession and incense master, but also its own opera, as do the other two nearby places that also celebrate on the sixteenth.

There are thus four levels of ritual organization expressed in the

structure of worship of Cieng-cui Co-su's birthday: the Anxi people of
the southern Taibei Basin, all of whom participate in the pig killing
and the local community celebrations; the areas around the market
towns of Sanxia and Yingge, which organize separate rotations of
local community festivities; the group of local communities, each of
which worships on a different day; and the local communities themselves, each of which has its own incense master, its own procession,
and its own opera. These four levels articulate into a neat, orderly
hierarchy. It would be tempting to see these as the relevant levels of
the socioeconomic systems in which Ploughshare participates. But
the reality is messier, as we have seen in chapter one, and though the
ritual organization always reflects some social reality, it reflects it in
very different ways.

If the ritual organization of local systems in the southern Taibei
Basin reflects the social organization of the area, and Ploughshare's
place in that organization, in an unpredictable and unsystematic way,
we can discern a much closer fit between the internal social organization of Ploughshare and the organization for the worship of the gods.
This fit becomes particularly evident when we compare Ploughshare's
internal ritual organization with its counterpart in two neighboring
localities, Hengxi and Shitouxi.

Ploughshare's organization for the worship of the gods reflects the
village's social organization. As there are no permanent discrete groups
into which the village is divided, so are there no internal divisions,
except into households, for the performance of rituals for the gods.
On the one hand, Ploughshare is clearly delineated as a ritual unit in
opposition to other communities. On the other hand, ritually as socially, it is internally undivided. Organized community worship in
Ploughshare takes place on three occasions, all shared with most other
communities in the Sanxia system. These are, as mentioned, the birthdays of Co-su Kong, in the first lunar month; Tho-te Kong, in the
eighth lunar month; and of the twin gods known as Ang Kong, in the
ninth lunar month. On each of these occasions, Ploughshare has its own
celebration, with a separate god's image, a separate procession, and a
separate opera. The internal organization for each of these celebrations
is based on actual membership of all households in the village as a ritual
community. At the previous year's festival, household heads gather in
or near the village's Tho-te Biou to choose the next year's *lo-cu* by
casting lots. The current year's incense master stands before the image
of the god in whose honor the festival is being celebrated, and throws a
pair of plano-convex, crescent-shaped divining blocks as the name of
the head of each household in the village is read from a list. If the
blocks land one down, one up, which in divining indicates a positive

answer, they are thrown again, and the process is repeated as long as positive answers come up. The household head with the longest streak of positive throws becomes the next year's incense master. Each year, the names of all the household heads are read from a master list, and one of them is eligible to become incense master.

Homogeneous participation in ritual is also indicated by the collection, each year, of a small amount of money known as *tien-ci: (ding money)*, from each household in the village on a per capita basis. This money goes to defray the expenses of renting the god's image from the temple, hiring a small band for the procession and, most important, the troupe that will present the opera for the god's pleasure.

In addition to organized, communal festivals, everyday worship of the earth spirit Tho-te Kong also reflects the lack of discrete groups making up Ploughshare as a community. Like many but not all villages, Ploughshare has one Tho-te Biou, symbolic of the ritual unity of the village. When villagers have business with Tho-te Kong, reporting births and deaths, taking their turn in cleaning the temple and lighting incense, or occasionally asking for specific favors that the earth god can perform, like rooting out dangerous ghosts, or searching out lost spirits, they inevitably worship Tho-te Kong at Ploughshare's temple. They would not ordinarily visit any other community's Tho-te Biou, nor would residents of any other community visit Ploughshare's.

The full significance of this simple ritual organization in Ploughshare does not appear until we examine comparable organization in two nearby communities, Xi'nan and Shitouxi. Xi'nan, as we have seen, consists of four discrete settlements, each one dominated and managed by members of a single, localized patrilineage. Although the residents of Xi'nan observe the same festivals as the residents of Ploughshare, the organization there is different, and reflects the differing social organization of the two communities. In Xi'nan, the position of *lo-cu* for both Co-su Kong's and Tho-te Kong's birthdays rotates yearly among the four lineage-based settlements (Ahern 1973, pp. 7-9). Thus only Ongs are eligible to be chosen one year, Lis the next year, Lous the third, and Uis the fourth. Similarly, the opera for the god is held each year in the settlement from which the *lo-cu* was chosen. For the birthday of Ang Kong, the responsibility for the arrangements does not always fall upon Xi'nan, but rotates among the three communities that make up the large unit of Hengxi (Xi'nan, Xibei, and Xidong). When it is Xi'nan's turn, every third year, responsibility is similarly rotated among the four settlements, so that each settlement chooses the *lo-cu* and hosts the opera only once in twelve years. Finally, rather than having only a single Tho-te Biou for the whole community, the Ongs have their own separate one, and ordinarily worship there. Thus the organization

After the procession, the gods and children are entertained with a puppet show. The adults will come when the story starts.

A man burns incense to the gods during the engagement of his brother's daughter, 1972. Note the two ancestral cabinets, separated by a board, on the stage right side of the altar.

of god worship in Xi'nan reflects both that the community is made up of four discrete settlements consisting of four rivalrous lineages, and that it is part of the larger unit of Hengxi (Ahern 1973, pp. 5-6).

Shitouxi presents a still different picture. As a geographic area containing one town but no rural villages, only scattered compounds and isolated houses, its ritual organization reflects the lack of nucleated communities. In the yearly festivals for Co-su Kong and Ang Kong, the area is divided into three subdivisions: Zhangshuku, Tauzijiao, now known as Nanyuan, and the remainder of Shitouxi, including Ganyuan and the rest of the rural area. Each of these divisions is but a district drawn on a map, with no physical basis in the clustering of houses. Each has a separate procession and opera for the gods, though they all worship on the same day. And the third and largest of these subdivisions is further carved up into four *ko,* or sections, one of which takes responsibility for choosing the *lo-cu* and organizing the opera one year in turn. If there are no communities, no discrete geographical groupings of households in Shitouxi, the area as a whole is still too large to have a single celebration. So the district is, rather arbitrarily, carved up into manageable units, none of which has much social importance outside these yearly celebrations.

The lack of village-level communities in Shitouxi is further reflected in its organization of Tho-te Kong's worship. In the western part of Shitouxi, known administratively as Xiyuan, and divided traditionally into the districts of Zhangshuku and Xiqiancuo, there is a Tho-te Biou. But it is small and decrepit, and seems neglected. When I asked people in this area where they went to worship Tho-te Kong, they ordinarily said "at home." If pressed, those in the western end of the district would name this small temple, and those farther east would cite the large Tho-te Biou in Ganyuan. Now Ganyuan, as a town, has a well-organized cult of Tho-te Kong, including an annual festival, but there is no such festival in the rural parts of Shitouxi. The small shrine in the western part of Xiyuan thus exists only to address the individual needs of local households. It is not the focus of a community, as are the Tho-te Bious in Ploughshare and Xi'nan, because there is no community there to be ritually focused.

From these comparative cases, we can see that, while Ploughshare villagers and their neighbors worship the same gods, they have organized differently for this purpose, according to the differences in the social organization in the particular locality. Internal ritual organization appears to reflect social organization very closely.

ANCESTORS

The differences in social organization between Ploughshare and other communities, both those described in the ethnographic literature on Taiwan and those in the immediate vicinity, are also illustrated by the form taken by ancestor worship in Ploughshare. Until recently, the study of ancestor worship in China has been concentrated in farming communities, most of them places with some lineage organization. Studies based on such communities have described a system of ancestral worship with several important features that heretofore have been taken as basic aspects of Chinese ancestor worship, but whose existence can be shown to depend on certain forms of social organization. For example, Chinese ancestor worship is seen as two separate cults, one called by Freedman the "cult of immediate jural superiors," or the "domestic cult," and the other known as the "hall cult" (Freedman 1958, p. 90). The first of these is concerned with memorializing or paying filial tribute to the recently deceased, and the second with rites of solidarity among the ancestors' agnatic descendants. While the two cults may not be physically distinct (Ahern 1973), they are functionally distinct: one expresses filial devotion and the other kin-group solidarity.

Another finding is that ancestor worship in China, or at least in the lineage-based communities described in most of the literature, is intimately connected with property inheritance. While every deceased person must receive offerings from at least one descendant to provide him or her with sustenance in the other world, once this obligation is fulfilled, it is not necessary for a particular living person to worship a particular ancestor unless he or she has inherited property, directly or indirectly, from that ancestor. Someone who personally feels an obligation to worship an ancestor may do so, but there is no requirement. In particular, an ancestral tablet need be erected only to an ancestor who has transmitted property to the descendant (Johnston 1910, pp. 284-85; Ahern 1973, pp. 141-42).

A third finding is that Chinese living in lineage communities tend to exclude from their ancestral shrines the tablets and incense burners of forebears who were members of lineages other than the principal one represented in the household and on its altar. Such ancestors as the parents and grandparents of uxorilocally married-in sons-in-law, the parents of virilocally married brides who have no daughters, or others, should not appear if they can possibly be excluded. Various exigencies may cause such tablets to appear on domestic altars, but people worship them only when their omission might cause some deceased person to go unworshipped altogether. Even then, such tablets are often placed in a subordinate shrine next to, and lower than, the main altar, or even on a shelf in a back room. This is particularly true of lineage communities like Xi'nan (Ahern 1973), and less true of communities where each family tends to have its own separate altar (A. Wolf 1974a, p. 158).

With such a bias toward lineage-based, landholding communities in the study of Chinese ancestor worship, particularly in Freedman's (1958, 1966) and Ahern's books (1973), it would seem particularly interesting to examine ancestor worship in Ploughshare. If ancestor worship ordinarily divides into a domestic cult and a lineage cult, Ploughshare has no traces of lineage organization. If ancestor worship is intimately connected with property, most of Ploughshare's families have never held agricultural land, and those few who do either have tea gardens that they no longer work, or own rice land that has been theirs only since the land reform of the 1950s. If agnatic solidarity often constrains people to exclude "outside tablets" from their ancestral altars, agnatic solidarity, while not absent in Ploughshare, is as weak as reported in any rural Chinese community that I know of. Yet Ploughshare villagers worship their ancestors with as much devotion, and attribute to them as much influence on the lives of the living, as do villagers everywhere in the Taibei Basin area. By examining Ploughshare ancestor worship, perhaps we can come closer to seeing what is basic to Chinese ancestor worship, what sustains the cult of the dead even in the absence of significant property and agnatic group organization.

The first thing we notice is that the absence of lineage organization means that ancestral rites in Ploughshare are reduced to the domestic cult pure and simple, with no trace of a hall or lineage cult. Freedman (1958, p. 84) described the domestic cult as rites of "memorialism, in which ancestors were cared for simply as forebears and independently of their status as ancestors of the agnates of the worshippers." This description accurately portrays ancestor worship in Ploughshare. Nearly every house in the village displays an ancestral altar prominently against the back wall of the front room. On the senior or stage left side of the altar are the images and incense burners of the gods, and on the junior or stage right side are the tablets and incense burners for the ancestors. In contrast to neighboring Xi'nan, where some domestic altars contain nothing but incense burners for Tho-te Kong, every single altar in Ploughshare, save one, contains ancestral tablets. And nearly every household has its own altar. For 101 households in the village in 1973, there were 85 altars, and 10 households who did not worship their ancestors in Ploughshare but in some other place. Two families, those of wretchedly poor Tiu: Pun and of Li Hong and her man Peq, worshipped their ancestors without the benefit of altars; the other 89 shared 85 altars. There were 4 altars shared by brothers, and none by agnates of a wider span than brothers. Even the four sets of brothers who shared tablets did so in special circumstances. Iu: Pun-iek and Iu: Ong-iong, for example, shared their altar in Pun-iek's house, because Ong-iong had no house of his own but used two small rooms in his brother's house. The Ciu brothers on the point also shared an altar. After all an ancestral altar must be in a geomantically correct and publicly visible position, and there was only one conceivable place for one in their rather ramshackle old house. The other two sets of brothers who shared altars were not constrained by such architectural difficulties, but had divided their households within the previous six years. The normal pattern in Ploughshare seems to be for brothers to erect separate altars very soon after they divide their *jia.* While I was living in Ploughshare the first time, three new altars were set up. One was erected a year and a half after division, one three years after, and one many years after, but by a man who had just built a new house and for the first time was free from the constraints of living with his brother in a house with only one good spot for an altar. Even the altar that was erected three years after division might have gone up sooner if its owner, Li Hieng, had not exhausted nearly all his financial resources in building his new house to escape his neurotic sister-in-law, who was driving his wife to desperation. As soon as they could afford any substantial furniture in their new house, they installed an ancestral altar, although it takes only a few minutes to walk from their original home at the lower end of the village to their new house at the top. By 1978, two of the four sets of brothers who had shared altars in 1973 now had separate altars.

That the domestic cult exists in its pure form in Ploughshare is also indicated by simplification of rites and offerings as ancestors recede farther from memory. Just as the filial obligation of obedience and respect is greatest to one's own parents, just as the grief expressed in funeral ceremonies and mourning dress is greatest when the deceased is of an immediately superior generation to the mourner (A. Wolf 1970), the obligations of ancestral worship are felt most strongly toward ancestors genealogically close to the worshipper. In Ploughshare people prepare extensive feasts for recently deceased ancestors—the Ongs and Huans on Front Street, all worshipping their grandmother on the third anniversary of her death, spent the entire day before the celebration preparing special foods, some of which are ordinarily cooked only for major holidays. In another case, Lou Kim-bi told me that now that her family is well off they can have a proper feast, with two or three tables of guests, for her father's and mother's deathdays (she is uxorilocally married), though of course they would do no such thing for any more distant ancestor. I once saw this contrast in two deathday offerings prepared by the Tiu: family only a few days apart.

The first was for the father-in-law of Lou Cng, mother of the Tiu:
brothers—they invited me and several other guests to a substantial meal.
A few days later, I was walking by their house and noticed that they
had some offerings set out, and upon inquiry they told me that they
were celebrating a deathday anniversary, but for a distant ancestor
whom none of them had ever known. The offerings were simpler and
their attitude was one of bored obligation rather than enthusiastic
celebration.

In this domestic cult, the villagers of Ploughshare not only simplify
their offerings as ancestors recede from memory, but many of them
cease celebrating the deathday anniversaries of distant ancestors altogether, and give them combined offerings on Tiong-iong ceq, the ninth
day of the ninth lunar month. Old Ong Chiu-tik, who knew everything,
told me this holiday should only be celebrated to commemorate victims
of large-scale slaughters, such as those arising from the sack of a village,
but the more common opinion is that Tiong-iong should be celebrated
whenever the exact date of an ancestor's death is unknown. Despite
even this belief, of the fifteen households who celebrated Tiong-iong
in 1972, only one family, which had been excessively poor and is
still one of the poorest in Ploughshare, did not know the dates of its
ancestors' deaths. Another celebrated Tiong-iong because they had no
suitable place to worship their ancestors properly.

Other villagers relegated to Tiong-iong ceq those ancestors they
considered least important. In two of these cases, the ancestors so
shunted are agnatic forebears of uxorilocally married-in men whose
virilocally married brothers also worship their ancestors at home on
their deathday anniversaries. In all the other thirteen cases, the Tiong-
iong ancestors are simply those who are more than one or two generations removed from the eldest living family members. Of these thirteen,
five stated that they had celebrated deathdays for the now-shunted
ancestors until a year or two ago, but that it was a lot less trouble
to relegate them to a single day. An Ong family, for example, had
tablets for three generations of ancestors of its own surname, plus
one set of parents of an uxorilocally married-in grandfather. Ong's
wife told me that when her mother-in-law was alive, they had worshipped them all, but now that she was dead and that none of them
had known any but her husband's parents and grandparents, they
only celebrated deathdays for these four, and had relegated the others
to Tiong-iong. Fifteen of eighty-five altars is, of course, a small percentage, but there is a definite trend toward consolidating the rites of
distant ancestors on Tiong-iong, and this seems a graphic illustration of
the principle that obligations to ancestors weaken along with their
memory. As Freedman (1958, p. 91) says, "people were involved

with the dead whom they had known in life and towards whose happiness in the other world they could make some contribution."

I should perhaps say a word about the practice of burning or burying the tablets of remote ancestors when they cease to receive individual offerings at the domestic altar (ibid., 1958, p. 85). Other observers of ancestor worship among Chinese in Taiwan (Ahern 1973; Gallin 1966a; Pasternak 1972a) make no mention of the practice, and my evidence tends to support their observations. Perhaps this departure from the customs reported for southern China (Freedman 1958, p. 85) is attributable to the physical form of the tablets found in most Taiwanese domestic shrines. While a few altars display the individual Chinese tablets, one for each ancestor or married pair of ancestors, the great majority support either Japanese-style tablet cabinets, containing wooden strips, one for each ancestor or pair of ancestors, or large wooden boards with all the ancestors' names written on them. Unlike the individual tablets, neither of these types takes up much room on the altar—it is not necessary to remove a wooden strip from a shrine box to add a new one, and a name board can accommodate several generations of ancestors before a fresh one is needed. So ancestors beyond the second or third generation remain on the altar, even though their deathdays are not celebrated. But remaining on the altar, they must be honored somehow, so people worship them on Tiong-iong ceq.

While the absence of lineages in Ploughshare has made ancestor worship a purely domestic cult, the lack of land ownership has helped to make ancestor worship much less closely connected with inheritance. Johnston (1910), reporting from distant Shandong, and Ahern (1973), reporting from nearby Xi'nan, have found that in communities where most families own rice land, many people have no tablets for lineal ascendants in the male line from whom they have not inherited rice land. Carried to its logical conclusion, this principle would imply that a great proportion of the deceased former residents of Ploughshare would have no ancestral tablets at all erected for them. Such is almost certainly not the case; although I only saw a few people's tablets, most villagers assured me that there were tablets on their altars for all ancestors in the primary line of descent. And I did examine the tablets on the altars of two families, one of which had never held either rice or mountain land, the other of which had only mountains—both these sets contained tablets for all direct ancestors since the families' arrival in Taiwan. On village head Ong Cin-hieng's altar, there were names on tablets that were completely unfamiliar to him. He did not know how many generations removed they were, and he certainly did not celebrate their deathday anniversaries.

Another aspect of the ancestor cult in Ploughshare that is perhaps connected with lack of property is the failure to divide responsibility for worship of different lines of ancestors. In many communities, the children of an uxorilocal marriage are divided between their two parents' lines of descent, some taking the father's surname and worshipping his ancestors, others taking the mother's surname and worshipping hers. Often those who take their descent from their father receive none of their mother's inheritance, so they feel no obligation to any of her forebears. Those who take descent from their mothers usually worship only their father in his line, as all their inheritance comes to them from their mother's line. But in Ploughshare, where there has traditionally been little property to inherit, the surnames are usually divided and that is all. The responsibility for ancestral worship remains undivided, all descendants worshipping all lines of ascent. For example, Ong Thuan-cin and his younger brother, Iu: Pun-iek, divided their *jia* in the summer of 1972. Before this time, they had both worshipped at an ancestral altar containing two sets of tablets, the senior one for their mother's ancestors, surnamed Ong, and the junior one for their uxorilocally married father's ancestors, the Iu:s. In accordance with Ploughshare practice, Iu: erected his own ancestral altar at the 1973 New Year. If he and his brother had, as seems to be the usual practice elsewhere, divided the responsibility for ancestral worship at this time, Ong would have worshipped the Ong ancestors as far back as there were tablets in the cabinet, but would include only his father in a Iu: tablet cabinet. In this case Iu: would need only one cabinet of tablets, since his mother, having married a Iu:, could legitimately be worshipped as a Iu: ancestress. But instead, both brothers seemed to regard the responsibilities of devotion to forebears as more important than the sorting out of agnatic obligations. Ong retained both of the original tablet cabinets on his own altar, and when Iu: erected his, he included a full set of Ong ancestors and a full set of Iu: ancestors. Property had come from neither side of the family, but filial devotion was still the due of both.

It is not surprising that, in the absence of property, Ploughshare villagers still worship their ancestors, but what is more interesting is that, where property does exist, Ploughshare villagers conform more closely to the rule outlined by Johnston and Ahern, that the making of ancestral tablets is contingent on the transmission of that property. Let me illustrate with Kou family's, in figure 5. Kou Phieng and his wife had no natural children, but adopted three offspring, two daughters, Phik-lien and Pou, and a son, Tieng. Phik-lien was never married, but bore two sons by her adoptive father's agnatic cousin, a relative that she could not marry because of the ban on marriage between

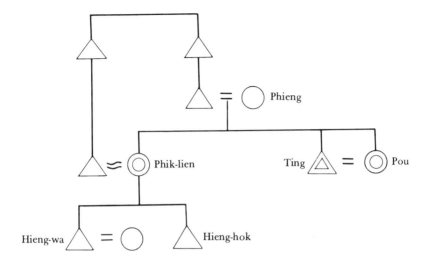

Fig. 5. Kou Phieng's family

members of adjacent generations. (Since she was an adopted daughter, she could have married her father's patrilineal nephew, as he would have been of the same generation.) Tieng and Pou, on the other hand, were married to each other in a variant of the "minor marriage" of an adopted daughter-in-law. The Kous had received their land in the 1950s land reform, and in the mid-sixties were living as a joint family. Phieng, however, was growing old by this time, and fell ill. According to Pou, she and her husband Tieng made every possible effort to see to the old man's comfort and care, while Phik-lien and her sons played around as usual and did little for the patriarch. Hieng-wa, Phik-lien's son, however, tells it differently. He says that while his mother, honest and hard-working as she was, was not much of a talker, his aunt, Pou, was good at talking and especially at flattery. When the old man got sick, he says, she won him over to her side in his confusion. Whatever the real story (and since Pou is generally known as a fast talker and something of a wheeler-dealer, I am inclined to believe Hieng-wa), the old man recovered, and when he did recover, he went to the township office to change the registration of his land to the names of Tieng and Pou, effectively disinheriting Phik-lien's sons. When he died and they divided their households, this left Tieng and Pou relatively well off and Hieng-wa and his brother quite poor. Tieng and Pou farm their land. In 1973, they lived in a nicely furnished new brick house, and together with some of their children, who were of working age, made a respectable living. Hieng-wa, by contrast, lived with his wife, their six children, and his younger brother in the old family house, built of mud-brick, and their sole source of support, at least until Hieng-hok returned from his army duty, was Hieng-wa's wages in the coal mine.

This family drama is clearly reflected in the ancestral worship of the two families. Tieng and Pou had a well-appointed altar, with the usual paraphernalia, including tablets for several generations of Kou ancestors. Hieng-wa, by contrast, had only an incense pot, no tablets, and worshipped only his mother.

This is only one case, but it suggests that Ahern's idea about ancestral tablets depending on property is somewhat incomplete. Her primary case of missing ancestral tablets concerns the Li lineage, whose ancestors lost the land they had originally held, forcing their descendants to take up less prestigious and profitable occupations than farming (Ahern 1973, pp. 140-43). To me this seems analogous to Kou Hieng-wa's situation. Both he and the Lis should have inherited property by rights, but did not. And in both cases it is clearly the ancestor's fault that they got none. In Ploughshare, however, the majority of villagers had ancestors with nothing to hand down to them in the first place, and thus they cannot be blamed for the lack. We might say more accurately, then, that Taiwanese make tablets for their ancestors if the ancestors have given them their due. What exactly their due is depends on what their ancestors had to give. If they had property, they must have transmitted it to their descendants. If not, it was not their fault that their descendants are poor. But if they had property and did not transmit it to their descendants, then they have failed in their obligations, and their descendants are not obligated to make ancestral tablets for them.

That the social organization of Ploughshare is based on many kinds of dyadic ties, rather than on unilineal organization, contributes to a third difference between the ancestor cult here and in other communities: the lesser extent to which ancestors of different surnames are excluded from, or separated on, domestic altars in Ploughshare. In Xi'nan, where Ahern worked, ancestor worship seems very exclusive. It is hardly surprising that in a community with strong lineage organization, no tablets for people of surnames other than the lineages are allowed to stand in the ancestral halls, but in Xi'nan even worship on domestic altars strongly reflects the lineage ideology of the community. Ahern states, for example, that "an uxorilocally married man, who would normally expect his brothers at home to worship his parents, would . . . be bound to make offerings to them if there were no other offspring" (Ahern 1973, p. 155). But in Ploughshare, where the social organization is based on dyadic ties only some of which are agnatic, people do not attempt to exclude from their altars ancestors with surnames other than the main line's. During my first stay in Ploughshare, I collected definite information about seventeen men who had married uxorilocally into or within the village. All of these men had brothers who remained at home, and it would have been possible for each of them to worship his own ancestors in his natal household. Of the seventeen, ten had ancestral tablets for their parents and seven worshipped them on their deathday anniversaries. Of the three who worshipped their parents on Tiong-iong only, one had recently moved his entire altar from a prominent place at the front of his house to a shelf in a back room, to convert the front room to a grocery store, and had changed all his deathday celebrations to Tiong-iong. Of the seven uxorilocally married-in men who had no tablets for their parents on their altars, four were from the mainland of China. One of these categorically refused to participate in any aspect of Taiwanese religion, one was not sure whether his parents were alive or not, a third thought it useless to worship his ancestors, since they could never cross such a wide stretch of water as the Taiwan Straits, and I have no information about the fourth. This leaves three Taiwanese men who were married uxorilocally and had no tablets for deceased parents, and of these, two specifically stated that they gave money to their brothers each year to pay for their parents' rites, which they attended. The third had made a marriage of the type called *pua:-ciu-chua,* in which it is understood that the married-in husband will take his wife home with him as soon as her younger brothers are old enough to earn money, so he does not consider Ploughshare to be his permanent residence. In short, the feeling that ancestors of outside surnames should be excluded from domestic altars, unless their exclusion means that nobody will worship them, is weak or absent in Ploughshare.

Not only do the villagers of Ploughshare seldom exclude ancestors of different lines or surnames from their domestic altars, but they often do not bother to separate two sets of ancestors on the same altar. Certainly there is a belief among many Taiwanese that ancestors of different surnames should not be worshipped together, and sometimes this restriction is carried so far that nonlineage ancestors are relegated to separate and subordinate altars, located in back rooms. In other instances, a subsidiary altar is built in the same room with the main one, but lower and on the junior side of the altar containing the primary set of ancestors. Failing this, if two or more sets of tablets must inhabit the same altar, they need to be separated by a board, and people often state that placing a board between tablets is a more convenient method, but that the proper way is to build a separate altar. In Xiyuan, my fieldwork in 1970 revealed eight houses that contained two lines of ancestors. One of these had the junior line on a separate altar in a back room, six had two sets on the same altar but separated by a board, and only one had two tablet cabinets sitting next to each other undivided. People explained the separation of their ancestors by saying that people of different surnames might get along all right in this world, but that they certainly could not live together in the next. Ahern (1973, pp. 130-31) describes a similar situation in Xi'nan. But in Ploughshare, the feeling that unrelated ancestors must be separated is much weaker. Of eighty-five ancestral shrines in the village in 1973, forty-one contained incense burners for more than one line of ancestors. Of these forty-one, only one had the junior incense burner in a different room, and all the others had their burners on the same altar. And among these remaining forty altars, only eleven had boards separating the unrelated ancestors. In six of the remaining twenty-nine cases, the two sets of ancestors bore the same surname (this situation arises when a childless couple adopts a daughter-in-law and then takes in for her a husband of their own surname), but this still leaves twenty-three cases where people did not deem it necessary to separate ancestors of different surnames. Whether the surnames of unrelated ancestors are the same or different is probably immaterial, as there was one altar where two sets bore the same surname but were still separated by a board. In some cases, people go so far as to purchase double cabinets for their ancestral tablets, which provide spaces to insert two sets of wooden slips side by side. The two sets of ancestors are in no sense merged, even in a double cabinet, as the incense burners are still separate and entail the burning of separate incense sticks. But neither is there any special effort to mark off one set of ancestors from another by the use of a conspicuous divider such as a board.

Examining Chinese ancestor worship in light of these data, we can perhaps see more clearly both the social and psychological supports of the ancestral worship system. Socially, the ancestor cult in Ploughshare serves no group but the family, or in a few cases the families of recently divided brothers. As such, its social manifestations are minimal compared to other places. It does not express the unity of extended kin groups, since there are none. In most cases, it does not reinforce the nature of reciprocal obligations of inheritance, because there has been no property to inherit. And it does not serve very significantly as a "boundary marker" between lines of descent because these are less important in the social organization generally, with many households containing representatives of different lines, through uxorilocal marriage. Even those containing a single line are neither property-holding corporations nor parts of politically or socially important patrilineal groups. Socially, then, ancestor worship is the religion not of the lineage, only partially of the descent line, but most important of the household. Each *jia* has its own ancestral altar and tablets, separate from those of its close agnates and combining to a great extent the worship of different lines of ancestors who have descendants in that household. In neighboring Xi'nan (Ahern 1973, p. 95), even the kitchen god, usually considered *the* household deity, is worshipped in the ancestral hall, thus emphasizing the household's subordination to the lineage. In Ploughshare, by contrast, the ancestors, who are usually thought to belong to the lineage, or at least to the direct patriline, become the responsibility of the household and the symbol of its corporate nature.

I would even say that in Ploughshare, the social significance of ancestral worship is weakened. It is all the more interesting, then, that its psychological dimension remains strong. To most villagers, the spiritual presence of the ancestors in the tablets is something to be reckoned with. It is true that they can rarely do much to aid their descendants, since, as A. Wolf (1974a, p. 160) points out, they are not very well-connected in the spirit world. But their potential for causing harm is much more important. Indeed the data from Ploughshare seem to support Ahern's contention (1973, pp. 201-3) that ancestors can be a dangerous, malevolent force, particularly if mistreated. When I asked Ploughshare villagers whether ancestors could cause harm, I invariably got one of two reactions: they either laughed and changed the subject, or assured me in no uncertain terms that the ancestors could indeed cause harm. The second response is unambiguous, but I think the first also expresses fear of the ancestors. People either felt embarrassed at admitting a fact that flew so in the face of ideas of filial devotion, or else were afraid to discuss the topic of the malevolent supernatural at all. In either case, I am absolutely sure that ancestors are seen as potentially malevolent. In fact, the severe mental illness of Tiu: Pun-a's granddaughter was first attributed to her decreased great-grandfather's anger at having no descendants in the line of descent of the eldest son. Other people told me stories of how ancestors, dissatisfied at any little slight, could *ciek-pi:-lang*—make people sick to get their attention and force them to right whatever slight they might have committed. Another example of the fear of ancestors is the belief that tablets can never be moved while the ancestral spirits inhabit them, except at certain predetermined auspicious times. Thus they can be disturbed only between the twenty-fourth of the twelfth lunar month, when the spirits are thought to depart, and the New Year, when they return. Disturbing them at any other time, I was repeatedly assured, would cause great harm to the descendants, and this belief was strong enough to prevent otherwise quite cooperative people from showing me their ancestral tablets.

In stripping ancestor worship of much of its social significance, the villagers of Ploughshare have taught us something important: they have explained the bare basics of the ancestral cult. From them we learn that Chinese ancestor worship, at bottom, is what Meyer Fortes long ago suggested about African ancestor worship, an expression both of the respect and of the ambivalence felt by members of junior generations for their seniors (Fortes 1959). That ancestor worship, or indeed any religious cult, can serve a social function depends in the end on its psychological validity for the majority of the worshippers. The fear and respect that Ploughshare villagers show toward their ancestors, ancestors with minimum significance in sociofunctional terms, are probably the same as the fear and respect shown to Chinese ancestors elsewhere. And, I would submit, it is because of these feelings, stemming from the relationship of juniors to seniors while they were both alive, that ancestral worship can be so powerful a symbol for group unity. But even without the group unity, agnatic exclusiveness, or property transmission, the fear and respect for ancestors is still there. That taking away the social functions of ancestor worship helps us to see its psychological foundations so much more clearly is another lesson about Chinese society that we can learn from the study of Ploughshare.

CONCLUSION

This chapter concentrates on differences in the organization of religious ritual, reflecting differences in the socioeconomic context of communities and in their internal social organization. As such it illustrates the point that aspects of behavior, such as ritual, are shaped by the context in which the behavior occurs. But again, this chapter should remind us that this is not the whole story. Despite all the differences in organization, which can ultimately be traced to differences in socioeconomic context, the villagers of Ploughshare worship the same gods as do their neighbors, and they worship the same kinds of gods and ancestors as do Chinese all over China. In religious ritual as in other aspects of behavior, there is common cultural ground upon which all these contextual influences work to produce differences in behavior.

Conclusion

THE CHOICE OF THEORY

The great conflict between materialism and idealism is played out on one of its minor battlefields—the anthropological one—as a conflict between culture and environment as explanatory factors. Either culture is purely derivative, something that can be explained, and possibly eventually predicted, from a conjunction of technology, environment, population, and perhaps even neurophysiology; or culture is something with a life of its own, a set of ideas passed down from generation to generation, which influences the way people act independently of technology, environment, and contextual factors. As a theoretical, rather than a factual dispute, this conflict will probably never be settled empirically—it is very difficult to test whether culture has an effect. Where this conflict shows signs of being resolvable, however, is at the level of usefulness. We ask not whether a particular theoretical position is correct or incorrect, but how useful it is in explaining observed phenomena. And if it is not particularly useful, we modify or discard the theoretical position and try another.

In this account of Ploughshare social organization, I have taken the theoretical position that to understand social organization in a particular community, one must consider that people carry with them a set of cultural or structural principles, and apply them in accordance with the limits set by the context in which they operate. If this theoretical position is useful, it should predict two things. First, that communities with an identical social structure but different contexts will differ in their social organization, and second, that communities with identical contexts but different social structures will also differ in their social organization. Furthermore, the differences observed should correspond to the differences in social structure (culture) or socioeconomic context. The empirical data presented here support the first of these two predictions unequivocally.

The people of Ploughshare, arriving from Anxi County or from nearby lowland areas of the Taibei Basin, carried the knowledge of Chinese social structural principles with them as they organized their lives in the community that became Ploughshare. But they had to adapt these principles to the particular context in which Ploughshare has existed for the last hundred and forty years—the context first of tea growing and wage labor on the periphery of an agricultural economy, then of increasing wage labor, particularly in the mines, and finally of absorption into the core of an industrial economy as wage earners and small-scale entrepreneurs. Adaptation to this context meant, above all, mobility of residence, lack of attachment to a particular place or property, and fluid, changing community membership. And the commercial/wage-labor context, together with the mobility as a necessary adaptation to it, made the people of Ploughshare apply the principles of Chinese social structure in a particular way. Of the wide range of polyadic groups and dyadic ties that form the social organization of various Chinese communities, they used only the dyadic ties. The polyadic groups, lineages and voluntary associations, did not need to form because the functions they served in other places were not necessary in Ploughshare, and could not form, in the case of lineages, because the necessary personnel were not available in the fluid, migratory population of the village. And of the dyadic ties, certain ones such as affinal ties tended to become more important because intravillage marriage allowed them and available agnatic connections were few. This particular application of Chinese structural principles to Ploughshare's context is evident both in the patterns of cooperation and conflict among the villagers. The contrast with other communities is nowhere clearer than in the comparison of Xi'nan, where followers of local political leaders line up according to lineage-branch membership (Ahern 1973), and Ploughshare, where they form factions according to a wide variety of dyadic links.

The same thing is true on the family level. Ploughshare villagers have applied Chinese social structure in a particular way. Their developmental cycle, when compared with those of other Taibei Basin communities, particularly those in the rice-growing lowlands where community membership has been stable and attachment to land an economic necessity, has shown earlier family division, a consequent smaller percentage of joint families at any one time, a lessening of tensions between generations, a higher incidence of uxorilocal marriage, and a weakening of sex-role distinctions. And the particular application of cultural principles in context carries over into the organization of religion. While the people of Ploughshare express the same tenets about the same gods as do their neighbors in Xi'nan or Shitouxi, for example, they organize worship of these gods differently, and the organization in each community reflects that community's social organization. Similarly, the people of Ploughshare express the same tenets about ancestors and the afterlife as do their rice-growing neighbors, but the organization of ancestor worship in Ploughshare reflects the emphasis on household, rather than on lineage, which is characteristic of Ploughshare's internal organization. It should be abundantly clear from the evidence presented throughout this book that context has made Ploughshare a particular village, with a particular organization different from its neighbors'.

In support of the second prediction, that communities with different structure in identical contexts will differ in their organization, I cannot offer the kind of empirical evidence presented in this study. Nevertheless, I believe the second prediction is also true. A weak form of evidence in its favor has been given: I have shown basic similarities in the social organization of Ploughshare and neighboring communities, even though their context, particularly their place within the local and regional systems of the southern Taibei Basin and North Taiwan, varies widely. But to really demonstrate the truth of this prediction, I would have to show how carriers of a different social structure—Japanese for instance, or Taiwan aborigines—inhabiting the area under the same socioeconomic conditions, would evolve a social organization different from Ploughshare's, and similar in certain ways to those of other communities bearing their own social structure. There is no proof that this is the case; however, there is a weak proof by exclusion. Consider the possibility that Japanese had settled on Ploughshare Point and evolved a social organization with only a loosely corporate village; equally important dyadic ties of agnation, affinity, sworn brotherhood, and neighborhood; a patrilocal-joint family cycle: around 35 percent minor marriage and around 15 percent uxorilocal marriage, with the surnames of the children divided between those of the mother and the father; and a lot of mixed-group socializing in the afternoons after the coal miners come home from work. In every known case in Japan, there is at least a nominal stem-family cycle, minor marriage is unknown, children of uxorilocal marriages take their mothers' surnames exclusively, and affinity and neighborhood tend to take precedence over other dyadic ties (Nakane 1967). A hypothetical Japanese Ploughshare would be different from any other village described in Japan, even though it bore resemblances in several respects to other villages described in China and particularly Taiwan. In adapting itself to this context, Chinese social structure has remained, and it has remained distinguishable from other peoples' social structures. The structure itself may well have been modified by its environment, but not to the extent that it would not be recognizably Chinese. Now in certain contexts, such modification would be impossible. Chinese villages, for example, never endured for long in the arid zone of Central Asia (Lattimore 1940), and overseas Chinese communities have lost much, if not quite all, of their characteristic Chinese social structure (Freedman 1979a, pp. 17-19). But Chinese social structure has remained where the context has allowed it, and it has shaped itself to that context. And the social organization that has developed in Ploughshare or any other Chinese community remains a recognizably Chinese adaptation to that community's context.

But the context itself is, of course, not static. It changes as people impose their own cultural or social structural rules upon it, in the same way as the rules change with the context. When we argue, as we have in these last few pages, about the primacy of culture or environment, we are missing the point. What is primary is history or process. Neither a cultural-determinist nor a material-determinist theory is very useful, because it is basically synchronic, and thus might be able to predict with reasonable statistical accuracy but can never explain anything. If we want to explain how social organization got to be the way it is, we have to look at the historical process of how it came to be. And that historical process is one of mutual interaction between a set of cultural rules and a set of contextual circumstances. I hope that this account of Ploughshare has demonstrated at least the usefulness of such an approach.

VILLAGE STUDIES

It may seem quaint, archaic, or even irrelevant to the substantive concerns of anthropology to study a village today. Are we not beyond a world of the little community, the microcosm, the society writ small, and the little tradition? Yes, we are, but this is no reason to ignore small-scale studies or intensive knowledge of particular communities. Once we recognize the relationship between the village community and the society of which it is a part, the study of each becomes necessary to the study of the other. To study the village in isolation or as a microcosm of the society is to explain nothing at all, though such study provides useful descriptive data that can later be used in explanatory attempts. But to actually try to explain the social organization of a village is to show how a society relates to some of its component parts, and how the component parts fit together to make up a society. The study of a place like Ploughshare can tell us several things about Taiwan and about China.

First, it can teach us about the range of variation within what we rather casually call Chinese social structure or even Chinese social organization. A study of a village of rice farmers can never tell us, by itself, which elements of its social organization are typically Chinese and which are explicable simply by the villagers' occupation as rice growers. When, however, we compare a rice-farming village with a fishing village or a workers' village, we can begin to learn what Chinese social structure is, and what variations in organization are possible within this structure. In short, a village study can be instructive because it is comparative.

Second, such a study can teach us about how the various levels of local systems in a society articulate with each other. If I spent a long time in the earlier chapters discussing the nature and history of the systems of which Ploughshare is a part, that was necessary to understand Ploughshare, to understand what it meant to the society of the Taibei Basin or of North Taiwan to encompass an upland zone with cash-cropping and wage-laboring villages; and also to understand how the aggregate figures presented by historians and economists worked themselves out at the level of individual families. The articulation of systems in Taiwan not only tells us about Ploughshare. Ploughshare and other similar communities must be studied in detail if we are going to understand the articulation of systems in Taiwan. A village study is thus also instructive because it is systemic.

As a study of Ploughshare in relation to its place in the larger systems, this study has some bearing on the current controversy over the nature of Taiwan as a component of the world economy, and of its effect on the internal organization of the island's political economy. Taiwan has been seen as a challenge to dependency theory (Amsden 1979) because, in spite of some aspects of its economy that make it "dependent" in certain conventional terms—its large-scale trade with the advanced industrial economies, in particular—it has not developed other characteristics thought to be inevitable in peripheral parts of the world economy: it has avoided dual development, extremes of wealth and poverty, and the formation of a "comprador elite." Whatever the ultimate causes of this difference from other countries (I do not intend to enter into the sterile debate of whether Taiwan is a "challenge to dependency theory" or merely a "special case"), it is clear that villages like Ploughshare have reacted to industrialization quite differently from villages in areas where long-term migration is the only alternative to increasing rural poverty. That Ploughshare's social organization has remained so remarkably stable across such major changes in Taiwan's political economy is surely a result of its place in the system of northern Taiwan—a place that has become part of the industrial economy's expanding core. At the same time, Taiwan's ability to expand the geographical extent of the core, to include places like Ploughshare in the economic benefits of industrialization, is largely responsible for the nonoccurrence of such typical peripheral phenomena as increasing diversity of income distribution, dual development, and the dominance of comprador capitalists. We can say that Taiwan's ability to organize its internal system in this particular way may have contributed to its ability to assume a less dependent position in the world economy.

Finally, a village study such as this one can teach us about how development and historical change in a society and economy affect certain ordinary people. In this sense, Ploughshare is nothing but a case study, but case studies of families in communities making decisions are important if we are going to translate such concepts as economic growth, import substitution, dispersed industry, rural-urban migration, and so forth, into terms that relate to actual human experience. I find that such terms, and the large-scale studies in which they are customarily used, are extremely useful, but not in the abstract. It is only when they are related to the particular experiences of particular communities that they become human, rather than abstract, terms. A village study can thus be useful because it is concrete.

A village study that is comparative, systemic, and concrete obviously differs from one in which a village is seen as the analogy of an isolated tribal community. Only the concreteness, the attention to individual detail and human experience, is carried over from the traditional study of the village. But with the addition of the comparison and the systemic context, the village study remains valuable for understanding a society in human terms. For this reason, village studies will not die out as long as villages do not. They will not, and should not, ever again be the single mainstay of anthropological writing, but will remain, along with other genres, an important vehicle for the anthropological message.

I do not intend to stop visiting Ploughshare village. I have friends and continuing interests there. I have learned a great deal about social process and organization simply by revisiting the village in the summer of 1978, five years after my first stay. I feel that subsequent trips will provide similar insights, not only into the life of a particular community, but into the effect of further economic and social change, which Taiwan is bound to undergo, on the organization of a place I already know well. And because I already know it well, I will be able to learn something about the way economic and social changes work in general—I will be able to control for the organization already there and thus see more clearly what change has done and why.

What, in particular, the changes will be, I hesitate to predict. Taiwan will undoubtedly become more industrial and less agricultural, and with Ploughshare's proximity to the city and its location in the industrial core of North Taiwan, its inhabitants will continue to be involved in industry. But the exact involvement is difficult to predict. Will they become strictly proletarians, as small businesses and cottage industry are forced out by more efficient large factories? Will they turn to education and the professions, areas in which they have fallen behind their neighbors in recent years? Will they in fact become more physically mobile, as transport continues to improve and jobs become more spread out geographically? Will they, in fact, remain a community, and for how long? Or will I live to see the day when Taibei has bedroom suburbs, and Ploughshare is one of them? I believe I have a good foundation upon which to base such further studies, and I only hope that I will have the opportunity to carry them out.

Glossary

Personal names are not included, except for historical figures. (H) indicates Hokkien, and (M) indicates Mandarin. Certain Hokkien terms have no known Chinese characters. The unknown or doubtful characters are indicated by question marks.

Ang Kong (H) 翁公

Ankeng (M) 暗坑（安坑）

Anxi (M) 安溪

a-so (H) 阿嫂

au-pia: (H) 後邊

Baiji (M) 白鷄

Banqiao (M) 板橋

Bazhang (M) 八張

be (H) 尾

Chajiao (M) 插角

cau (H) 灶

Chengfu (M) 成福

chi:-m (H) 親姆

Cieng-cui Co-su (H) 清水祖師

chua (H) 娶

ciek-pi lang (H) 責備人

ciu (H) 招

co-chan-lang (H) 作田人

co-sua: (H) 作山

co-sua:-lang (H) 作山人

Co-su Kong (H) 祖師公

Dadaocheng (M) 大稻埕

Dagou (M) 打狗

Dakekan (M) 大嵙崁

215

Dapu (M) 大埔

Daxi (M) 大溪

dazu (M) 大租

ding (M) 丁

Dingpu (M) 頂埔

e-kang (H) 下港

Erjia (M) 二鬮

fang (M) 房

fen (M) 分

fenjia (M) 分家

ganqing (M) 感情

Ganyuan (M) 柑園

Gaoxiong (M) 高雄

Guishan dao (M) 龜山島

Guomindang (M) 國民黨

Hoing-kang chai (H) 香港菜

hou-kia: (H) 好額 ?

hu (H) 户

jia (M) 家

Jiaoxi (M) 礁溪

jiaozi (M) 餃子

Jiantian li (M) 嘉添里

jin (M) 斤

Jinguashi (M) 金瓜石

Jinmin (M) 金敏

kang-kho (H) 工苦

ke-pang kia: (H) 過房囝

Khei-ciu-a (H) 溪洲仔

khieng-pian-chia (H) 輕便車

kho (H) 箍 ?

ko (H) 股

Lei-ci-be (H) 犁舌尾

li (M) 里

Liu Mingchuan (M) 劉銘傳

lizhang (M) 里長

lo-cu (H) 爐主

Longenpu (M) 龍恩埔

Luku (M) 鹿窟

Ma-co (H) 媽祖

Mayuan (M) 麻園

Mazutian (M) 媽祖田

Meinong (M) 美濃

Mengjia (M) 艋舺

mo-tha (H) ?

Nanyuan (M) 南園

Pengcuo (M) 彭厝

Penglai (M) 蓬萊

Pha-thi-khi: (H) 打鐵坑

pho-tong (H) 普通

pieng (H) 坪

pua:-ciu-chua (H) 半招娶

Pueq-lang Kong (H) 八人公

Quanzhou (M) 泉州

Quanzitou (M) 圳仔頭

Sanchong (M) 三重

Sanxia (M) 三峽

Sanyi (M) 三邑

Shanyuantanzi (M) 山員潭仔

Shanzijiao (M) 山仔脚

shequ (M) 社區

Shisantian (M) 十三添

Shitouxi (M) 石頭溪

Shuangxi (M) 雙溪

Shulin (M) 樹林

siou:-ma (H) 相罵

siou:-pha (H) 相打

siou:-thai (H) 相刣

Taibei (M) 台北

Taizhong (M) 台中

Taoyuan (M) 桃園

Taozijiao (M) 桃仔脚

than-ciaq-lang (H) 賺食人

thau (H) 頭

thau-cieng (H) 頭前

thau-lang (H) 頭人

thia: (M) 廳

thit-thou (H) 迌迌 ?

tho-ke (H) 土雞

Tho-te Biou (H) 土地廟

Tho-te Kong (H) 土地公

tia: (H) 鼎

tiam-khi (H) 店起

Tianfu li (M) 添福里

tieng-ci: (H) 丁錢

ti-kha mi:-sua: (H) 猪脚麵線

Tiong-cng cap-si: (H) 中庄雜姓

Tiong-hok Giam (H) 長福巖

Tiong-iong ceq (H) 重陽節

Tongan (M) 同安

tua cap-si: (H) 大雜姓

Tudigongkeng (M) 土地公坑

Wanhua (M) 萬華

wa:-thiap (H) 換牒

Wujia (M) 五鬮

Wuliao (M) 五寮

xiangpian (M) 香片

xiao (M) 孝

xiaozu (M) 小祖

Xibei (Ch'i-pei) (M) 溪北

Xi'nan (Ch'i-nan) (M) 溪南

Xindian (M) 新店

Xinzhuang (M) 新莊

Xiongkong (M) 熊空

Xiqiancuo (M) 溪墘厝

Xiyuan (M) 西園

Xizhou (M) 溪洲

Yilan (M) 宜蘭

Yingge (M) 鶯歌

Yongchun ting (M) 永春廳

Youmu (M) 有木

Zhangshuku (M) 樟樹窟

Zhangzhou (M) 漳州

zhen (M) 鎮

Zheng Chenggong (M) 鄭成功

Zhonghe (M) 中和

Zhongli (M) 中壢

Zhongqiu jie (M) 中秋節

Zhongpu (M) 中甫

Zhongshe (Chung-she) 中社

Zhongzhuang (M) 中庄

Zhulun (M) 竹崙

zi (M) 慈

Bibliography

Ahern, Emily M.

    1973. *The Cult of the Dead in a Chinese Village.* Stanford: Stanford University Press.

    1976. "Segmentation in Chinese Lineages: A View Through Written Genealogies." *American Ethnologist* 3, no. 1:1-16.

Amsden, Alice H.

    1979. "Taiwan's Economic History: A Case of Etatisme and a Challenge to Dependency Theory." *Modern China* 5, no. 3:341-80.

Baker, Hugh D. R.

    1968. *Sheung Shui: A Chinese Lineage Village.* Stanford: Stanford University Press.

Banfield, Edward C.

    1958. *The Moral Basis of a Backward Society.* New York: Free Press.

Barclay, George W.

    1954. *Colonial Development and Population in Taiwan.* Princeton: Princeton University Press.

Brim, John A.

    1974. "Village Alliance Temples in Hong Kong." In *Religion and Ritual in Chinese Society*, ed. Arthur P. Wolf, pp. 93-104. Stanford: Stanford University Press.

Chirot, Daniel M.

    1977. *Social Change in the Twentieth Century.* New York: Harcourt Brace Jovanovich.

Cohen, Myron L.
    1968. "A Case Study of Chinese Family Economy and Development." *Journal
        of Asian and African Studies* 3, nos. 3-4:161-80.
    1969. "Agnatic Kinship in South Taiwan." *Ethnology* 15, no. 3:167-82.
    1970. "Developmental Process in the Chinese Family Group." In *Family and
        Kinship in Chinese Society,* ed. Maurice Freedman, pp. 21-36. Stan-
        ford: Stanford University Press.
    1976. *House United, House Divided: The Chinese Family in Taiwan.* New
        York: Columbia University Press.
Davidson, James W.
    1903. *The Island of Formosa.* New York: Macmillan.
De Glopper, Donald R.
    1972. "Doing Business in Lukang." In *Economic Organization in Chinese
        Society,* ed. W. E. Willmott, pp. 297-326. Stanford: Stanford Uni-
        versity Press.
Diamond, Norma
    1969. *K'un Shen: A Taiwan Village.* New York: Holt, Rinehart, and Winston.
    1979. "Women and Industry in Taiwan." *Modern China* 5, no. 3:317-40.
Directorate General of the Budget, Accounting and Statistics, Republic of China
    1978. *Statistical Yearbook of the Republic of China.*
Elvin, Mark
    1973. *The Pattern of the Chinese Past.* Stanford: Stanford University Press.
Evans-Pritchard, E. E.
    1965. *Theories of Primitive Religion.* Oxford: Oxford University Press.
Fei Hsiao-t'ung [Fei Xiaotong]
    1939. *Peasant Life in China.* London: Routledge and Kegan Paul.
Fortes, Meyer
    1959. *Oedipus and Job in West African Religion.* Cambridge: Cambridge
        University Press.
Freedman, Maurice
    1958. *Lineage Organization in Southeastern China.* London: Athlone Press.
    1966. *Chinese Lineage and Society: Fukien and Kwantung.* London: Athlone
        Press.
    1979a (1965). "The Chinese in Southeast Asia." Reprinted in *The Study of
        Chinese Society,* pp. 3-21. Stanford: Stanford University Press.
    1979b (1969). "Geomancy." Reprinted in *The Study of Chinese Society,*
        pp. 313-33. Stanford: Stanford University Press.
Fried, Morton H.
    1953. *Fabric of Chinese Society.* New York: Praeger.
Galenson, Walter
    1979. "The Labor Force, Wages, and Living Standards." In *Economic Growth
        and Structural Change in Taiwan,* ed. Walter Galenson, pp. 384-447.
        Ithaca: Cornell University Press.
Gallin, Bernard
    1966a. *Hsin Hsing, Taiwan: A Chinese Village in Change.* Berkeley and Los
        Angeles: University of California Press.
    1966b. "Political Factionalism and its Impact on Chinese Village Social Organi-
        zation in Taiwan." In *Local-Level Politics,* ed. Marc J. Swartz, pp. 377-400.
        Chicago: Aldine.

Gallin, Bernard and Rita S. Gallin

1974. "The Integration of Village Migrants in Taipei." In *The Chinese City between Two Worlds*, eds. Mark Elvin and G. William Skinner, pp. 331-58. Stanford: Stanford University Press.

Gamble, Sidney

1954. *Ting Hsien: A North China Rural Community*. Stanford: Stanford University Press.

1963. *North China Villages*. Berkeley and Los Angeles: University of California Press.

Gates, Hill

1979. "Dependency and the Part-time Proletariat in Taiwan." *Modern China* 5, no. 3:381-407.

1981 "Ethnicity and Social Class." In *The Anthropology of Taiwanese Society*, ed. Emily M. Ahern and Hill Gates, pp. 241-81. Stanford: Stanford University Press.

Geertz, Clifford

1959. "Form and Variation in Balinese Village Structure." *American Anthropologist* 61, no. 6:991-1012.

Giddens, Anthony

1973. *The Class Structure of the Advanced Societies*. New York: Harper.

Harrell, Stevan

1974a. "Belief and Unbelief in a Taiwan Village." Ph.D. dissertation, Stanford University.

1974b. "When a Ghost Becomes a God." In *Religion and Ritual in Chinese Society*, ed. Arthur P. Wolf, pp. 193-206. Stanford: Stanford University Press.

1981a. "The Effects of Economic Change on Two Taiwan Villages." *Modern China* 7, no. 1:31-54.

1981b. "Growing Old in Rural Taiwan." In *Other Ways of Growing Old*, ed. Pamela T. Amoss and Stevan Harrell, pp. 193-210. Stanford: Stanford University Press.

1981c. "Social Organization in Haishan." In *The Anthropology of Taiwanese Society*, ed. Emily M. Ahern and Hill Gates, pp. 125-47. Stanford: Stanford University Press.

n.d. "The Rich Get Children: Segmentation, Stratification, and Population in Three Zhejiang Lineages, 1550-1850." Paper presented at the ACLS-SSRC Conference on Historical Demography and Family History in East Asia, Wadham College, Oxford, August 1978.

Harris, Marvin

1968. *The Rise of Anthropological Theory*. New York: Crowell.

1979. *Cultural Materialism: The Struggle for a Science of Culture*. New York: Random House.

Ho, Samuel P. S.

1978. *Economic Development of Taiwan, 1860-1970*. New Haven: Yale University Press.

1979. "Decentralized Industrialization and Rural Development: Evidence from Taiwan." *Economic Development and Cultural Change* 27:77-96.

Hsieh Chiao-min

1964. *Taiwan—Ilha Formosa: A Geography in Perspective*. Washington, D.C.: Butterworth.

Hu Hsien-chin
  1948. *The Common-Descent Group in China and its Functions*. New York: Viking Fund.
Johnston, R. F.
  1910. *Lion and Dragon in Northern China*. New York: Dutton.
Jordan, David K.
  1972. *Gods, Ghosts and Ancestors*. Berkeley and Los Angeles: University of California Press.
Kelly, Raymond
  1977. *Etoro Social Structure: A Study in Structural Contradiction*. Ann Arbor: University of Michigan Press.
Kraus, Richard Kurt
  1979. "Two Models of Social Stratification." Unpublished paper.
Kuhn, Philip A.
  1970. *Rebellion and Its Enemies in Late Imperial China*. Cambridge, Mass.: Harvard University Press.
Kulp, Daniel H.
  1924. *Country Life in South China: The Sociology of Familism*. New York: Teachers College, Columbia University.
Kung, Lydia
  1981. "Perceptions of Work among Factory Women." In *The Anthropology of Taiwanese Society*, ed. Emily M. Ahern and Hill Gates, pp. 184-211. Stanford: Stanford University Press.
Kuznets, Simon
  1979. "Growth and Structural Shifts." In *Economic Growth and Structural Change in Taiwan*, ed. Walter Galenson, pp. 15-131. Ithaca: Cornell University Press.
Lamley, Harry J.
  1981. "Patterns of Interethnic Conflict in 19th Century Taiwan." In *The Anthropology of Taiwanese Society*, ed. Emily M. Ahern and Hill Gates, pp. 282-318. Stanford: Stanford University Press.
Lang, Olga
  1946. *Chinese Family and Society*. New Haven: Yale University Press.
Lattimore, Owen
  1940. *Inner Asian Frontiers of China*. New York: American Geographical Society.
Little, Ian M. D.
  1979. "An Economic Reconnaissance." In *Economic Growth and Structural Change in Taiwan*, ed. Walter Galenson, pp. 448-508. Ithaca: Cornell University Press.
Meskill, Johanna Menzel.
  1970. "The Lins of Wufeng: The Rise of a Taiwanese Gentry Family," in *Taiwan: Studies in Chinese Local History*, ed. Leonard M. P. Gordon, pp. 6-22. New York: Columbia University Press.
Mote, Frederick W.
  1971. *Intellectual Foundations of China*. New York: Alfred A. Knopf.
Nakane, Chie
  1967. *Kinship and Economic Organization in Rural Japan*. London: Athlone.

Ossowski, Stanislaw
    1963. *Class Structure in the Social Consciousness.* New York: Free Press.
Parish, William, and Martin King Whyte
    1978. *Village and Family in Contemporary China.* Chicago: University of Chicago Press.
Pasternak, Burton
    1972a. *Kinship and Community in Two Chinese Villages.* Stanford: Stanford University Press.
    1972b. "The Sociology of Irrigation: Two Taiwanese Villages." In *Economic Organization in Chinese Society,* ed. W. E. Willmott, pp. 193-214. Stanford: Stanford University Press.
    n.d.   "Causes and Demographic Consequences of Uxorilocal Marriage: Three Chinese Communities Compared." Paper prepared for the ACLS-SSRC Conference on Historical Demography and Family History in East Asia, Wadham College, Oxford, 1978.
Pepper, Suzanne
    1978. *Civil War in China: The Political Struggle, 1945-1949.* Berkeley and Los Angeles: University of California Press.
Perkins, Dwight H.
    1969. *Agricultural Development in China, 1368-1968.* Chicago: Aldine.
Popkin, Samuel
    1979. *The Rational Peasant.* Berkeley and Los Angeles: University of California Press.
Potter, Jack M.
    1968. *Capitalism and the Chinese Peasant.* Berkeley and Los Angeles: University of California Press.
Ranis, Gustav
    1979. "Industrial Development." In *Economic Growth and Structural Change in Taiwan,* ed. Walter Galenson, pp. 206-62. Ithaca: Cornell University Press.
Sahlins, Marshall
    1976. *Culture and Practical Reason.* Chicago: University of Chicago Press.
Schneider, Jane and Peter Schneider
    1976. *Culture and Political Economy in Western Sicily.* New York: Academic Press.
Scott, James C.
    1976. *The Moral Economy of the Peasant.* New Haven: Yale University Press.
Shryock, John
    1931. *The Temples of Anking and Their Cults.* Privately printed, Paris.
Silin, Robert H.
    1972. "Marketing and Credit in a Hong Kong Wholesale Market." In *Economic Organization in Chinese Society,* ed. W. E. Willmott, pp. 327-53. Stanford: Stanford University Press.
Silverman, Sydel
    1968. "Agricultural Organization, Social Structure, and Values in Italy: Amoral Familism Reconsidered." *American Anthropologist* 70: 1-20.
Skinner, G. William
    1957. *Chinese Society in Thailand: An Analytical History.* Ithaca: Cornell University Press.

1971. "Chinese Peasants and the Closed Community: An Open and Shut Case." *Comparative Studies in Society and History* 13, no. 3:270-81.

1976. "Mobility Strategies in Late Imperial China." In *Regional Systems,* ed. Carol Smith, pp. 327-64. New York: Academic Press.

1978a. "Introduction: Urban and Rural in Chinese Society." In *The City in Late Imperial China,* ed. G. William Skinner. Stanford: Stanford University Press.

1978b. "Cities and the Hierarchy of Local Systems." In *The City in Late Imperial China,* ed. G. William Skinner, pp. 275-352. Stanford: Stanford University Press.

Smith, Arthur H.

1894. *Chinese Characteristics.* New York: Revell.

1970 (1894). *Village Life in China.* Boston: Little, Brown.

Speare, Alden Jr.

1974. "Migration and Family Change in Central Taiwan." In *The Chinese City Between Two Worlds,* ed. Mark Elvin and G. William Skinner, pp. 303-30. Stanford: Stanford University Press.

Stavenhagen, Rodolfo

1975. *Class Structure in Agrarian Societies.* Garden City: Doubleday.

Stover, Leon

1974. *The Cultural Ecology of Chinese Civilization.* New York: Mentor Books.

Van Der Sprenkel, Sybille

1962. *Legal Institutions in Manchu China.* London: Athlone.

Wallerstein, Immanuel

1974. "The Rise and Future Demise of the World Capitalist System: Concepts for Comparative Analysis." *Comparative Studies in Society and History* 16:387-415.

Wang Shih-ch'ing

1974. "Religious Organization in the History of a Chinese Town." In *Religion and Ritual in Chinese Society,* ed. Arthur P. Wolf, pp. 71-92. Stanford: Stanford University Press.

1976. "Hai-shan Shihua (Shang)" [The History of Haishan—first part]. *Taibei Wenxian* 37:49-132.

Wang Sung-hsing

1971. "Pooling and Sharing in a Chinese Fishing Economy: Kuei-shan Tao." Ph.D. dissertation, University of Tokyo.

Wang Sung-hsing and Raymond Apthorpe

1974. *Rice Farming in Taiwan.* Nankang: Institute of Ethnology, Academia Sinica.

Warner, W. Lloyd, Marchia Meeker, and Kenneth Eells.

1949. *Social Class in America.* Chicago: Science Research Associates.

Watson, James L.

1974. *Emigration and the Chinese Lineage.* Berkeley and Los Angeles: University of California Press.

Wickberg, Edgar

1970. "Late Nineteenth Century Land Tenure in North Taiwan." In *Taiwan: Studies in Chinese Local History,* ed. Leonard Gordon, pp. 78-92. New York: Columbia University Press.

1981. "Continuities in Land Tenure, 1900-1940," In *The Anthropology of Taiwanese Society,* eds. Emily M. Ahern and Hill Gates, pp. 212-38. Stanford: Stanford University Press.

Wolf, Arthur P.
  1966. "Childhood Association, Sexual Attraction, and the Incest Taboo: A Chinese Case." *American Anthropologist* 68, no. 4:883-98.
  1968. "Adopt a Daughter-in-law, Marry a Sister: A Chinese Solution to the Problem of the Incest Taboo." *American Anthropologist* 70, no. 5: 866-74.
  1970. "Chinese Kinship and Mourning Dress." In *Family and Kinship in Chinese Society*, ed. Maurice Freedman, pp. 189-207. Stanford: Stanford University Press.
  1974a. "Gods, Ghosts, and Ancestors." In *Religion and Ritual in Chinese Society*, ed. Arthur P. Wolf, pp. 131-82. Stanford: Stanford University Press.
  1974b. "Marriage and Adoption in Northern Taiwan," in *Social Organization and the Applications of Anthropology*, ed. Robert J. Smith, pp. 128-60. Ithaca: Cornell University Press.
Wolf, Arthur P. and Chieh-shan Huang
  1980. *Marriage and Adoption in China, 1845-1945*. Stanford: Stanford University Press.
Wolf, Eric R.
  1967. *Peasants*. Englewood Cliffs, N.J.: Prentice-Hall.
Wolf, Margery
  1972. *Women and the Family in Rural Taiwan*. Stanford: Stanford University Press.
Yang, C. K.
  1958. *A Chinese Village in the Early Communist Transition*. Cambridge, Mass.: M.I.T. Press.
  1961. *Religion in Chinese Society*. Berkeley and Los Angeles: University of California Press.
Yang, Martin C.
  1945. *A Chinese Village*. New York: Columbia University Press.

Index

Aborigines: and Chinese, 21, 26; as landholders, 23; "pacification" of, 121

Adoption, 130; of daughter-in-law, 160, 200; and lineages, 174; of males, 174, 200

Adultery, 144

Affinal ties: importance of, 126-27; and women, 127; hostility in, 128; as basis of political power, 144

Agnatic groups. *See* Lineages

Agnatic ties, 124-26

Agriculture: improvements in under Japanese, 29; surplus and industrialization of, 43-44; decline in importance of, 45; as occupation, 78-82

Ahern, Emily Martin, 123-24, 171, 199, 202

Aid, United States: and industrialization, 44

Alcoholism, 101; and conflict, 143-44; and violence, 146

Altars, ancestral. *See* Ancestral altars

Ancestors: as potentially malevolent, 205

Ancestor worship, 194-206; women's participation in, 178; and farming communities, 195; and property, 195, 199-202; as domestic cult in Ploughshare, 196-99; and filial obligation, 197; of different lines, 200, 202-4; and inheritance, 200-202; social function of, 204; psychological dimension of, 205

Ancestral altars, 195-96; and family division, 197; of subordinate lines, 203-4

Ancestral tablets: and property, 195; of subordinate lines, 195, 203-4; physical form of, 199; burning and burying of, 199

Ang Kong (local twin gods,), 184, 188

Anxi: dialect, 3-4; communities in Taiwan, 184

PUBLICATIONS ON ASIA OF THE SCHOOL OF
INTERNATIONAL STUDIES (formerly the Institute
for Comparative and Foreign Area Studies)

1. Boyd, Compton, trans. and ed. *Mao's China: Party Reform Documents, 1942-44.* 1952. Reissued 1966. Washington Paperback-4, 1966. 330 pp., map.
2. Siang-tseh Chiang. *The Nien Rebellion.* 1954. 177 pp., bibliog., index, maps.
3. Chung-li Chang. *The Chinese Gentry: Studies on Their Role in Nineteenth-Century Chinese Society.* Introduction by Franz Michael. 1955. Reissued 1967. Washington Paperback on Russia and Asia-4. 277 pp., bibliog., index, tables.
4. *Guide to the Memorials of Seven Leading Officials of Nineteenth-Century China.* Summaries and indexes of memorials to Hu Lin-i, Tseng Kuo-fan, Tso Tsung-tang, Kuo Sung-tao, Tseng Kuo-ch'üan, Li Hung-chang, Chang Chih-tung. 1955. 457 pp., mimeographed. Out of print.
5. Marc Raeff. *Siberia and the Reforms of 1822.* 1956. 228 pp., maps, bibliog., index. Out of print.
6. Li Chi. *The Beginnings of Chinese Civilization: Three Lectures Illustrated with Finds of Anyang.* 1957. Reissued 1968. Washington Paperback on Russia and Asia-6. 141 pp., illus., bibliog., index.
7. Pedro Carrasco. *Land and Polity in Tibet.* 1959. 318 pp., maps, bibliog., index.
8. Kung-chuan Hsiao. *Rural China: Imperial Control in the Nineteenth Century.* 1960. Reissued 1967. Washington Paperback on Russia and Asia-3. 797 pp., tables, bibliog., index.
9. Tso-liang Hsiao. *Power Relations within the Chinese Communist Movement, 1930-34.* Vol. 1: *A Study of Documents.* 1961. 416 pp., bibliog., index, glossary. Vol. 2: *The Chinese Documents.* 1967. 856 pp.
10. Chung-li Chang. *The Income of the Chinese Gentry.* Introduction by Franz Michael. 1962. 387 pp., tables, bibliog., index.
11. John M. Maki. *Court and Constitution in Japan: Selected Supreme Court Decisions, 1948-60.* 1964. 491 pp., bibliog., index.
12. Nicholas Poppe, Leon Hurvitz, and Hidehiro Okada. *Catalogue of the Manchu-Mongol Section of the Toyo Bunko.* 1964. 391 pp., index.
13. Stanley Spector. *Li Hung-chang and the Huai Army: A Study in Nineteenth-Century Chinese Regionalism.* Introduction by Franz Michael. 1964. 399 pp., maps, tables, bibliog., glossary, index.

14. Franz Michael and Chung-li Chang. *The Taiping Rebellion: History and Documents*. Vol. 1: *History*. 1966. 256 pp., maps, index. Vols. 2 and 3: *Documents and Comments*. 1971. 756 and 1,107 pp.

15. Vincent Y. C. Shih. *The Taiping Ideology: Its Sources, Interpretations, and Influences*. 1967. 576 pp., bibliog., index.

16. Nicholas Poppe. *The Twelve Deeds of Buddha: A Mongolian Version of the Lalitavistara*. 1967. 241 pp., illus. Paper.

17. Tsi-an Hsia. *The Gate of Darkness: Studies on the Leftist Literary Movement in China*. Preface by Franz Michael. Introduction by C. T. Hsia. 1968. 298 pp., index.

18. Tso-liang Hsiao. *The Land Revolution in China, 1930-34: A Study of Documents*. 1969. 374 pp., tables, glossary, bibliog., index.

19. Michael Gasster. *Chinese Intellectuals and the Revolution of 1911: The Birth of Modern Chinese Radicalism*. 1969. 320 pp., glossary, bibliog., index.

20. Richard C. Thornton. *The Comintern and the Chinese Communists, 1928-31*. 1969. 266 pp., bibliog., index.

21. Julia C. Lin. *Modern Chinese Poetry: An Introduction*. 1972. 278 pp., bibliog., index.

22. Philip C. Huang, *Liang Ch'i-ch'ao and Modern Chinese Liberalism*. 1972. 200 pp., illus., glossary, bibliog., index.

23. Edwin Gerow and Margery Lang, eds. *Studies in the Language and Culture of South Asia*. 1974. 174 pp.

24. Barrie M. Morrison. *Lalmai, A Cultural Center of Early Bengal*. 1974. 190 pp., maps, drawings, tables.

25. Kung-chuan Hsiao. *A Modern China and a New World: K'ang Yu-Wei, Reformer and Utopian, 1858-1927*. 1975. 669 pp., transliteration table, bibliog., index.

26. Marleigh Grayer Ryan. *The Development of Realism in the Fiction of Tsubochi Shōyō*. 1975. 133 pp., index.

27. Dae-Sook Suh and Chae-Jin Lee, eds. *Political Leadership in Korea*. 1976. 272 pp., tables, figures, index.

28. Hellmut Wilhelm. *Heaven, Earth, and Man in the Book of Changes: Seven Eranos Lectures*. 1976. 230 pp., index.

29. Jing-shen Tao. *The Jurchen in Twelfth-Century China: A Study of Sinicization*. 1976. 217 pp., map, illus., appendix, glossary, bibliog., index.

30. Byung-joon Ahn. *Chinese Politics and the Cultural Revolution: Dynamics of Policy Processes*. 1976. 392 pp., appendixes, bibliog., index.

31. Margaret Nowak and Stephen Durrant. *The Tale of the Nišan Shamaness: A Manchu Folk Epic*. 1977. 182 pp., bibliog., index.

32. Jerry Norman. *A Manchu-English Lexicon.* 1978. 318 pp., appendix, bibliog.
33. James Brow. *Vedda Villages of Anuradhapura: The Historical Anthropology of a Community in Sri Lanka.* 1978. 268 pp., tables, figures, bibliog., index.
34. Roy Andrew Miller. *Origins of the Japanese Language.* 1980. 217 pp., maps, bibliog., index.
35. Stevan Harrell, *Ploughshare Village: Culture and Context in Taiwan.* Forthcoming.
36. Kozo Yamamura, ed. *Policy and Trade Issues of the Japanese Economy: American and Japanese Perspectives.* Forthcoming.
37. Bruce Cumings, ed. *Child of Conflict: The Korean-American Relationship, 1945-1953.* Forthcoming.
38. Chan Hok-lam. *Theories of Legitimacy in Imperial China: Discussions on "Legitimate Succession" under the Jurchen-Chin Dynasty (1115-1234).* Forthcoming.